# Cat Got Your Tongue?

Paul McPherron and
Patrick T. Randolph

Recent Research
and Classroom
Practices for
Teaching Idioms
to English
Learners Around
the World

Typeset in Janson and Frutiger
by Capitol Communications, LLC, Crofton, Maryland USA
and printed by Gasch Printing, LLC, Odenton, Maryland USA

TESOL International Association
1925 Ballenger Avenue
Alexandria, Virginia 22314 USA
Tel 703-836-0774 • Fax 703-836-7864

Publishing Manager: Carol Edwards
Cover Design: Citrine Sky Design
Copyeditor: Sarah J. Duffy
Project reviewers: Gilda Martinez-Alba and Margarita Mitevska

TESOL Book Publications Committee
John I. Liontas, Chair
Robyn L. Brinks Lockwood, Co-chair      Guofang Li
Jennifer Lebedev                        Deoksoon Kim
Gail Schafers                           Gilda Martinez-Alba
Lynn Zimmerman                          Adrian J. Wurr

ISBN 9781942223221
Library of Congress Control Number 2014940100

# *Praise for* Cat Got Your Tongue?
## Recent Research and Classroom Practices for Teaching Idioms to English Learners Around the World

*Paul McPherron and Patrick T. Randolph*

The number of English learners continues to grow across the world, raising dilemmas about how best to teach a language born and nurtured in a small corner of Europe, transported across the Atlantic to take firm root on American shores and then expanding exponentially to lodge in the homes, classrooms, offices, and networks, both professional and personal, of almost two billion people all across the globe. All languages contain literal dimensions and figurative/metaphorical ones, allowing creativity and fostering language arts while permitting transactional exchange. Teaching languages involves addressing all aspects of the complex resources different languages deploy to make meaning, but how is this best done for the world's auxiliary language? This insightful, brilliant, yet highly practical book is rare among the many that claim to assist teachers to teach and learners to learn not just communication, grammar, and the literal lexicon, but many aspects of the cultural residue of English, and specifically here, the approximately 10,000 idioms contained in English. I thoroughly recommend its lucid treatment of the challenge of idiomatic expression, based solidly in scholarly traditions of language analysis, brain research, and especially experimental psycholinguistic examination of the processing and retention of idioms, while always present in the classroom, with teacher and learner, supporting them both in a creative, balanced, realistic, and ultimately more successful engagement with contemporary English.

*—Joseph Lo Bianco, PhD*
*Chair Professor of Language and Literacy Education*
*Graduate School of Education, University of Melbourne*

Too often, ES/FL teachers have explained anything they didn't understand in our language as "Oh, that's just an idiom." This book does the worldwide TESOL community a great service by demystifying idioms, placing them within the continuum of collocations, phrasal verbs, multiword expressions, and other formulaic forms by helping identify important issues in the learning, teaching, and understanding of idioms. In a truly easy-to-understand but solid treatment of all of these types of formulaic or "fixed" language, this book brings together research on vocabulary and language analysis, neuroscience and cognitive processing, second language acquisition, student interlanguage, corpus research, and applications to learning and teaching all in one place. What a marvelous resource for teachers! Bravo! I recommend it highly to ESL and EFL teachers at all levels, and in language teaching contexts from K–12 to college and university.

*—Anne Ediger, PhD*
*Coordinator and Professor, Hunter College,*
*City University of New York, MA in TESOL Program*

Defining "idiom" broadly, this helpful book shines a useful light on multiword units of many types. A great basic guide to recognizing, analyzing, and teaching these vital vocabulary items.

*—Lawrence J. Zwier*
*Associate Director of Curriculum*
*English Language Center, Michigan State University*

*Cat Got Your Tongue?* welcomes the reader to a practical and relevant guide in the learning and teaching of idioms that aligns science with compassionate, responsive classroom teaching—Illuminating! Insightful! and Instructive!

*—Joseph Slick, PhD*
*Director of the ESL Program, LaRoche College*

Are you and your students tiptoeing around idioms? In *Cat Got Your Tongue?*, McPherron and Randolph shed some light on roadblocks and avenues to idiom learning. In addition, they successfully build a bridge between research findings and classroom practice.

*—Gina Giamei*
*Senior Lecturer, The Center for English Language and*
*Orientation Programs, Boston University*

# Contents

## Part 1: Theoretical and Pedagogical Research Into Learning and Teaching Idioms

## Part 2: Teaching Idioms to English Language Learners Around the World

# Dedication

This book is humbly and proudly dedicated to our inspiring students, dedicated colleagues, and loving families.

# Acknowledgments

I am, because of you.

—*Ubuntu Philosophy*

Hermann Ebbinghaus (1885/1913) writes in his seminal work on memory, "All sorts of ideas, if left to themselves, are gradually forgotten" (p. 62). Unfortunately, with the hustle and bustle of life, the people who help us are often forgotten as well, unless, of course, we make a sincere effort to remember, honor, and thank them for their contributions on a page such as this one.

It is often a tradition to mention family in the final portion of the acknowledgments. This is one tradition we wish to disregard, for our families provided the core inspiration that helped make this project possible and bring it to its successful completion.

Paul would like to thank his wife, Jessica, and son, Robbie, for their unwavering support and understanding of all his late nights and working weekends at his office. Quite simply, the book would not be possible without them. Also, Paul thanks the diligent students who took his Vocabulary and Idioms class over many English for Foreign Students summer programs at Stanford University. It was their enthusiasm and joy in discussing English idioms that was his inspiration for this book.

Patrick offers his undying gratitude and heartfelt appreciation to his wife, Gamze, for her enthusiastic support, help in reviewing the manuscript, and insightful suggestions for clarity in the writing of this book. Her presence is a genuine blessing. He also would like to thank his daughter, Aylene, for her contributions of humor and keeping life in perspective while working on this project. And many thanks to his parents, Darlene and Joe, who lent support throughout the various stages of the book. He also offers a wink of thanks to his cat, Gable, who helped inspire the title of the book. Patrick would also like to to acknowledge a special nod of gratitude to his Turkish in-laws, Haluk and Ayfer. Their presence is always felt.

Chapters 6 and 7 would not have been possible without the assistance and willingness of the editors of TESOL-affiliated journals and newsletters to post our surveys. Much thanks to Krista Bittenbender Royal, editor of the *TESOL IEPIS Newsletter*; Karen Bleske, editor of *CATESOL News*; Emily Cripps, former editor of the *ARKTESOL Post*; Kelly J. Cunningham, former editor of the *ITBE Link*; Allison Piippo, editor of the *MITESOL Messages*; and Heather Torrie, current editor of the *ITBE Link*.

We are truly grateful for the instructors who helped make Chapter 9 a colossal feast of eclectic lesson plans: Jean L. Arnold, University of Nebraska at Lincoln; Veronica Csorvasi, Richland Community College in Dallas, Texas; Regina Dahlgren Ardini, Culinary Institute of America; Sohani Gandhioke, Shantou University, China; Hillary Gardner, The City University of New York Adult Literacy Programs; Michael Gilmore, Southern Illinois University Carbondale; Emily Green, Toledo, Ohio; Feifei Han, University of Sydney; Michelle Jackson, University of Texas at El Paso; Michelle Lam, Lucas Detech International Education, Tuy Hoa, Vietnam; Nadezda Pimenova, Ball State University; Chanchal Sigh, Shantou University, China; and Samantha Weekes, Burma Education Partnership in Thailand.

We would also like to extend special thanks to our colleagues near and far for their continued support, faithful assistance, and kind hearts: the ever-supportive and inspiring educators, Doug and Linda Plath; the exceptional Joseph Lo Bianco, chair of language and literary education at The University of Melbourne; the insightful Davide Secchi, senior lecturer in organizational behavior at Bournemouth University; our diligent teachers from Japan, Miho Nose and Manami Higa; and our grateful one-man sounding board at Western Michigan University: Joseph Ruppert. We also must say thanks to the staff at the Leon & Toby Cooperman Library at Hunter College and Michael McDonnell and Megan Brown of the Waldo Library on the Western Michigan University campus for their support and the use of their facilities.

And finally, we would like to give special thanks to Carol Edwards, publishing manager at TESOL Press, for her guidance and motivation from day one. And lest we forget, we must also thank Robyn Brinks Lockwood of Stanford University for her confidence in recommending us for this book project. At times, we did not think we could finish this book, but we are happy both Carol and Robyn always did.

In concluding these reflections of gratitude and respect, we would like to sincerely say, "We are, because of you."

# About the Authors

 **Paul McPherron** is an assistant professor of English at Hunter College of the City University of New York (CUNY), where he directs the undergraduate ESL program and teaches ESL and linguistics courses. His research projects include examinations of identity, globalization, and language teaching methods in China and the United States.

 **Patrick T. Randolph** has taught English language learners for the past 20 years, specializing in creative and academic writing, speech, debate, vocabulary pedagogy, and drama. His research interests include applying recent findings in neuroscience to the language classroom. Patrick lives in the upper Midwest with his soul-inspiring wife, Gamze; his cheerfully bilingual daughter, Aylene; and his wise, comical cat, Gable.

# CHAPTER 1

# Introduction: Who Is Afraid of Teaching Idioms?

We are. Idioms and idiomatic language are some of the most interesting and creative vocabulary terms to learn in any language. It is estimated that there are over 10,000 idioms in English, some relatively recent and some that have been used for more than 2,000 years (Brenner, 2011). Most linguists, language teachers, language learners, writers, poets, or anyone who has ever thought much about their language will freely admit that idioms provide vivid descriptions and expressions that are more powerful and effective than literal and nonidiomatic language. For example, consider the following interaction between Captain Kirk and Dr. Spock in the film *Star Trek IV: The Voyage Home* (Nimoy, 1986).

> Captain Kirk: If we play our cards right, we may be able to find out when those whales are being released.
>
> Dr. Spock: How will playing cards help?

Captain Kirk could have simply stated something such as, "If we proceed in the correct manner, we will be able to ascertain when the whales are being released." In fact, the aforementioned sentence resembles something Dr. Spock would probably say. Thus, it is certain

*Figure 1-1. Raining Cats and Dogs*
Source: http://openclipart.org/homepage

that idioms and idiomatic language make our language more color-ful, and they easily provide learners with a way to subtly express their thoughts and sound more proficient; however, at the same time, idioms stubbornly resist easy classification and are some of the most difficult vocabulary terms to teach. Numerous English teachers, including the co-authors of this text, have been left "tongue-tied" when English learners come up with questions such as, "How can a fat chance and a slim chance be the same?" or "What do cats and dogs have to do with the rain anyway?" (Figure 1-1).

In fact, the motivation for writing this book comes directly from our own experiences as English language teachers[1] in a variety of settings coupled with our desire to find effective ways to address idioms, collocations, multiword phrases, and other types of formulaic language in our classrooms.

Putting aside the complex definitions of idioms and formulaic language for a moment, consider the following self-evaluation written by one of McPherron's university students in southern China about what he learned as a member of a team that created a business. Also putting aside the global verb and sentence structure errors (cf. Lange & Lane, 2011), notice the underlined terms and phrases that show the student's attempts at idioms and formulaic expressions.

> After several weeks' <u>hard work</u>, we created out a company of ourselves. It's exciting that we were the first time to do such a big project. Though we met a lot of problems in the time, we had learned a lot.
>
> To be successful is not so easy. Today's world go very fast. People found companies as a fashion. When we got the assignment, we think it's <u>a piece of cake</u>. But truly, it's <u>easier say than done</u>. We had to take all situations and details during our company working. Leaving a little thing, the project would possibly fail. For example, when we assigned the money, we argued that how much to each department. <u>No more, no less</u>, and we had to think the market supply and demand, and what would the same industry affect us. Problems not only lived in the capital assignment, but also in the persons' choices, like how to spend less money to employ the high-quality person must to be thinking. It's very important to a new company and we <u>spent a lot of time</u> on it.
>
> <u>In a word,</u> as a college student, I think that leaning is important, but we could do something more than that. We should <u>open our eyes to the outside world</u> as to adapt the society in future.

---

[1] We hesitate here to use the term *second language* or *foreign language* because many of our students are learning English as their third or fourth language or have learned English at the same time as another "first" language. Further, few places in the world can accurately be described as second or foreign language contexts, so we use the terms *English language learner* (ELL) and *English language teaching* (ELT) throughout the book.

During the project I felt the real fortune is not money but friendships. When we work with friends, maybe we <u>pay much work,</u> but we gain more happiness.

This project let me know more about the business and the difficulties of it. It helps me a lot.

Second language acquisition researchers and pedagogists have noted that formulaic language makes up a large portion of linguistic competence (Zyzik, 2011), and as illustrated here, even a novice writer with many errors has also learned and attempted to use a great number of idioms and formulaic language, some correctly, some not. For example, the student draws on his knowledge of collocations (*hard work*), multiword phrases (*in a word*), idioms (*piece of cake*), and idiomatic language (*open our eyes to the outside world*). Clearly, the student has studied and acquired many types of formulaic language, and McPherron felt that he needed to address idioms and formulaic language in his writing class, but where should he start? Should he only address idioms post hoc and focus on their infelicitous use on writing assignments, or should he start with some basic description of what idioms are and how they are used in different contexts (e.g., spoken versus written idioms, formal versus informal idioms)? Alternatively, many language researchers argue that idioms can largely be grouped according to a shared conceptual metaphor (King, 1999; Kövecses & Szabó, 1996; Lakoff & Johnson, 2003), and perhaps the instructor should begin with teaching idioms as vocabulary items before focusing on their use. In this way, he could explain the base metaphors (e.g., light is knowledge) and then move toward more functional and register-based considerations of academic and informal idiomatic language use.

In addition to considerations of how to address idioms in a writing class, Randolph noticed the following pattern of idiom learning when he taught a speech and debate course at a North American university. Unfortunately, there were no idioms in the textbook, so he taught a list of useful phrasal verbs and idioms as vocabulary, such as *at first blush, drive the point home, in a nutshell, come up with,* and *boil down to.* Initially, these and other terms were taught as daily vocabulary items. Although the students scored high on the quizzes given to check meaning and correct usage, they rarely used this vocabulary in their speeches and debates. Randolph explained that these idioms are used naturally and that sometimes they are even more fitting than their single-word counterparts. He went on to explain that the single-word counterparts often seem contrived when used in speeches and that the phrasal verbs and idioms are more natural sounding.

The result of the use, or rather non-use, of the taught idioms and phrasal verbs was a clear case of avoidance, similar to the case study by Dagut and Laufer (1985) concerning Hebrew-speaking students of English. The Hebrew-speaking students did not have certain phrasal verbs in their own language and preferred to use the one-word equivalent. Although Randolph's students did have phrasal verbs and idioms in their respective languages, they reverted back to the one-word equivalents while giving their speeches. For example, instead of saying, "Finally, I'd like to drive my last point home," they said, "Finally, let me emphasize my last point." Instead of "There are many arguments that I have come up with regarding this point," the students reverted back to "There are many arguments I have produced regarding this point."

When asked why they did not incorporate the new vocabulary in their speeches, the majority of the students said that they were not comfortable with using "nonacademic" or "informal" English. Others claimed they couldn't remember the phrases, so they used what was "safe." In short, the desire to take risks was decreased because they were not confident in how to use these, despite their high scores on the quizzes, which required both a definition and natural use of the terms. Certain questions then arose in Randolph's mind: Do idioms and phrasal verbs inhibit the desire to take risks in the second language? Are these wonderful semantic tools unnecessary to teach?

These are just a few of the questions and concerns that have arisen in our own English courses, and in the following chapters we continue to ask these pedagogical questions about teaching and learning idioms and formulaic language. In this way, we draw on our own teaching experience as well as illustrations from a variety of classrooms around the world.

## An Increasingly Popular and Infuriating Topic

> If natural language had been designed by a logician, idioms would not exist. They are a feature of discourse that frustrates any simple logical account of how the meanings of utterances depend on the meanings of their parts and on the syntactic relation among those parts. (Johnson-Laird, 1993, p. vii)

From even a cursory glance at work in linguistics, applied linguistics, and TESOL, for quite some time, idioms and figurative language have been a popular but contentious topic (Chomsky, 1980; Fernando, 1996; Grant & Bauer, 2004; Katz & Postal, 1963; Liu, 2008; Moon, 1998; Nunberg, Sag, & Wasow, 1994). The contentiousness stems in large part from what linguists call the noncompositional feature of most idioms; that is, the meanings of most idioms and idiomatic phrases cannot be determined and are not predictable based on the sum of smaller word units within the idiom. As Katz (1973) writes, idioms "do not get their meanings from the meanings of their syntactic parts" (p. 358). To take an example from earlier, an English language learner (ELL) can know the meaning of *fat* and *chance*, but not the meaning of *fat chance*. This difficulty in defining and analyzing idioms may contribute to the reluctance of some ELL teachers and textbook writers to explicitly teach idioms or idiomatic language.

At the same time, as idioms have gained prominence as a theoretical linguistics topic, there has also been a heightened awareness in the field of English language teaching (ELT) of the critical role of vocabulary learning and teaching, and within the broad topic of vocabulary acquisition, most scholars agree that collocations, idioms, and lexical patterns make up as much or more of vocabulary competence than individual words (Biber, Conrad, & Leech, 2002; Lewis, 1993). Taking this basic insight about the patterns inherent in all language use, many linguists have built and refined large corpora of authentic language use in order to study the collocations and related strings of words in discourse, and, as described in later chapters in this book, these corpora have become increasingly available and useful in the English language classroom, particularly when teaching idioms (Reppen, 2010, 2011).

Thus, in recent years, idioms and idiom learning have received more and more attention from ELT researchers and textbook writers

(Grant, 2007; Irujo, 1986; King, 1999; Liu, 2003; Simpson & Mendis, 2003). Much of this work, however, has been narrowly focused on either the goal of surveying the most common idioms in spoken English (Liu, 2003) or proposing lessons and activities for idiom learning in the classroom (King, 1999). Psycholinguists have also focused their research on the processing and cognitive features associated with the use and acquisition of idioms (Abel, 2003; Boers, Demecheleer, & Eyckmans, 2004; Prodromou, 2003), but for English language teachers, outside of Liu (2008), there have been few resources that collect and analyze various theoretical and pedagogical research studies on idiom learning and relate them to actual classroom practices. The field seems to be able to do one or the other: experimental/discourse studies *or* teacher lessons. What is needed, however, is a balanced analysis and presentation of the two.

Therefore, in addressing the complex questions around teaching idioms, our main goal for this book is to never stray far from the classroom, but to inform all of our classroom discussion with theoretical and experimental studies of idioms and formulaic language. We are both English teachers and draw on our many years of teaching English in diverse settings throughout the world—from Japan and Romania to Carbondale, Illinois, and Stanford, California. And we also draw on the perspectives of teachers and learners from these and other learning contexts around the world.

Zyzik (2011) notes that psycholinguistic researchers have made advances in experimental knowledge of how idioms are processed and retained by learners, but "we are still in the initial stages of understanding the acquisition of idioms by non-native speakers" (p. 414). Similarly, it has been our experience that much of the research, discussion, and writing on idioms in applied linguistics and education journals has taken a narrow, experimental approach to studying idiom acquisition, and outside of lesson plans and shared learning activities in teacher blogs and journals—all important sources, of course—little work has drawn together research findings with actual classroom and teacher perspectives on learning. As teachers know intuitively, any research finding or theory looks very different when viewed through the perspective of actual classroom and student activity. Further, we have noticed that a great deal of recent research into how the brain works and processes language, including idioms, has direct connections to our classrooms, but much of this work is only reported as scientific reports for neuroscientists or made into popular culture books on how to improve your brain's functions, bypassing important links that can be made between neuroscience discoveries and English language teaching. Thus, it is our hope that this book can summarize and relate recent advances in research about idioms and idiom learning to actual classroom practices and perspectives, with the understanding that we are all still in the initial stages of developing both research and pedagogical understandings of how best to teach and learn idioms.

## Three Important Caveats

One of the main goals with this book is to move between classroom practice and research on learning and teaching idioms; therefore, the chapters are organized around the following two perspectives. In the first section, "Theoretical and Pedagogical Research Into Learning and Teaching Idioms," we survey recent work on learning and teaching idioms from diverse perspectives in the linguistics and educational research literature. We focus on various definitions of idioms from theoretical and pedagogical literature, in particular, cognitive, neurolinguistic, cross-linguistic, and social-constructionist research. In the second section, "Teaching Idioms to English Language Learners Around the World," we summarize and critique idiom learning from teacher, student, and classroom perspectives by presenting results of our own surveys on how students and teachers address learning idioms, a collection of lessons from around the world, and a review of textbooks and other resources for teaching idioms.

The division of the book into the two sections is somewhat misleading in that all of the chapters offer both classroom teacher and language researcher perspectives. We decided to start the book with an extensive review of recent theoretical and pedagogical research into learning and teaching idioms in order to clear the ground for the second part of the book's more concentrated focus on illustrations from classrooms around the world. However, in each chapter in the first section, we end with a "Pedagogical Perspective" on the research presented in the chapter, and at the end of Chapters 6, 7, and 8, in the second section of the book, we include an "Implications for Future

Research on Teaching and Learning Idioms" section to connect the teacher, student, and classroom perspectives presented in these chapters to research projects and themes from the first section of the book.

Also, it is important to note that the book is designed primarily for practicing teachers who are interested in learning about recent research into teaching idioms while simultaneously gaining practical suggestions and lessons that they can use in the their classrooms. The book, however, should also appeal to graduate students in teacher education classes (particularly MA-TESOL courses) as well as other linguistics, psychology, and education students and researchers who are interested in examining research and pedagogical perspectives on learning idioms in English. In addition, the book is not necessarily designed for language learners as a textbook or guide to learning idioms, but we feel that advanced English language learners, particularly graduate students who are learning English as an additional or multiple language, may find the background information in the first section interesting and use the resources in Chapter 9. Overall, in mixing research and pedagogical perspectives throughout the book, our aim is that no one view or theme dominates or appears more important and integral to teaching and learning idioms; instead, we hope that the book offers something for many members in the TESOL professional community.

Finally, before you delve into the book chapters, we want to draw your attention to our glossary of key terms (Appendix A). Although we make every effort to provide examples, definitions, and explanations for key terms throughout the book, we realize that there may be passages in which we use a term that is unfamiliar to our audience. In order to clarify the terms, we added a definition and example. Thus, we highlighted in bold the first time we use terms that are included in the glossary. Most of the terms are in the first five chapters.

## Sections of the Book

Adopting the above outline and goal of moving the line between research and practice, in Chapter 2, we discuss the variety of perspectives on how to define idioms and what implications different definitions have for teaching. This chapter also surveys corpus and sociolinguistic research on the roles of idioms in spoken and written discourse and analyzes various lists of idioms from different written and spoken contexts.

In Chapter 3, we survey important parts of the brain and discuss significant areas and functions that teachers ought to be aware of, and we offer suggestions on the best ways to activate the key functions of our brains for optimal idioms learning. We also present cognitive and neurolinguistic research on how vocabulary, idioms, and figurative language are processed, stored, and retrieved by both native and non-native speakers of English.

In Chapter 4, we review research about methods and materials for teaching idioms. We present the findings from both experimental research on idiom learning and classroom-based studies and reviews of pedagogical methods. In particular, we summarize the different best practices and recommendations that TESOL and applied linguistics researchers have made in regard to choosing, organizing, and presenting idioms in textbooks, dictionaries, and class lists.

In the final chapter of the first section, Chapter 5, we connect the literature on materials and methods from Chapter 4 to a review of best practices for classroom and learner-based activities for acquiring idioms. In this chapter, we offer more of our own thoughts on what could, if at all, be considered a best practice for teaching idioms. We pay special attention to the variety of teaching and learning contexts and cultures around the world. We emphasize an eclectic and **postmethod approach** (cf. Kumaravadivelu, 2003, 2006) to teaching idioms in which teachers draw on the work of theorists, researchers, and other teachers, but ultimately make pedagogical choices that fit with their own teaching context.

In the second part of the book, we focus on teacher and classroom perspectives from learning contexts around the world. In Chapter 6, we present findings from our survey of and interviews with English language teachers in a variety of countries and teaching contexts. We present and analyze both the fears and problems encountered by teachers as well as their best practices and effective methods. In Chapter 7, we present findings from our survey of and interviews with English language students in a variety of countries and contexts, and we compare these student perspectives with the results of the teacher surveys in the previous chapter. Chapter 8 is the most "hands-on" and practical as we outline lessons from around the world that address idiom learning and use. We connect these lessons to the previous summaries of research and our findings from teacher and student surveys as well as offer example work produced by students in these diverse settings. Finally, in Chapter 9, we offer practical suggestions for teachers looking for textbooks and curricula to use in their classrooms. We summarize textbooks, dictionaries, and online resources, and we offer critiques of the best and most useful materials for teaching and learning idioms.

In the final chapter of the book, we end with a brief overview of the key aspects and themes in the book: (1) the need to address idioms and idiom learning in the English language classroom, (2) the importance of developing idiom learning materials that are appropriate to specific classroom and learning needs, and (3) the development of an eclectic and postmethod approach to teaching and learning idioms.

## The Mythos and Logos of Language

The ancient Greeks developed an understanding of language and discourse as a dichotomy between *mythos* and *logos*, in which the former expressed poetic, cultural, religious, and even spiritual experiences, and the latter was considered to express facts and the "real" world that can be verified. Western understandings of scientific discourse and rationalism have emphasized logos discourse over the seemingly more subjective mythos discourse, associated with poetry, allusions, metaphors, proverbs, idioms, irony, and other imaginative and nonrational ways of speaking. Work by cognitive linguists such as George Lakoff, Mark Johnson, and Raymond Gibbs (Gibbs, 1994; Lakoff & Johnson, 1980), however, reveals the figurative and metaphorical aspects of all daily and scientific language use. They argue against a simple subjective versus objective dichotomy, and as Berendt (2008) points out, the study of figurative language has revealed the power of conceptual schemata and metaphors that constrain "how we think and express our ideas in both our everyday, technical, and literary discourses" (p. 3). Thus, teaching idioms and other forms of figurative and formulaic language, as discussed throughout this book, may reveal a host of definitional questions and usage problems for students, but we deal with some of the fundamental aspects of human communication and thought. And, as Berendt further notes, these elements of language or mythos discourse can "give contexts of meaning to make our mundane lives worthwhile" (p. 2). Making the mundane into the sublime, or at least elevating the literal into the poetic—we cannot think of a better reason to teach idioms.

# PART 1

# Theoretical and Pedagogical Research Into Learning and Teaching Idioms

CHAPTER 2

# What Is an Idiom?

What's in a name?
That which we call a rose
By any other name would
Smell as sweet.

*—William Shakespeare,*
Romeo & Juliet, *Act II, Scene 1*

What is an idiom? It seems like such a simple question, or one that linguists, teachers, and language researchers should come to some sort of consensus on, at least in order to make teaching materials more uniform. Strässler (1982) points out that the root of the word *idiom* is the Greek lexeme *idios*, which means "own, private, peculiar" (p. 13); and while the word *idiot* has the same root, it has become a pejorative term for being "peculiar" in a bad way, whereas *idiom* has become a term for almost any type of new or unique concept. As Moon (1998) notes, an idiom varies from (1) a term for "a particular manner of expressing something in language, music, art, and so on" to (2) a term for "a particular lexical collocation or phrasal lexeme, peculiar to a language" (p. 3). So, for example, "idiom" in the phrase "the show's own cliché-riddled idiom" is referring to the characteristics of the dialogue on a popular television show, whereas "idiom" in the sentence "the translator was unfamiliar with some out-of-the-way English idiom I had used" is referring to a peculiar phrase in English that may not be directly translatable into another language (Moon, 1998, p. 3). In this book, we are primarily concerned with the second understanding of idiom, and as this book is geared toward teachers who are trying to make sense of the diversity of views on defining and teaching idioms, we begin this introduction to the question of "what is an idiom" with perspectives from ESOL dictionaries and textbooks.

To start, *Webster's New World American Idioms Handbook* (Brenner, 2011) introduces idioms as "two or more words together that, as a unit, have a special meaning that is different from the literal meaning of the words separately" (p. 2). The *Longman Student Grammar of Spoken and Written English* (Biber, Conrad, & Leech, 2002) follows this focus on nonliteralness and introduces the notion of different degrees of "transparency":

> Idioms vary in "transparency": that is, whether their meaning can be derived from the literal meanings of the individual words. For example, *make up [one's] mind* is rather transparent in suggesting the meaning "reach a decision," while *kick the bucket* is far from transparent in representing the meaning "die." (p. xi)

Similarly, the *Cambridge Dictionary of American Idioms* (Heacock, 2003) defines idioms as phrases "whose meaning is different from the meanings of each word considered separately" (p. ix), and this definition is operationalized in the Cambridge-published textbook *English Idioms in Use* (O'Dell & McCarthy, 2010) with a similar definition that focuses on the transparency of idioms.

> Idioms are fixed combinations of words whose meaning is often difficult to guess from the meaning of each individual word. For example, if I say "I put my foot in it the other day at Linda's house—I asked her if she was going to marry Simon," what does it mean? If you do not know that put your foot in it means *something accidentally which upsets or embarrasses someone*, it is difficult to know exactly what the sentence means. It has a non-literal or idiomatic meaning. (p. 6)

The *Oxford Dictionary of English Idioms* (Ayto, 2009) also begins its definition of idioms with examples of what it calls the *semantic opaqueness* of idioms such as *kick the bucket* and *get down to brass tacks* that cannot be understood from their literal meanings, and the author extends the definition of idioms by noting that in idioms "the elements (words) of which they are made up are more or less firmly fixed and in most cases there is little or no leeway for changing them" (p. vii). For example, you can say, "Fred kicked the bucket," but you cannot say, "The bucket was kicked by Fred," nor is it possible to substitute chicken for hen in the phrase "rare as hen's teeth" (p. vii).

Thus, the above definitions all stress the transparency or opaqueness of idioms and idiomatic expressions as well as—to a lesser degree—the fixedness of the parts that make up an idiom. In fact, Liu (2008) notes that these two characteristics are the most difficult aspects of learning idioms and the proper starting points to define and teach them to language learners. He writes,

> When learners approach a new language form, the level of difficulty in understanding its meaning and the effort required to grasp its structure are two extremely important issues they have to consider in deciding whether the item deserves their special attention. (p. 13)

Perhaps the focus on transparency, or what linguists have often referred to as **compositionality** (Katz & Postal, 1963), and **fixedness**, or what linguistics have commonly referred to as *restricted variance* (Fernando, 1996), is illustrated in one of the first lists of criteria for determining idioms for pedagogical and research purposes as proposed by Fernando and Flavell (1981):

1. The meaning of an idiom is not the result of the compositional function of its constituents.

2. An idiom is a unit that either has a homonymous literal counterpart or at least individual constituents that are literal, though the expression as a whole would not be interpreted literally.

3. Idioms are transformationally deficient in one way or another.

4. Idioms constitute set expressions in a given language.

5. Idioms are institutionalized.[1]

---

[1] Institutionalization refers to "the process by which a string or formulation becomes recognized and accepted as a lexical item of the language" (Bauer, 1983, as cited in Moon, 1998, p. 7).

Similar to the above list, the degree of noncompositionality (as related to criteria 1 and 2) and fixedness in form (as related to 3 and 4) have become central criteria used for many teaching materials and much experimental language research. But for teachers hoping to determine exactly how to define idioms for students and determine the best way to organize and teach idioms, we have to ask: How figurative or semi-literal must the meaning of the phrase be in order to consider it an idiom? Further, in terms of fixedness, how many options or changes in structure are permitted for the phrase to still count as an idiom? For example, the adjective in the phrase *break new ground* can be changed to *break fresh ground* or even the verb changed to *clear new ground*, but clearly the phrases *break new field* and *break new dirt* are unacceptable. This first point about compositionality was alluded to above in the discussion of *kick the can*, reinforcing the point that a simple definition of idioms as noncompositional is complicated by the fact that phrases such as *make up one's mind* can be determined by knowledge of the component parts. Zyzik (2011) notes this spectrum in stating "it is supposed that decomposability (measured by speakers' intuitions) is a gradient concept, with some idioms being classified as more decomposable than others" (p. 414), but we still have to ask how to introduce a term like *idiom* or a term such as *decomposable* to students when there is such a variety of examples.

Discussed in more detail below, this fuzzy boundary between fixedness and transparency has led researchers such as Grant and Bauer (2004) to propose a strict distinction between what they call *core idioms* and other *figuratives*. They argue that by focusing only on phrases that cannot be reinterpreted to convey the intended truth (e.g., *It's a red herring*), teachers will help students distinguish the more difficult phrases (the core idioms) from phrases that are easier to process and acquire (the figuratives such as *He's a big fish in a small pond*). This distinction of core idioms is useful and, as also discussed later, there is pedagogical value in categorizing phrases according to their degree of difficulty, but the label *core idioms* seems to recognize the fact that teachers and students are using the term *idiom* to address a range of idiomatic and formulaic language. And we need to develop a working definition that addresses all idioms and idiomatic language which we can use to build curriculum and teaching objectives.

In addition to debates about how literal or compositional an expression needs to be in order to be considered an idiom, further complicating matters are questions of whether teachers should include formulaic expressions such as greetings (*see you*), proverbs/sayings (*Give a man a fish and he eats for a day*), phrasal verbs (*turn on*), or even common collocations (*black coffee*) in a definition of idioms. Just as they vary in terms of degree of literalness, linguists vary in what types of formulaic expressions can be included as idioms; for example, Fernando (1996) and Makkai (1972) include **phrasal verbs** as idioms, but Moon (1998) and Grant and Bauer (2004) do not. Grant and Bauer do, however, include formulae and fixed expressions as core idioms as long as the expression is completely nonliteral (e.g., *of course*). Due to this variety of idioms and how to define them, Moon prefers to avoid using the term *idiom*, except for "clearly semi-transparent and opaque metaphorical expressions" (p. 5), but she does include idioms as a type of fixed expression that includes phrases such as frozen collocations, proverbs, and similes. For simplicity's sake and to draw attention to idioms as the most important category of fixed expressions, Moon conflates all of these expressions into the term *fixed expressions and idioms*.

Although linguists may differ on the inclusion of certain types of formulaic expressions, Jaeger (1999) notes that the overall trend is clearly toward "all-inclusiveness of the class of linguistic objects called idioms" (p. 35), a trend that is also apparent in the variety of examples of idioms in ESOL textbooks. For example, the textbook *English Idioms in Use* begins its first chapter "What Is an Idiom?," by stating that idioms are one type of formulaic language similar but apparently different from fixed expressions, phrasal verbs, collocations, preposition phrases, and compounds. The introduction goes on to offer a general description of the syntax and sentence position of idiomatic expressions:

Tim took a shine to [immediately liked] his teacher. (verb + object + preposition)

The band's number one hit was just a flash in the pan [something that happens only once]. (idiomatic noun phrase)

Little Jimmy has been as quiet as a mouse [extremely quiet] all day. (simile)

We arrived safe and sound [safely]. (binomial; O'Dell & McCarthy, 2010, p. 1)

In the second chapter, "Types of Idioms," it is clear that all formulaic language is included in the authors' definition of idioms as they detail types of idioms from similes and euphemisms to proverbs. Similarly, in introducing idioms to students, the textbook *The Big Picture* (King, 1999) does not directly address what types of phrases are included in a definition of idioms, only stating generally that idioms are "a word or group of words whose meaning is not literal," with the emphasis on the use of idioms in "informal contexts" (p. xi). In the lists of idioms in the book, however, the author does include phrasal verbs, proverbs, greetings, and many one-word idioms.

One-word idioms (either compounds of free morphemes or single, free morphemes) pose a further problem for linguists and dictionary writers. Some linguistics—such as Katz and Postal (1963) in an influential account of idioms—argue that single words and even the bound morphemes of a word count as idioms, claiming that the overall meaning of the word is not based compositionally on its parts. For example, *telephone* literally means *tele* (far) and *phone* (sound), thus literally "far sound" and not the actual meaning of "long distance talk device" (Katz & Postal, 1963, p. 275). Other linguistics, including Moon (1998) and Grant and Bauer (2004), while not explicitly ruling out one-word idioms, focus their definitions and discussions of idioms exclusively on multiword phrases, and Kövecses (2002) specifically sets up the condition that idioms must be multiword phrases. Textbooks and dictionaries generally do not make a distinction between single- or multiword idioms in their working definitions of idioms, and they do generally include one-word idioms in their lists. One exception is Brenner (2011), who argues in the introduction to *Webster's New World American Idioms Handbook* that there are numerous one-word idioms such as *scratch* or *dough* for *money*, and she proposes perhaps the most general definition of idioms as a starting point for learners and teachers, one that we also use as our basic criteria in this book about what makes an idiom:

- Idioms have a meaning that is different from or extends the literal meaning of the individual word or words.

- Idioms break or stretch the rules of grammar, word order (syntax), and semantics to a certain degree.

- Idioms change meaning when translated word for word into another language. (p. 3)

In summary, from this initial survey of definitions of idioms used in ESOL textbooks as well as references to key linguistic studies in the past decades, it is clear that the core aspects of idioms include degrees of compositionality and fixedness. Further questions remain, however, including where to place the line between literal and nonliteral expressions, what types of expressions should be included in a definition of idioms, and what metaphoric and pragmatic aspects of idioms are useful in a pedagogical definition of idioms. As noted above, ESOL textbooks vary widely in their working definition of what an idiom is, and they often do not differentiate or explicitly tell students and teachers how they have chosen the terms or organization of their textbooks. Thus, the next sections of this chapter further engage with research and ideas about these definitional questions to help English language teachers better define idioms for students and select textbooks that mirror their own beliefs about how to define and organize idioms. For simplicity and clarity, note that in the sections below, we place attention on one or two key studies or authors who are often associated with a particular aspect of a definition of idioms. This by no means implies that these authors are alone in their particular positions, nor does it imply that they do not also include other attributes in their definitions of idioms.

## Idioms as Noncompositional Phrases

In his influential study of idioms in English, Makkai (1972) makes noncompositionality a key aspect of his study of idioms when he draws a distinction between the narrower category of *idioms of decoding* and the wider category of *idioms of encoding*. For Makkai, idioms of decoding are phrases and expressions that have nonliteral meanings and have "disinformation potential" for first and second language users (p. 122), while he defines idioms of encoding as stable collocations in a language including phrasal verbs. For example, Makkai would consider the phrase "cat got your tongue" as an idiom of decoding because of the difference between the literal and figurative meanings and the potential for errors by language learners.

Idioms of encoding are any phrases or terms that are fixed in some way, for example, the specific combination of the verb *bounce* and *back* in order to form the phrasal verb and its meaning in *She bounced back from her initial disappointment* and the choice of the preposition *at* in the expression *drive at 70 mph*. Since idioms of decoding are generally fixed in form, all idioms of decoding are also considered idioms of encoding for Makkai (1972). Thus, just as Fernando and Flavell (1981) make the *compositional function* of a phrase the first aspect in a definition of idioms, Makkai draws attention to the opacity and nonliteralness of idioms, and although he still uses the term *idioms* for the more general notion of fixed collocations, his focus on the more opaque and noncompositional idioms of decoding has continued in much of the research into the learning and teaching of idioms (Fernando, 1996; Grant & Bauer, 2004).

Furthering the work of Makkai (1972), Fernando (1996) offers an important discussion and categorization of idioms according to the key aspect of compositionality or opacity. She proposes a three-tier system of classifying idioms: pure, semi-literal, and literal. In her classification, a pure idiom is similar to a core idiom (cf. Grant & Bauer, 2004) in which a phrase's meaning cannot be understood by combining the meanings of the words that make up the phrase. As noted above, common examples of pure idioms include *spill the beans, kick the bucket*, and *pull someone's leg*. Related, a semi-literal idiom has at least one nonliteral word or element combined with at least one literal expression. Drawing on Fernando's distinction, Liu (2003) offers examples of semi-literal idioms such as *fat chance* and *use something as a stepping stone* in which the terms such as *use* and *chance* are literal elements, whereas the words *fat* and *stepping stone* have nonliteral meanings. Finally, literal idioms are easier to understand than pure and semi-literal idioms, and these are only considered idioms because either they are completely fixed or they allow restricted variation. Examples of these idioms include *on foot*, *in sum*, and *throw away*. Fernando admits throughout her work that these boundaries are not always clear, and many researchers would not include phrasal verbs as idioms that constitute a large portion of the literal idioms (Moon, 1998; Simpson & Mendis, 2003).

Thus, Fernando (1996) and Makkai (1972), two widely cited works on idioms, offer noncompositionality as a key component of their definition of idioms, and we find that an initial introduction of idioms and idiomatic language to students can easily start from this definition of compositionality. For example, Helen Fragiadakis (1992), in the textbook *All Clear: Idioms in Context*, begins her introduction to students by displaying two pictures, one showing two people literally running into each other, or as she writes, "They crashed into each other" (p. xi). Next to this image, she places a picture of the same two friends meeting on the street and waving to each other. She labels this picture, "They met without planning" to explain the idiomatic meaning of the phrase "to run into someone" (p. xi). She writes:

> In both pictures, we can say that "Steve ran into Melissa yesterday." In the first picture, that sentence means that Steve was running and then crashed into Melissa and maybe even hurt her. In the second picture, that sentence means that Steve and Melissa met each other without planning to meet. When they saw each other they were surprised. (p. xi)

Using a similar starting point to introduce the literal (compositional) and idiomatic (noncompositional) meaning of an idiom, we often show students images such as the representations of *tie the knot* in Figure 2-1 on the first day of a unit on idioms.

## Idioms as Fixed Expressions

Moon (1998) describes the lexicogrammatical fixedness of idioms as "formal rigidity" in which idioms show a range of "preferred realizations and often restrictions on aspect, mood, or voice" (p. 7). As cited above, a common example of fixedness is the inability (or extreme awkwardness) of realizing many idioms in the passive voice once they have become fixed in the active voice (*the breeze was shot by us*).[2] This type of error based on breaking the rigidity of idioms and fixed expressions is common among ELLs. In particular, they often use unidiomatic constructions and replacements that seem logical based

---

[2] The asterisk indicates that a phrase or word is ungrammatical and would not be allowed or sound correct to speakers of a language.

*Figure 2-1. Tie the Knot*
Source: http://pixabay.com

on literal interpretations of idioms but are ungrammatical or pragmatically incorrect in English. For example, McPherron, while teaching in China, often confused the Chinese students when using formulaic greetings such as *What's up?* or *What's cooking?*; students would often look around or attempt to guess literally what was cooking. Similarly, they tried to reconstruct the expressions into unidiomatic expressions such as *\*What's high?* or *\*How it cooks?* As with the notion of compositionality, Moon points out that fixedness is a complex characteristic of idioms, and just because two words occur often or even always together does not make them an idiom or fixed expression. Instead, Moon distinguishes between simple co-occurrence of terms such as *industrial revolution* and *center divider* (from Nunberg, Sag, & Wasow, 1994) from anomalous collocations which she considers idioms. Anomalous conventions either break conventional grammar rules (e.g., *by and large*) or represent unique strings of words (e.g., *kith and kin*).

Further, not all idioms are completely fixed, and some may allow more transformations and replacements than others. In fact, Moon (1998) shows that 40% of English fixed expressions and idioms allow some transformation and 14% have at least two or more established variations. For example, Fernando (1996) offers the terms *invariant idioms* and *idioms of restricted variance* to compare a more fixed expression in which no word can be changed (e.g., *smell a rat*) to idioms that allow only one or more words to be changed (e.g., *get cold feet, have cold feet*). Thus, fixedness is a necessary criterion for defining idioms, but it is not sufficient without the other criteria of compositionality and figurativeness.

Useful for teaching ELLs about idioms, Fernando (1996) lists specific aspects of fixedness that can be added to a definition of idioms and incorporated into lessons about what constitutes an idiom. She focuses particular attention on varying degrees of fixedness (or transformation ability) according to each aspect, and her criteria for defining fixedness are as follows:

*Replacements or substitutions (tense, number, lexical)*
   Example: You can vary the tense of the idiom *He smells a rat* from present to past *He smelt a rat* but you cannot change the tense of *A stitch in time saves nine* to the past *A stitch in time saved nine*. (p. 49)

*Additions*
   Example: You are not typically allowed to change a word in an idiom (e.g., *\*raining cats and mice*), but you can "introduce extraneous elements into idioms" such as *with his tongue only partly in his cheek*. (p. 48)

*Permutations*
Many idioms do not allow any permutations of their internal structure or grammar.

   Example: *Kick the can* is not equal to *the can was kicked*. And the particle cannot be moved in three-part phrasal verbs such as *He came up with an idea* (*\*He came up an idea with*).

But other idioms do allow permutations, such as movement from a verb phrase to a compound noun.

   Example: *To blow smoke* can be made into *smoke-blower*. And the particle can be moved in *They looked up the word* to *They looked the word up*.

*Deletions*

Some idioms that have been in use for years and are well established have become truncated and are better known in a reduced form.

> Example: The sentence *A rolling stone gathers no moss* is more commonly known in its reduced noun phrase form as simply *a rolling stone*.

(Examples above are ours except those followed by a page number, which are paraphrased from Fernando, 1996.)

Language learners who may have learned idioms primarily from textbooks and dictionaries will need particular help and practice with understanding the idiosyncrasies of these aspects of idiom usage. In addition, we have found it very important to illustrate the variety of fixedness in different idioms as part of a general introduction to what idioms are, and as discussed further in later chapters, we recommend having students record the individual aspects of each idiom when creating word lists and definitions.

## Idioms as Shared Knowledge and Core Concepts

Based on but moving beyond the common understanding of idioms as nonliteral language use, work in cognitive linguistics by Lakoff (1987), Lakoff and Johnson (2003), Kövecses (1990, 2002), and Kövecses and Szabo (1996) has shown that many idioms are not completely arbitrary and may, in fact, be motivated by or based on core **metaphors** and human experiences. Szczepaniak and Lew (2011) write that this notion of motivation is very different than the "arbitrary-predictable" dichotomy that was presented in the definitions above because it places emphasis on the image and cultural knowledge that link an idiom with its figurative meaning; in this way, idioms are not simply unpredictable strings of words, but they are made up of "motivating links" between "conventional images, knowledge about the image (often culture-specific), and the conceptual metaphors" (p. 325). Further, from a cognitive linguistics perspective, teachers should draw on these motivating links when they teach idioms because, as Lakoff writes, "it is easier to *remember* and *use* motivated knowledge than arbitrary knowledge" (p. 346, original emphasis).

The metaphors that motivate the idioms are not literary or poetic metaphors used to vividly describe an emotion or feeling, as in artistic work, but they are conceptual metaphors that, according to Kövecses (2002), "bring into correspondence two domains of knowledge" (p. 4). The source domain is "the conceptual domain from which we draw metaphorical expressions to understand another conceptual domain," and the target domain is "the domain that we try to understand through the use of the source domain" (p. 4). So, for example, the conceptual metaphor of light as knowledge equates the presence of light (source domain) with the ability to know or understand something (target domain). This metaphor helps to explain idioms such as *to see the light, to dawn on,* and *to see in a whole new light.* As Kövecses and others further explain, this ability to draw on conceptual metaphors to determine an idiom's literal meaning does not mean that an idiom's meaning is entirely predictable, but "the derivation from that literal sense can nonetheless be 'explained'" (Boers, Eyckmans, & Stengers, 2007, p. 44). In addition to being based on core, conceptual metaphors, cognitive linguists emphasize that many idioms are based on shared human experiences, as illustrated in the phrase *get a grip,* which is based on the metaphor *mental control is physical control* and draws on the physical feeling of losing one's grip on a physical object.

As a definition and pedagogical explanation of what idioms are, Kövecses (2002) adds two further, overlapping conceptual processes (what he calls *cognitive mechanisms*) to the concept of the metaphor: **metonymy** and conventional knowledge (p. 211). Similar to the idea of a metaphor, metonymy is typically thought of as a literary device in which a figure of speech or phrase is referred to by something that is a part of or related to the larger concept (e.g., *the crown* often refers to the royal family in Great Britain). For Kövecses and other cognitive linguists, metonymy or a metonymic relationship is revealed in idioms such as *we need more hands* in which *the hand* stands for the person. In the same way as metaphors, many idioms can be related to one basic metonymy, and as described in more detail in Chapters 4 and 5, teaching these conceptual relationships can help students learn idioms.

Kövecses (2002) writes that the other aspect of a cognitive understanding of idioms, conventional knowledge, is the shared knowledge that people in a given culture have concerning a conceptual domain like the human hand. This shared everyday knowledge includes standard information about the parts, shape, size, use, and function of the human hand, as well as the larger hierarchy of which it forms a part (hand as a part of the arm, etc.). (p. 207)

For example, the idioms *with open hands* and *tight-fisted* can be understood based on the image of how easy it is to give something to someone with an open hand versus a closed fist. It is important to note that these three aspects of idioms—metaphor, metonymy, and conventional knowledge—from a cognitive perspective, are not distinct and often overlap in the same metaphor, such as *to do something in an underhanded way*, which is based on the metonymy of *the hand stands for the activity* and the metaphor that *ethical/moral is up*.

Thus, Kövecses (2002) and others advocate that drawing on these overlapping cognitive mechanisms can help learners organize, memorize, and use idioms. At the same time, this aspect of a definition of idioms can be difficult for students to understand. We have found that using this aspect of idioms is particularly useful for advanced learners and graduate students, but it may be too abstract and confusing for beginners and younger students who may not be as interested in the underlying semantic features of idioms. Further, not all idioms are clearly based on an underlying concept. For example, the textbook *The Big Picture* (King, 1999) includes the idiom *blanket statement* as based on the underlying concept *knowledge is territory*; the term is defined as "a broad generalization, usually not justified in its extent," but it is not clear how that meaning is generated from the core concept (p. 30). As discussed further in later chapters, organizing idioms around core concepts is an effective way to draw student attention to similar semantic features and relationships between idioms as well as introduce very interesting and intellectual aspects of idioms and their linguistic attributes. Teachers, however, should be careful not to overemphasize this part of a definition with students who are not able to understand that not every idiom will fit perfectly into a core concept and who need a more concrete and operational definition of idioms.

## Idioms as Pragmatic and Discourse Resources

Thus far, the work summarized above—while contributing to the semantic, syntactic, and cognitive aspects of a definition of idioms—has primarily been experimental and theory based, without any use of language data from actual interlocutors, and as conversation analysts often point out, authors rarely incorporate natural spoken language and contexts of use into their discussions and analyses of idioms. This gap in the literature is particularly glaring as so much of what makes idioms difficult for language users is their actual use in conversation. In response to these more theory-driven studies, recent work in applied linguistics and speech communication has examined idioms from a more pragmatic perspective to identify how idioms structure and organize real, "authentic" written and spoken language. A common characteristic of these investigations is the importance not only of the semantic and structural features of idioms but also the discourse features of idioms and their role as pivot markers in conversation. As Moon (1998) notes, idioms are "not simply a matter of the lexical realization of meaning, but part of the ongoing dynamic interaction between speaker/writer and hearer/reader within the discoursal context" (p. 244).

Two of the early researchers from this discourse and conversation analysis perspective on idioms were Harvey Sacks and Jurg Strässler, who, in looking at the pragmatic aspects of idiomatic expressions, both discovered that idioms play a very powerful role in conversation and that their use is highly predictable. In his 1970 spring lecture, "Poetics: Spatialized Characteristics," Sacks discussed the insightful observation that speakers unknowingly influence others naturally by using idioms. The example he gave in his lecture is a conversation between a patient and a doctor. The patient initially used spatially influenced idioms such as *I got to a point where, you go through a period, somewhere along the line, scare the daylights out of them,* and *hiding under a paper bag* (Sacks, 1995). What is of interest is that as the patient-doctor conversation continued, the doctor seemed to be unconsciously aligning himself with the patient and began to use spatialized idioms as well. For example, he used *you are in a spot now, make some kind of move, I've gone through it,* and *come out the other side* (Sacks, 1995). In short, without realizing that the patient was influencing the doctor with spatialized idioms, she was "getting in his head" and orienting him to use similarly focused idioms. In his pragmatic account of idioms, Strässler (1982) also showed how idiom use assumed or created similar orientations to the conversation subject: "idioms contain information on the one hand, but they also provide a method of handling special situations" (p. 134), an aspect of idiom usage that is very important for ELLs to grasp and one we return to in Chapters 4 and 5.

Since this initial broad research, several other studies have examined, in a more narrow sense, the discourse features of idiom use, most of them making use of large written and/or spoken corpora as their database (Fernando, 1996; Holt & Drew, 2005; McCarthy, 1998; Moon, 1998; Schmitt, 2004; Wray, 2002). Surveying this work, three specific functions of idioms in a conversation appear useful to mention here: first, they help in topic termination and topic transition; second, they assist in evaluating storytelling situations; and third, they create a sense of social bonding. For an example of the first usage, consider the following transcript adapted for use in our classes from Holt and Drew (2005, pp. 37–38) in which D is discussing bumping into an acquaintance she went to school with who she thought was a poor student but who is now a lawyer.

D:  And I- You know it- for some reason he struck me as never even being able to get out of high school. Well I's talking to him well he's go- he's got a year left at SMU in law school.

M:  Mmmmm

D:  and he's real cute now

M:  Well see that just goes to show you he's a late bloomer

D:  Yeah he was real handsome

M:  You know sometimes the late bloomers'll fool you

D:  Yeah that's true

M:  I told you about my friend who's graduated and he went straight to law school all that kind of stuff and now he's

D:  and now he's workin' as a painter

M:  driving a trailer or something

Holt and Drew (2005) comment that the speakers in this conversation use the figurative expression *late bloomer* to refer to the man D knew in high school, met again recently, and found to have achieved much more in life than she expected. M then uses the expression to tell a story about someone from her past that did well in school but then did not follow through on his initial potential. Holt and Drew write that M is not using *late bloomer* to refer to the specific man in D's story but to late bloomers in general, "thus providing an explicit link to a related story" (p. 38).

In addition to topic transition, idioms are used pragmatically to evaluate stories, as evidenced in the following examples adapted from McCarthy (1998, pp. 134, 142):

> I said, "What would you like to do this afternoon?" And she said, "Oh Mary, let's go to bingo." Now, bingo was never ever *my cup of tea*, but seeing that I was supposed to be with her I'd say, "All right then, where do we go now to bingo?"

> I think that she ought to be *told the time of day*. When I was 21, I didn't have a car.

Liu (2008) notes that the use of idioms in the above examples helps speakers communicate their ideas or express their viewpoints, and they can be categorized as *ideational* according to Halliday's (1973) classic work on **systemic functional linguistics (SFL)**. In total, Halliday defines three key functions of language: ideational, interpersonal, and textual. The earlier examples from Holt and Drew (2005) and others in which idioms are used to align interactions between speakers fall under the interpersonal function of language (e.g., *you made my day*). The textual function of language refers to language that is used to organize information or highlight an idea either from within a sentence (intra-sentential), within a longer paragraph (intersentential), or between sections of a text by introducing new topics (metadiscoursal). Textual idioms not only are used in writing, but can organize information in any spoken or written text. For example, Liu provides examples of idioms such as *by the way* or *on the contrary* in spoken texts such as Barbara Walters stating, "By the way, koalas are not bears at all" and "On the contrary, we've given them every indication that they will be held to the high standards of international law" (p. 31).

As evidenced in the above examples from linguists working from a conversation analysis perspective, it is important to add a discourse aspect of idioms and idiom use to a classroom definition of idioms because language users

> do not form their utterances solely by applying grammatical rules on the one hand and creating original, ad hoc expressions on the other. . . . They also constantly bear in mind the socio-pragmatic conventions of the linguistic and cultural community they are part of in that precise historical moment; such factors are crucially exemplified in fixed, routinized expressions. (Eerdmans & Di Candia, 2007, pp. 579–580)

Thus, language teachers need to draw students' attention to the functional (i.e., interpersonal, evaluative, ideational, and textual) resources that idioms provide to speakers. Just as the notion of a core semantic concept is difficult to introduce to younger students and beginning learners, teachers need to be careful how much they draw on conversation analysis and the linguistic terms and approaches introduced in this section. Perhaps the most successful way that we can illustrate a discourse and conversational definition of idioms for students is by (1) bringing in a transcript of a dialogue from a television show in which an idiom is used, (2) discussing with students both the meaning of the idiom and why the speaker chose to use the idiom at that point in the conversation (i.e., the pragmatic and functional reason for using the idiom), and (3) asking students to look for and write down an example of an idiom they hear in a television show and bring the transcript to class. In this way, students can begin to both listen for idioms in the media they consume and think through the different reasons idioms are used at different times in a conversation. We discuss similar activities to this in Chapter 5 as well as in some of the lessons in Chapter 8.

## Pedagogical Perspective: A "Fuzzy" Category

> Attempts to provide categorical, single-criterion definitions of idioms are always to some degree misleading and after the fact. In actual linguistic discourse and lexicographical practice, "idiom" is applied to a fuzzy category. (Nunberg et al., 1994, p. 492)

Just as students and teachers are often frustrated by the difficulty and "fuzziness" of defining exactly what an idiom means, linguists and language researchers have noted the futility of determining an all-inclusive definition of the idiom itself, particularly if only one criterion is to be applied. Instead, teachers should draw on the many aspects of idioms outlined above in introducing idioms to students. Table 2-1 summarizes the four key aspects of idioms that we have introduced as well as examples of how theses definitions are used in textbooks on idioms.

In addition to understanding the multiple aspects of idiom definitions in textbooks and research studies, we have also found it helpful to present charts to students with example idioms based on the different aspects of the definition of idioms presented above (or at least to keep the following examples in mind when presenting the types of idioms students will encounter and use). For example, Figures 2-2 and 2-3 are based on categories and examples we have adapted for our classrooms from Nation (2001, pp. 229–332).

Showing students these lists allows us to introduce the variety and range of idioms as well as similarities among groups of idioms that students can draw on when confronted with new idioms. We should note here that by presenting these charts, we are adopting a very general definition of idioms. For example, in Figure 2-3, under "semantically opaque," we include the one "true" idiom according to Grant and Bauer (2004): *a red herring*. But we also include other idioms that they would define as figurative because we feel that these are all idi-

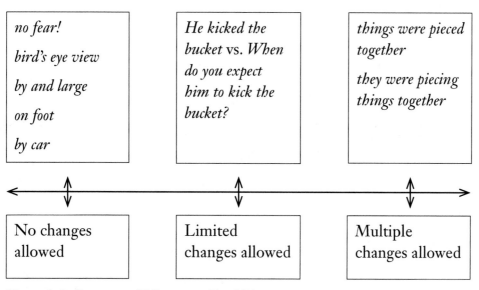

*Figure 2-2. Spectrum of Idioms as a Fixed Phrase*

## Table 2-1. Summary of Definitions of Idioms From Linguistic and Pedagogical Materials

| Definition | Key Linguistic Works That Draw on This Definition |
|---|---|
| Noncompositionality | Katz and Postal (1963); Makkai (1972); Fernando and Flavell (1981) |
| Fixed expressions | Fernando (1996); Moon (1998) |
| Shared knowledge/core concept | Lakoff and Johnson (2003); Kövecses (2002); and Kövecses and Szabo (1996) |
| Pragmatic/discourse resource | McCarthy (1998); Sacks (1995); Strässler (1982) |

| Key Quote Illustrating This Definition | Quote From Textbook That Draws on This Definition |
|---|---|
| The essential feature of an idiom is that its full meaning . . . is not a compositional function of the meanings of the idiom's elementary parts. (Katz & Postal, 1963, p. 275) | An idiom is a group of words that has a special meaning. The meaning of the group of words is different from the meanings of the individual words together. For example, the group of words "What's up?" means "What's new?" or "What's happening?" (McPartland, 1989, p. vi) |
| Idioms are indivisible units whose components cannot be varied or varied only within definable limits. No other words can be substituted for those comprising, for example, *smell a rat* or *seize/grasp the nettle*, which take either these two verbs but not others: thus *grab* is unacceptable. Nor are the words of an idiom usually recombinable. (Fernando, 1996, p. 30) | Idioms are a type of formulaic language. Formulaic language consists of fixed expressions which you learn and understand as units rather than as individual words. (O'Dell & McCarthy, 2010, p. 6) |
| Many, or perhaps most, idioms are products of our conceptual system and not simply a matter of language (i.e., a matter of the lexicon). An idiom is not just an expression that has a meaning that is somehow special in relation to the meanings of its constituting parts, but it arises from our more general knowledge of the world embodied in our conceptual system. In other words, idioms (or, at least, the majority of them) are conceptual, and not linguistic, in nature. (Kövecses, 2002, p. 201) | We could simply tell students that bouncing an idea off someone means to get a person's feedback. But students will have a deeper grasp of the meaning, and the idiom will be much more memorable if we inform them that this and numerous other idioms can be explained via the same basic metaphor: Ideas Are Balls. (King, 1999, p. xii) |
| Idioms are never just the neutral alternatives to literal, transparent, semantically equivalent expression. Idioms always comment on the world in some way, rather than simply describe it. They are evaluative and frequently involve potential threats to face.<br><br>Idioms are communal tokens that enable speakers to express cultural and social solidarity. (McCarthy, 1998, p. 145) | You will see and hear idioms in all sorts of speaking and writing. They are particularly common in everyday conversation and in popular journalism. For example, they are often found in magazine horoscopes. . . . However, idioms are also used in more formal contexts, such as lectures, academic essays, and business reports. (O'Dell & McCarthy, 2010, p. 8) |

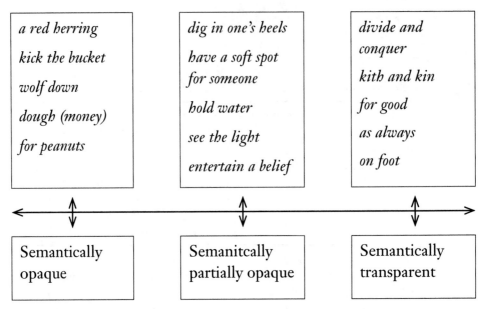

| a red herring<br>kick the bucket<br>wolf down<br>dough (money)<br>for peanuts | dig in one's heels<br>have a soft spot<br>for someone<br>hold water<br>see the light<br>entertain a belief | divide and<br>conquer<br>kith and kin<br>for good<br>as always<br>on foot |
| --- | --- | --- |
| Semantically<br>opaque | Semanitcally<br>partially opaque | Semantically<br>transparent |

*Figure 2-3. Spectrum of Idioms as Noncompositional (Opaque) Phrases*

oms in which the entire meaning is noncompositional, and students will have a very difficult time inferring their meanings in comparison to the meanings of "partially opaque" idioms in which only one term can be considered noncompositional. Further, under "semantically transparent," we include mostly stable collocations that are included in Moon's (1998) category of literal idioms, and we include phrasal verbs throughout Figures 2-2 and 2-3.[3]

Thus, for teachers asking, "Is there a pedagogically sound definition of idioms or do the 'fuzzy' definitions of idioms make teaching idioms impossible?," we "beat around the bush" and answer "yes and no," and we do not adopt one definition of idioms in the following chapters. There is clearly no one definition that we can point to that will work in all contexts, but idioms or terms and phrases that we can call idioms, based on a combination of definitions, clearly exist as a category of

---

[3] We typically address phrasal verbs in connection to learning idioms in our classroom (as we do in the following chapters), but some teachers and many textbooks prefer to treat phrasal verbs as separate categories, as discussed above. We argue that many of the activities and topics that we discuss in the following chapters can be adapted for teaching phrasal verbs as well as other types of idioms described here, but there are certainly many sources that can provide a much more in-depth treatment of phrasal verbs than we have space for in this book.

language that is instructive for students, and teachers should draw students' attention to the aspects of a definition of idioms that will make the most sense to learners and motivate them to learn and use idioms. If this definition includes phrasal verbs and literal expressions as well as "true" idioms, teachers should feel empowered to explain idioms and idiomatic language in whatever way opens students' eyes to the importance of this aspect of vocabulary learning. As many scholars and teachers note, it is through the use of idioms that students will sound more fluent in both their spoken and written English, and without knowledge of idioms, much of the creativity and beauty of English will be missing from student comprehension of everything from a conversation with a peer to the enjoyment of a film. Moreover, teachers need to disprove the often-thought student idea that all idioms are informal and not to be used in academic writing. For example, *according to* and *at first glance* are idioms often employed in scholarly writing, to be sure.

Some teachers may argue that the lack of a consistent definition of idioms makes them impossible to classify and organize for students, thus we should not address them as a pedagogical topic in language classrooms. However, in addition to the value of idioms as an integral part of language fluency, students already notice idioms, ask questions about idioms, and use and misuse them. In fact, it is often when a student asks us about a particular idiom that we begin to investigate how we can address idioms in our classrooms. Ruhl (1989) even argues that idioms do not exist for fluent speakers (what he calls *mature native speakers*) because once you are fluent in a language, you do not notice idioms as different from any other terms and phrases in the language, and it is only language learners who experience and learn idioms. Liu (2008) calls this idea controversial because there are idioms in a variety of English dialects that any native speaker would not understand; regardless, we argue that this is exactly the way to view idioms and how to go about defining them for students. In other words, we must continually ask ourselves questions about how students view the language they are learning and what definitions and explanations work the best from their perspectives.

# CHAPTER 3

# How Are Idioms Acquired? On the Brain and Idiom Acquisition

> Your life changes when you have a
> working knowledge of your brain.
> —*John J. Ratey*

Would teaching methods change if English language instructors had a better understanding of the different definitions of idioms as outlined in the previous chapter? Would teaching methods change if English language instructors had better insights into how the brain works? We think they would, and we think that such knowledge matters, not only for teaching idioms, but for the general instruction of vocabulary and all language skills. With that in mind, this chapter takes a look at one of the most incredible miracles known to us—the wondrous and ever-developing human brain! We begin by reviewing parts of the brain that function in language use and memory. Next, we summarize theories and models on how the brain processes and stores figurative vocabulary such as idioms, and we offer insights into research on key aspects of what the brain needs to function well. We end the chapter with key points on how all of this new information about the brain can inform our teaching of idioms.

But first a caveat on the limitlessness and limitedness of research into the brain and how it processes and stores new vocabulary; the *Tao*

*Te Ching* rightly claims, "The more you know the less you understand." This notion is amplified regarding the inner worlds and complicated webbing of the brain. There have been a myriad of fantastic discoveries in the past two decades alone that have shed light on certain areas of the brain, and these have played a significant role in learning and memory. However, there is still limitless room for a deeper and better understanding of how the brain learns in the manner it does and how it retains old and new information.

It seems our desire to jump on the science bandwagon and oversimplify the functions of the various parts of the brain has kept us from learning more about it (Eagleman, 2011; Iacoboni, 2009). For example, in the field of educational theory, Howard Gardner's (1983) theory of nine multiple intelligences has influenced many teachers, including us, but new research in neuroscience argues that there could be as many as seven billion different types of intelligences, one unique to each human being (Medina, 2009). In this sense, Sigmund Freud's insights into the id, ego, superego, and the idea of consciousness, unconsciousness, and subconsciousness ring true to what modern neuroscientists are discovering—the brain is a highly complex universe of unbelievable intricacies, each part having an astounding ability to help us think, feel, reflect, judge, intuit, learn, and remember countless facts, figures, songs, events, and life-enhancing skills, and we should be careful not to limit any students by thinking of them—and the way their brains are processing information in our classes—in simply one way.

Everyone from scientists to language instructors, therefore, is limited in their knowledge of the workings of the brain, and any findings and interpretations of those findings must be qualified. Similarly, this chapter does not attempt to offer a new paradigm for how the brain works or how we learn and use languages. It does, however, offer a view of what we currently know about the brain according to recent research and how that information can help teachers become better aware of how to help students learn and retain new language such as idioms. Also of importance, we refrain from employing the frequently overused computer analogy for the brain. Such a limited device pales in comparison to the infinite depths of the brain. A far better analogy for the brain would be the universe itself, for it is simply mindboggling to think that the average adult brain has 100 billion (100,000,000,000) **neurons,** and the average neuron can create up to 10,000 connections with other neurons. If we do the math, we can calculate that "there are as many connections in a single cubic centimeter of brain tissue as there are stars in the Milky Way galaxy" (Eagleman, 2011, p. 2). Moreover, what also makes the brain so fascinating, according to neuroplastician Michael Merzenich, is that "the cerebral cortex is actually selectively refining its processing capacities to fit each task at hand" (as cited in Doidge, 2007, p. 47); that is to say, it is perpetually "learning how to learn" (p. 47). The brain, claims Merzenich, is not like a computer—far from it—it is like a living organism capable of changing its own wiring, growing more neurons, and building better connections for learning and memory.

To summarize, the brain is not a limited creature, but rather an unlimited one far more superior than we once thought (Doidge, 2007), and in the following sections, we hope to shed some light on just how complex and limitless the brain is. But before moving on to look at how the brain learns idioms and picks up a language, a review of the brain's parts is needed in order to illuminate recent research findings and classroom applications.

## Key Parts of the Brain That All Teachers Should Know a Little Bit About

### The Brain Stem

The brain stem is the lowest physical part of the brain, and it is the oldest. This is sometimes called the "lizard brain" or the "reptilian brain." The neurons in this part of the brain help control vital functions such as digestion, heart rate, breathing, body temperature, and sleeping and waking states.

### The Cerebellum

The cerebellum is just below the back part of the cerebrum and directly behind the brain stem. This area is concerned with motor control, posture, balance, and the memory of routine or automated movements such as typing on a keyboard or tying a necktie (Sousa, 2011). Some claim that this region may be the most complex region of the brain, with 40 million nerve fibers (Jensen, 2008). Moreover, the circuits from this region highly influence the rest of the brain, including memory, attention, and spatial perception (Middleton & Strick,

1994). Unfortunately, for too long a time, this area was overlooked, but recently recognition of its importance has grown. Neuroscientists believe that it also supports cognitive processes by working with the senses, emotions, memories, and thoughts (Sousa, 2011). And what makes this area so powerful is that these skills can be done automatically, thus requiring no conscious effort and demanding only small amounts of energy.

## The Limbic System

The limbic system is an area of several functionally and structurally connected structures that are located in the telencephalon and diencephalon regions of the brain. The members of this system include the thalamus, the hypothalamus, the **hippocampus**, and the **amygdala**—constituting a fab four in terms of learning and memory. The thalamus receives almost all the incoming sensory information and then redirects it to the various other parts of the brain. It works tirelessly with both the cerebrum and the cerebellum. The thalamus is highly involved in the brain's cognitive activities, how the senses get processed, and how that information gets redistributed. See Appendix E for diagram of amygdala and hippocampus.

The hypothalamus is the great monitor of the body's internal systems, making sure that the body temperature and other systems, including nutrition intake and sleep, are working smoothly. If any of the systems that the hypothalamus is in charge of do not function correctly, learning and memory will suffer.

The hippocampus is a critical player in memory formation and is located at the base of the limbic region. One of its main functions is to convert short-term information from working memory to long-term memory and life-long learning. This process of consolidation can take days, months, or even years (Medina, 2009). If it is our memory that makes us human, then the hippocampus is a crucial component in making us human. Its influence on learning and creating meaning is remarkable. Another vital element of the hippocampus is its ability to generate new neurons, which has a significant impact on learning and memory processes (Balu & Lucki, 2009). The production of new neurons—called neurogenesis—is paramount in learning and memory formation. One way to facilitate this is through exercise, which we discuss later in this chapter.

The last of the fab four is the amygdala. This is connected to the end of the hippocampus. The amygdala is almost mature at birth, which goes to show how important it is in the overall functioning of the brain. The main job of the amygdala is to create and maintain human emotions—both positive and negative. The amygdala is also responsible for releasing **neurotransmitters** like dopamine—a great help in memory formation and learning. It is currently unknown whether emotional memories are stored in the amygdala, but more research is being done on that even as you are reading this. There is one theory that emotional memories are stored exclusively in the amygdala, and nonemotional memories are stored in other locations (Squire & Kandel, 1999). As we will see later, emotion is a key element in acquiring new information. So the amygdala, in helping to both form emotional experiences and maintain our memories, seems to be a vital component in the learning process.

## The Cerebrum

The cerebrum is the last major part we would like to focus on here. This is the section most people are acquainted with as it houses the four areas referred to as the lobes. The cerebrum's left and right hemispheres are covered by the cortex, which is quite astonishing in its own right. The cortex is the ultimate stage in the brain's evolution and what many argue is the part which separates us from other species (Horstman, 2009). The cortex controls our imagination, thoughts, reasoning, and, most important, language capabilities. The cortex has around six different layers of neurons connected in about 10,000 miles of connected fibers per cubic inch (Sousa, 2011). What's more is that it makes up roughly 70% of our nervous system, and the neurons that run through its whole system constitute one million miles of nerve fibers (Jensen, 2008). Now you are beginning to see why we want to compare the brain to the universe and not a finite limited toy like a computer!

The four well-known lobes of the cerebrum are the frontal, parietal, temporal, and occipital. The frontal lobe is responsible for speech, creativity, self-will, planning, problem solving, and judgment, and it is the home of working memory. Unfortunately, this area matures rather slowly; in fact, in most men it isn't fully developed until after they have turned 22. The parietal lobe is responsible for movement, touch, taste, temperature, calculation, various types of recognition, and language functions. The temporal lobe detects sound, hearing, music, and face recognition, and it is responsible for some long-term memory and speech centers (on the left side of the brain). The occipital lobe houses our center for vision, that crucial sense used so hungrily by the brain in memory and learning. See Appendix E for diagram of lobes.

## Neurons and Glial Cells

All of the above parts of the brain are vital for learning, and yet the most important parts are the tiniest—the neurons and the glial cells that underlie all functions in the brain. It is hard to state precisely, but neuroscientists estimate that the brain has over 100 billion neurons that pump electricity through it at an astonishing 250 miles per hour (Medina, 2009), helping us learn new and exciting things every hour. Supporting these neurons are glial cells. When a human child is born, its brain has up to one thousand billion glial cells—"one hundred times the number of known stars in the Milky Way" (Jensen, 2008, p. 12). Glial cells help in producing myelin for the axons of our neurons (which help the neurons communicate information smoothly and quickly), they assist in transferring nutrients, and they also help in regulating the immune system. In the past, like so many other parts of the brain, glial cells were overlooked and not held in as high regard as neurons. That is currently changing, as Jensen (2008) notes: "Today, we know that they are equal to neurons in their capacity, function, and importance" (p. 12).

The neuron cannot be seen with the naked eye; in fact, the body of a neuron is about one hundredth the size of a period mark. But what it lacks in size, it makes up in number and power; for without the neuron, learning would never happen and the wondrous multifunctions of the brain would not communicate with each other. It is the neuron which is the processing entity for the brain and the nervous system. In addition to having over 100 billion neurons in our brain—which means "a single cubic millimeter of brain tissue has over one million neurons" (Jensen, 2008, p. 13)—each tiny neuron can have as many as 10,000 dendrite branches (the branch-like extensions that receive input). In essence, this means that our brains can "have up to one quadrillion synaptic connections" (Sousa, 2011, p. 22). And the number of neurons and connections isn't the only mind-blowing feature about neurons; the speed with which they register and transmit impulses is astonishing—between 250 and 2,500 impulses per second at a phenomenal 250 miles per hour.

It is the miracle of the neuron and its vast web of connections which allow us to process great amounts of information that bombard our senses each minute, and it is the neuron and its vast web of connections that allow us to store volumes upon volumes of memories and knowledge and to learn that beautiful thing we call language!

## Mirror Neurons

Before moving on to memory and looking at how the brain learns, we think it is significant to draw attention to a specific kind of neuron first discovered some twenty years ago in Parma, Italy, in Giacomo Rizzolatti's lab. It was there that **mirror neurons** were first observed and later studied. This particular kind of neuron seems to be a key element in language acquisition and in learning in general. Let us turn, then, to the world of mirror neurons.

One day, in Rizzolatti's lab, the scientists were on break from examining the motor neural activity of a monkey. Gallase, one of Rizzolatti's valued researchers, stepped back into the lab and reached for a snack in a dish. At that moment, according to the computer screen, the neurons in the monkey's premotor cortex fired with considerable excitement. The readout on the screen shocked the researcher because the monkey was only sitting in her seat, hooked up to the electrodes. She was not doing any physical activity. She was merely watching the scientist's actions. From this the question arose: Are there certain neurons that fire at the mere sight of another individual performing an action? The answer was yes! These mirror neurons fire in the brain of the observer as if the observer were actually performing the said action. For example, when you watch a football game on TV, and you see Adrian Peterson score a touchdown, the mirror neurons in your brain are firing as if you were actually running and scoring the touchdown.

That is, these neurons are activated when you see someone kick a ball, hear someone kick it, or just hear the actual word *kick* (Iacoboni, 2009). According to Iacoboni, "When you see me perform an action—such as picking up a baseball—you automatically simulate the action in your own brain" (as cited in Blakeslee, 2006, para. 18). As one can easily imagine, the activation of these neurons has intriguing consequences in the classroom and even deeper ramifications for the teaching and learning of English idioms, especially those idioms which are easily visualized or have visceral implications.

We hereby use the term *mirror neurons* to define the general category of brain cells that fire at the sight of watching someone make a gesture with meaning, make a facial expression, or perform some kind of action. According to Rizzolatti and his colleagues, there are four distinct subcategories of mirror neurons: (1) strictly congruent, (2) broadly congruent, (3) logically related, and (4) audiovisual. We would like to include a fifth category: word-elicited mirror neurons (Randolph, 2013c).

Rizzolatti and Craighero (2004) discovered that *strictly congruent* mirror neurons have a very specific function in that they bring together both action and perception. A decade before, most neuroscientists claimed that perception, action, and cognition were, for the most part, separate from each other. With the discovery of these kinds of mirror neurons, we now know that perception and action work together. These neurons fire and code experiences in the neural network. As action and perception are stored in the memory, we can now add cognition to this process. In short, all three facilities, once thought to be autonomous, actually work in unison. What makes the strictly congruent mirror neurons so interesting is that they fire when an agent performs a specific action and also when the agent perceives another performing the same specific action. Moreover, these neurons will fire if someone watches another complete a precision grasp with just the fingers or with a whole-hand grasp (Iacoboni, 2009). For instance, they fire if one person watches another person pick up a teacup by the handle with his fingers or if another person picks up a whole apple.

*Broadly congruent* mirror neurons are broad in the sense that they fire when observing any number of actions related to a specific goal. There is no sense of a strict correlation of actions like the aforementioned subset. For example, broadly congruent mirror neurons will fire when one is holding a pencil and begins to write and when one sees someone giving her friend a pencil to write with. They share a goal, and the neurons react to this. These neurons consequently fire "at the sight of an action that is not necessarily identical to the executed action but achieves a similar goal" (Iacoboni, 2009, p. 25).

*Logically related* mirror neurons seem to be more advanced than their neural siblings in that they react to the observed intention in question. These neurons require the agent to have had certain experiences so that the neurons can relate to the patterns and sequences at a high cognitive or logical level. One could argue that broadly congruent mirror neurons also work off of the same underpinnings; that is, the goal is the key factor. However, that is not exactly the case. Logically related mirror neurons fire rapidly for specific scenes of preparation or logically related events. For instance, they fire at the mere sight of a pencil being placed on a desk. The logical implication of this is that ultimately the pencil will be used for writing. So these types of neurons fire at the expectation of what will come. In this sense, we could also call them *harbinger* mirror neurons.

*Audiovisual* mirror neurons fire at not only the observation of actions but also the sound of actions. They fire equally as intensely when the action is only heard and not seen (Kohler et al., 2002). So let's say a student closes his eyes and hears the teacher take out a book from her book bag by unzipping the bag. She then places it on the table in front of the class. All during this process, the student's audiovisual mirror neurons are firing as if the student himself were doing the actions; this is all based on hearing and not seeing the action. It is fascinating to know that these neurons respond to sounds and transfer them to a corresponding action. The brain's mirror neuron network is, in essence, going through the motions of sight and sound by merely being aware of particular perceptions.

We call the final set of mirror neurons (that we are aware of) *word-elicited* mirror neurons (Randolph, 2013c). These neurons fire when we simply hear, read, or say words. Perhaps that is why visually based idioms are so predominant in languages; they create visual representations in our mind and elicit mental participation on the part of the agent involved. One study conducted by Lisa Aziz-Zadeh "suggests that when we read a novel, our mirror neurons simulate the actions described in the novel, as if we were doing those actions ourselves" (Iacoboni, 2009, pp. 94–95). This means, then, that reading and using idioms stimulate this set of mirror neurons and that, in turn, simulates and reinforces the learning of idioms, especially if they elicit visual or emotive-based images, as in *bark up the wrong tree* or *cat got your tongue*. The more we activate these neurons, the more we reinforce deeper neural connections and transfer information to long-term memory.

Mirror neurons seem to be very prevalent in Broca's area—the crucial area for language. Various brain-imaging experiments have continually shown that Broca's area is significantly stimulated during both the observation and imitation of various actions. This leads us to what so many others have argued: that gestures and actions have played an essential part in human language (Arbib, 2002; Armstrong, Stokoe, & Wilcox, 1995; Corballis, 2002; Hewes, 1973). From this we can further the argument that imitation is a vital element in learning. The well-known child psychologist Jean Piaget claimed that babies "learn" to imitate. However, Andrew Meltzoff's experiments with babies in the 1970s seemed to show a rather different phenomenon; his idea is that babies "learn *by* imitating" (Iacoboni, 2009 p. 48). In a sense, this should come as no surprise, for just think how the average adult imitates a friend or colleague—sometimes unconsciously, sometimes consciously. There is learning or neural connection reinforcement going on in these moments of imitation. Other studies have shown that when we listen to our friends talk, we imitate them with our tongues (Fadiga, Craighero, Buccino, & Rizzolatti, 2002).

Does this mean we learn everything via the fascinating world of mirror neurons? The answer to such a question cannot be attempted currently; however, it will be exciting to see what the research shows us in the coming years. In the meantime, we as teachers need to be aware how we physically conduct ourselves in the classroom, for each student is simultaneously mirroring what we do in their brains. At the same time, it is exciting to know that the more we use gestures to explain idioms, the likelihood of the students learning them will increase substantially due to the influence of their mirror neurons.

But how does the brain retain what we learn? How do these neurons decide what goes into long-term memory? How can we best condition the brain to function at its optimum? These are questions we now turn to.

## Vocabulary Learning: How the Brain Processes and Stores New Information

Moving from the specific parts of the brain to the more general notions of processing and storing new information, the next two sections address research about the models and hypotheses that guide our understanding of how the mirror neurons in the brain process new information—in this case idioms—and how that information is encoded into long-term memory in the hippocampus and other regions of the brain. As with our earlier caveats, we are not attempting to summarize all research in language processing and memory as it relates to our knowledge of the brain, nor are we attempting to advocate for one model or explanation for how mirror neurons receive, store, and retrieve new information such as idioms. Our purpose here is to provide some insights into research on the brain processing and storing new vocabulary that will be most useful for teaching new vocabulary and idioms.

### The Great Debate: Literal Versus Figurative Processing of Idioms

One of the central questions in both first (L1) and second language (L2) idiom acquisition research has been which meaning of an idiom—literal or figurative—is retrieved first by the brain or whether the two meanings are processed at the same time. Much of this work has focused on L1 idiom comprehension, and according to Pimenova (2011), the work falls into two broad categories that can be labeled as hypotheses—such as the idiom list hypothesis (Bobrow & Bell, 1973) or the direct access hypothesis (Gibbs, 1980; Schweigert, 1986)—or models—such as the configuration model (Cacciari & Glucksberg, 1991; Cacciari & Tabossi, 1988) or the phrase-induced polysemy model (McGlone, Glucksberg, & Cacciari, 1994). We first summarize a few of the models and hypotheses that are most relevant to L2 English idioms learning. We then offer more recent work illustrating the limitations of these models in understanding how L2 learners process idioms and what this means for teaching idioms in our classrooms. See Cacciari and Tabossi (1988, 1993), Cieślicka (2006), or T. C. Cooper (1999) for more extended summaries of important L1 and L2 idiom processing models and hypotheses.

One of the first theories that attempted to describe how L1 speakers process idioms was the *idiom-list hypothesis* (Bobrow & Bell, 1973), which states that a native speaker first interprets an idiom literally. Once the speaker has identified this meaning as incorrect, the figurative meaning of the idiom is chosen from a different mental lexicon. As T. C. Cooper (1999) and others have pointed out, this model and others based in generative linguistic theory—models Cieślicka (2006) calls *standard pragmatic models*—have been rejected in many later studies in which participants in their L1 have processed the figurative meanings of idioms just as quickly as the literal ones and appear to have direct access to the figurative meanings of idioms (see Glucksberg, 1993). As we illustrated in our discussion of the parts of the brain, there is clearly much more overlap in how we process information than we previously thought, but one value of these early models was to draw attention to the interplay of literal and figurative processes in the brain.

Two models that came after the idiom-list hypothesis but still focused on the interaction of literal and figurative processing were the *idiom decomposition model* (Gibbs & Nayak, 1989; Gibbs, Nayak, & Cutting, 1989) and the *configuration model* (Cacciari & Glucksberg, 1991; Cacciari & Tabossi, 1988). The idiom decomposition model argues that speakers need less time to process idioms that are more decomposable—that is, as described in Chapter 2, idioms in which the literal and figurative meaning are close, such as *pop the question*, will be more quickly processed in a speaker's mind than idioms in which the literal and figurative meanings are not very close, such as *a red herring*. This model was not comprehensive as a processing model, but through multiple experiments, Raymond Gibbs and his colleagues were able to illustrate the importance of decompositionality and how much longer it takes the brain to process idioms that are not easily decompositional, an important feature of idiom processing that can have direct effects for English language learners.

Attempting for the first time to view the roles of literal and figurative meanings of idioms as connected and occurring at similar times, the configuration model argues that the literal meaning and figurative meanings are both available in a speaker's lexicon as the idiom is encountered, but the literal meaning is discarded as soon as the brain recognizes that the idiomatic meaning is necessary for comprehension.

Connecting with the idiom decomposition model, this model points out that some idiom phrases trigger the idiomatic meaning earlier than others.

A final hypothesis based on L1 processing of idioms that is relevant to L2 idiom learning is the *graded salience hypothesis* (Giora, 2003). Instead of focusing on literal versus figurative meaning processing, this hypothesis contends that salient meanings—defined as those which "enjoy prominence due to their conventionality, frequency, familiarity, or prototypicality" (Giora, 2003, p. 490)—will be more quickly and directly processed by the brain. For example, an idiom whose figurative meaning is more familiar to speakers and is used more often than its literal meaning will more likely be processed by listeners as figurative, even in a context that biases the literal meaning. For example, Giora (2003) offers the anecdote of a couple living in England, and the wife is always complaining about the cold weather. One evening, the wife complains about how she has such cold feet. Despite the fact that the literal interpretation is heavily biased, her husband first processes the phrase as the idiom *to get cold feet* and begins to make a joke by asking his wife what she is so nervous about. Alternatively, less familiar and less salient idioms, perhaps a phrase such as *bite the bullet*, will be processed literally first before the idiomatic meaning is activated. This model is thus a hybrid approach combining aspects of the idiom decomposition model and the configuration model.

In addition to the inherent limitations of all of the above models and hypotheses for explaining L1 idiom processing, notions such as decompositionality, salience, and familiarity are even more difficult to define and judge in the language ability and processing of L2 learners. To start, as Irujo (1986) has shown, second and multiple language learners will be influenced by their knowledge of the idioms in their first languages when processing English idioms. In her influential study, Irujo showed that English idioms identical to the Spanish idioms that participants knew from their L1 were easiest to comprehend and produce, revealing an extra dimension when determining which idioms would be most difficult for learners.

In reviewing the above studies, we continue to examine which idioms will be the most difficult for students: Will it be the least decomposable idioms, the least salient idioms, or the idioms most different from the learners' L1?

At least two models of L2 idioms processing have attempted to help teachers understand what is happening when students learn new idioms in a second or multiple language and are worth reviewing here: the model of dual L2 idiom representation and the literal-salience resonant model. In the *model of dual L2 idiom representation*, Abel (2003) argues that nondecomposable idioms require an idiom entry in L1 and L2 mental lexicons, but decomposable idioms can be represented as their constituent parts; the more frequently occurring idioms gain their own representation. In this way, the model draws on the graded salience hypothesis in focusing on the roles of familiarity and salience in idiom processing. Abel argues that "because nonnative speakers encounter idioms less often than native speakers, the first language and second language lexicon vary with regard to the number of idiom entries" (p. 329). Returning to the argument first made by the idiom-list hypothesis, Cieślicka (2006) argues that native speakers may process idioms figuratively and have a separate figurative meaning encoded in their mental lexicons, but L2 processing of idioms is fundamentally different, and her *literal-salience resonant model* posits that

> Since L2 learners who undergo formal L2 instruction most typically encounter new L2 idiomatic expressions when they are already familiar with literal meanings of words making up those idiomatic phrases, it is these literal meanings that are likely to be much better established in their mental lexicons than the newly acquired figurative ones. (p. 121)

Thus, the model argues that, even when a learner is highly proficient and the idioms have been automatized, the literal meanings "will continue to enjoy a more salient status than their figurative meanings, irrespective of whether an L2 idiom is highly familiar or less familiar to the L2 user" (Cieślicka, 2006, p. 121).

By debating the importance of the literal versus figurative meanings in the way idioms are processed by language learners, the models surveyed above reinforce for teachers that the brain is constantly functioning on multiple levels and, as teachers, we need to present information, especially new idioms, in ways that activate both literal and figurative connections in students' brains, showing as much as telling students the meanings of new idioms. Clearly, as with much of how the brain's neurons and various parts function, there is still much to learn about how our brains process idioms in our L1 and L2, but these studies, models, and hypotheses are important for teachers because even inconclusive results and hypotheses can be used as guides and reference points for how we present idioms and what idioms students will have the most difficulty encoding, remembering, and recalling.

## Memory: The Ebbinghaus Curse

Moving from how language users process and recognize idioms in their first, second, and additional languages, we now turn to how these idioms are encoded and stored in our memories. It is every educator's goal to somehow do nothing more than to break the foreboding and ever daunting *Ebbinghaus curse*.[1] Hermann Ebbinghaus (1885/1913), the great 19th century German researcher, showed us that students forget up to 90% of what they learn within a mere 30 days after the initial encoding. The even more surprising fact is that most of that forgetting happens just hours after the material is first learned. Although recent studies have modified and updated Ebbinghaus's findings (e.g., Sousa, 2011), the majority of them are still true today (Medina, 2009). If students forget such an unprecedented amount of information, how can we get them to remember all things equally? And for this, there is no easy answer. There are, however, a number of ways that can help students better encode, store, and retrieve information and ultimately transfer more learned material from their short-term to long-term memories. Before we discuss how to better help develop students' ability to remember what they learn, let's look at the stages and the basic types of memory.

Memory is perhaps the most important tool that our brains have developed, for without it, we would have perished long, long ago in our nomadic hunter-gatherer societies. Without memory, we simply would not have survived as long as we have. Without memory, we would not know who we are, nor would we know what we are capable of doing, thinking, or creating. Memory, simply put, is what makes us who we are.

The whole network of memory and how it functions is, as we stated at the beginning of this chapter, like the brain itself—far more

---

[1] This is a term coined by coauthor Randolph.

complex and intricate than the once parsimonious views held. Memories, we are learning, are "dynamic and not fixed" (Jensen, 2008, p. 155). The analogies of a filing cabinet, library, or computer have been tossed out. Our brains do not remember things in a simplistic, ordered, compartmentalized, linear fashion. According to recent neuroscience research, there are numerous locations in the brain devoted to memory (Jensen, 2008; Sousa, 2011). For example, the amygdala (it is thought) stores emotional memories; the hippocampus is crucially responsible for long-term memory; the temporal lobe engages in long-term semantic memory; the parietal lobe works with short-term memory along with the prefrontal cortex in the frontal lobe; and, as the Chinese have believed for hundreds of years, scientists are now compiling data that "suggests memories may be stored in peptide molecules that circulate throughout the entire body via the bloodstream" (Jensen, 2008, p. 157). Yes, memories literally seem to be everywhere!

The basic stages of memory, at least the ones we are currently aware of, are the immediate memory, working and short-term memory, and long-term memory. The immediate memory and working and short-term memory are, for the most part, temporary; long-term memory is permanent, but changeable. It is our goal as instructors to transfer significant short-term memories to long-term ones.

There are essentially two major kinds of long-term memory, and each one has its respective subcategories. Declarative or explicit (also referred to sometimes as conscious) memory seems to be processed primarily in the hippocampus and the cerebrum. Declarative memory deals with such things as music, emotions, objects, faces, and factual data. If you recall your favorite teacher's face, voice, manners, the kind of relationship you had, and the year you were in his or her class, then you are using declarative memory. The subcategories of declarative memory are episodic or autobiographical memory and semantic or factual memory. Episodic memory is the memory of the self; it refers to the events in one's own life. It helps you recall getting your first pet, receiving your first romantic phone call, or going on a road trip. It is the kind of memory that makes you who you are. Semantic or factual memory is the memory of words, faces, objects, and facts; it is essentially the memory of all facts related to oneself. Flashbulb memories (Willis, 2006) can also be categorized under declarative memory. These are memories that are tied to a specific event and what you were doing when that specific event occurred. For example, where were you when Pope Francis was voted in or when you first heard the news about the 9/11 attacks? Relational memory (Willis, 2006) is also a kind of declarative memory. This is a type of memory that ties old and new information together; it takes the newly remembered information and adds it to what is already in the memory or what has already been mastered.

Nondeclarative memory, also known as nonconscious or implicit memory, is the other important kind of long-term memory. These are unconscious types of memories; for example, remembering how to play tennis or drive a car are nondeclarative memories. The major subcategory of nondeclarative memories is procedural memory. These memories relate to the acquisition of cognitive or motor skills and how to perform them. The more they are practiced, the more natural they become and thus develop into almost unconscious actions or thoughts; language, for example, is one of these.

How, then, are these long-term memories formed? They require three steps: **encoding**, **storage**, and **retrieval**. There is a fourth step involved—forgetting—but we are not interested in that one. Encoding, storage, and retrieval are at the heart of how we can help students perform to their potential and master the world of idioms. Encoding is the period of initial learning. It is the moment the new information is first embraced by the vast network of neurons, and two theories from psychology that have been taken up by cognitive linguistics—levels of processing theory and dual-coding theory—illustrate aspects of effective activities for successful encoding of new information in the brain.

Craik and Lockhart (1972) first proposed levels of processing theory as a framework to explain how processing quality and/or processing efforts affect memory. In short, the theory argues that the depth of processing that is undertaken when learning new information will have differential effects on short- and long-term memory. Specifically, deeper levels of processing refer to activities in which meaning, implication, or inference are required to process the new information. More shallow levels of processing refer to activities that engage in surface details such as color, brightness, or form. For example, Kane and Anderson (1978) reveal that participants who were required to generate the last word of a sentence in order to complete the sentence remembered more of the information in a text than those who read the text already completed. In other words, long-term memory is enhanced when learning new information if the learner has to work harder when presented with the information. Research on brain imaging has even revealed that there is a higher level of neuron activity when the brain is working at a deeper level when learning new information (Kapur et al., 1994), offering further evidence in support of the levels of processing theory and the need for teachers to present new vocabulary in complex and cognitively challenging ways for learners.

Similar to levels of processing theory, dual-coding theory (Clark & Paivio, 1991; Paivio, 1986) is an information processing model. Its main idea is that the formation of mental images aids in learning and memory. Dual-coding theory postulates that both visual and verbal information is used to represent information, creating separate representations for information processed in each channel, and both visual and verbal codes can be used when recalling information. For example, if someone has stored the concept *ball* as both the word and image, when the word comes up in a text or conversation, the person can retrieve either the word or the image or both at the same time. This ability to encode the term in two different ways increases the person's ability to remember the word than if it were only encoded in one way. In terms of encoding and recalling new idioms, these theories challenge teachers to present new idioms in ways that require students to think deeply about the new words in both verbal and visual ways, in other words, to activate more neurons. We discuss this further in Chapter 4.

It is clear that what helps encoding run smoothly is the involvement of all of our senses, and it is our senses that help create solid memories to be transferred to the storage, where they are kept until we need to retrieve them at a later time. As Medina (2009) notes, "The more elaborately we encode information at the moment of learning, the stronger the memory" (p. 110). Encoding, for teachers, is really the most important part of our relationship to that moment we impart a skill, concept, or question to students. How we do that will determine whether the neurons will fire and start a new memory in students' brains. Encoding is the magical moment that a new idea or piece of knowledge either is born and develops or dies in the 100 billion neural network of learners' minds.

## What the Brain Needs to Function:
## The Roles of Stress, Sleep, and Exercise

### Stress

In order for the brain to be at its best, we first need to make sure that its stress levels are low and that it has had enough sleep. Granted, a small amount of stress is healthy for the brain before learning, taking quizzes, going on a date, or participating in a sports competition. Chronic stress, however, that hazardous kind, can actually kill existing brain cells and keep new ones from developing (Medina, 2009; Sapolsky, 2004).

What's particularly troubling is the fact that stress hormones like to attack the cells in the hippocampus. Why this is the case is still unknown. Neurobiologists are at a loss as to the reason behind this hippocampal invasion. Why this is troubling is simple: The hippocampus is highly involved in neurogenesis, learning, and memory formation. In addition, stress is also related to low serotonin levels (Casolini et al., 1993). So if their stress levels are high, students won't be able to experience the joy of learning idioms, nor will they be able to encode the idioms and transfer them to long-term memory.

### Sleep

Sleep is fundamentally involved with learning, and sleep deprivation is a great way to keep the brain from functioning normally and from learning anything. Moreover, the less sleep we get, the more the mind and body suffer. This is obvious to anyone who has driven across northern Utah. There are signs posted that rightly claim that driving while experiencing sleep loss is equated to driving while intoxicated, and these lifesaving signs encourage sleep-deprived drivers to pull over and rest awhile.

Why is sleep loss so critical? There are a number of issues at stake, but the central one is that it inhibits the process of extracting energy from glucose, one of the brain's necessary ingredients to function at full force. Sleep loss also damages attention, memory, critical thinking, judgment processes, and, in the case of driving, motor skills.

Another factor that comes into play is that if one does not get a sufficient amount of sleep, then that sleep debt can easily carry over into the following week (Medina, 2009), so students must get that well-needed vacation of rest and beauty sleep if they wish to perform at an optimum level in school.

## Exercise

Assuming that the brain is well rested and running on a comfortable level of stress, what is the next most important thing required for it to be at a heightened level of attentiveness, ready to learn anything we throw its way? The answer is the phenomenon that is at the core of our evolutionary history—exercise! You have heard and perhaps adhere to the idiomatic expression *I think better on my feet*. This idiom is actually grounded in fact and is seen throughout human history. Take, for example, the ancient Greek proverb "A sound mind in a sound body." This is echoed in Plato's (360 BCE/1985) *Republic* time and time again: "If we bring men of sound body and mind to undergo so rigorous a training and to undertake such difficult studies, justice itself will find no fault with us" (pp. 229–230). Soon after this passage he writes, "Moreover, athletic prowess will any case be one of the tests they must pass, and by no means the least" (p. 230). Hippocrates (380 BCE/1931) also included exercise at the core of his philosophy: "Eating alone will not keep a man well; he must also take exercise. For food and exercise, while possessing opposite qualities, yet work together to produce health" (p. 229).

This idea of exercise being at the core of our mental and physical health makes complete sense. Our history on this planet evolved as we walked the forests, coasts, and deserts of the earth, hunting and gathering, moving from place to place to survive. Our brains did not evolve by sitting behind the new brain-numbing device of the 21st century—the computer! As John J. Ratey (2008), a professor of psychiatry at Harvard Medical School, explains, "Learning and memory evolved in concert with the motor functions that allowed our ancestors to track down food, so as far as our brains are concerned, if we're not moving, there's no real need to learn anything" (p. 53).

How often have you had a block in thinking while you were trying to write something? How often have you gotten up from your desk, walked around, and magically solved the problem after a stroll around the house, block, or a local park? Here is what is going on: When we walk, our cerebellum, the motor cortex in our cerebrum, and our midbrain are all working together to help us walk smoothly. But what they are also doing is coordinating and stimulating thoughts and ideas by setting off neurons to fire and connect thoughts and ideas throughout their amazing universe of neural webbing (Sousa, 2011). It makes perfect sense, then, that walking helps us think—it has been doing this for tens of thousands of years. It has made us who we are.

Neurobiologist John Medina (2009) claims that "physical activity is cognitive candy" (p. 22). And Ratey (2008) argues that "the point of exercise is to build and condition the brain" (p. 3); what it does for other parts of the body, he claims, are only considered to be side effects. Ratey goes on to show in his book *Spark! How Exercise Will Improve the Performance of Your Brain* that "physical activity is crucial to the way we think and feel" (p. 4). Eric Jensen (2008) insightfully points out that a good physical workout uses 100% of the brain and helps create new brain cells. Such developments in the brain under the assistance of physical activity are mindboggling, and not one class in the academic world can lay such a claim to neural development as physical exercise can (see also Pereira et al., 2007).

The brain, as we have come to understand it, works 24/7; even when we sleep it is working away, developing ideas, solving problems, and embarking on new challenges. As a result, it is in constant need of energy. It is almost incomprehensible to think that our three-pound thinking muscle is a mere 2% of our body's weight but burns about 20% of our body's total energy reserve.

Two great sources of brain fuel are glucose and oxygen. Foods with natural sugars, like fruits or grains, are a wonderful source of glucose. Moreover, glucose helps in focusing the brain's attention, assists in certain motor functions, and develops long-term memory (Korol & Gold, 1998; Sünram-Lea, Dewhurst, & Foster, 2008). And, of course, oxygen is supplied by exercise—that activity that keeps your brain in picture-perfect condition.

The impact of exercise on the brain seems endless, for it enhances cognitive performance, long-term memory, problem solving, creativity, reasoning, attention, and ultimately learning. But how does this all happen? First, exercise is responsible for the release of neurotransmitters. To date, the neuroscience community has detected approximately 50 different kinds of neurotransmitters. Among these are serotonin, dopamine, and norepinephrine. These three are significantly related to learning. Serotonin helps control brain activity and regulates mood, impulses, and anger. Dopamine regulates movement, learning, attention, and satisfaction. Norepinephrine is also a mood neurotransmitter and regulates attention, arousal, motivation, and perception. As we can see, these three neurotransmitters are paramount in the learning process, and when we exercise, these come flooding into the blood and help the neurons create stronger bonds. Moreover, they balance the brain. If what we learn depends on the firing and wiring of neurons, then we are equally dependent on a balanced brain with the healthy release of these neurotransmitters.

In addition to the release of neurotransmitters, exercise also helps produce neurotrophins; these proteins help build and maintain the circuitry in neurons. One of the most powerful is **brain-derived neurotrophic factor (BDNF)**. This factor gives neurons incredible amounts of nourishment and is one amazing brain fertilizer. Ratey (2008) calls it "Miracle-Gro for the brain" (p. 40). When neuroresearchers put BDNF on neurons in a controlled environment, the neurons sprouted an overwhelming amount of dendrites (Ratey, 2008). Now imagine a whole brain under the magical power of exercise, and just think of how powerful this protein is and how it can help in producing more connections for learning. In fact, BDNF can even activate genes that produce more BDNF and other proteins that create stronger synaptic connections.

Another vastly important aspect of BDNF is that it helps in the process of cell growth called *neurogenesis*. That means the myth perpetuated by the science community for decades which was after a certain age—around 30 or so—the brain stops producing neurons is absolutely false. Thanks to exercise and BDNF, we can continue to produce baby neurons into adulthood and beyond.

The discovery that BDNF is produced and present in the hippocampus is even more exciting because, as mentioned earlier, that is the area related to learning and memory. For instructors, this is truly exciting news and will hopefully inspire more teachers to do more exercise in the classroom. In 2007, German researchers put BDNF to the test and had students exercise and then study vocabulary. The people who exercised learned 20% faster after exercising than before exercising. What's more is that their rate of learning the new vocabulary was matched directly with the amount of BDNF in their systems (Ratey, 2008).

This notion of exercise and its immediate benefits in the classroom is refreshing. What, then, are some ways that we can get students up and moving to help them better acquire language skills, in particular, idioms? Studies in neuroscience have shown that we actually do not need to do much exercise to affect the learning brain in a positive way (Medina, 2009; Ratey, 2008). A very effective way to get students exercising while studying idioms is to pair them up and have them take turns pantomiming or gesturing the idioms: While one gestures, the other guesses the idiom and defines it. For example,

A:   (Gesturing: The student tries to bend over backward and then touches her heart to show emotion.)

B:   Bend over backwards! (To try very hard to help someone.)

A:   Yes, you got it.

This serves three very important purposes: (1) it gets students to exercise and consequently create the optimal learning brain; (2) it puts actions to words, which is a very powerful form of learning (Iacoboni, 2009); and (3) it helps reinforce the learning via the firing of students' mirror neuron system.

Another very simple and effective way to increase oxygen and memory is by doing simple stretches and minimal exercises at the beginning of and during class. An example of a fun and relatively easy in-class exercise can be found at www.youtube.com/watch?v =E65StVJTzVU. Another way to keep students alert is to create an **exercise station** in class (see Randolph, 2013a). Designate a back corner of the classroom as the exercise station. Any student in need of an oxygen boost can simply go to this corner of the room and do stretches or run in place for a few seconds without disrupting class. The student will return from this with a fresh mind ready to absorb idioms like a sponge.

Exercise clearly helps us learn, remember things, and just plain keeps us healthy. It facilitates the production of neurotransmitters to help us focus, attend to learning, and aid in developing a better, sharper, cleaner memory; it helps pull in more oxygen to the brain for fuel, and it creates the all-powerful BDNF, which produces new neurons and helps maintain the existing ones. In addition, it helps BDNF produce new cells in the hippocampus—the great center for learning and memory. Not to mention the fact that exercise makes us feel refreshed and cuts down on stress. In short, exercise is the key for success and the great facilitator of enhanced memory.[2]

## Pedagogical Perspective: R.E.S.T

What, then, is the perfect recipe to make sure that information gets encoded? To start with, as discussed above, teachers need to use exercise as an everyday companion in their classes. It is recommended to get students up and energized every 20 minutes (Jensen, 2008). While this may seem too often, it is not an unrealistic goal to set. Short spurts of stretching exercises can be done at the beginning of class and then at 20-minute intervals, just before you start a new teaching point. This will keep students focused, alert, and better prepared to analyze material and come up with creative and insightful answers to various questions.

Second, the learning environment should be one that fosters what we call *the great endorphin release environment.* It is crucial to have a healthy rapport with students, and this will create a happy and positive feeling in the classroom. When this occurs, learners' brains will release endorphins, which stimulate their brains, particularly the frontal lobe, thereby assisting their brains in decision making, creating that initial blast of attention to the new information, and ultimately making those encoding neurons fire away like the Fourth of July.

Also remember that, due to the extensive mirror neuron network, each student is mirroring his or her instructor all throughout the lesson. The better the rapport between the instructor and the students, the better the relationship and the more the students will mirror or concentrate on the information at hand (La France, 1982). This, too, will help in achieving optimal encoding.

Assuming that the above elements have set the stage, the next significant ingredient is how the topic is introduced to students. Medina (2009) claims that this might be the most important single factor in successful securing, encoding, storage, and retrieval. If your introduction to the new topic or even a review of old information is exciting and stimulating, then you have won the battle because emotionally charged

---

[2] For a full set of physical classroom activities, see Randolph (2013b).

events (ECEs) immediately get students' attention and draw them into the infectious learning environment of your classroom. Starting the lesson with a short narrative or question is very effective. Or, in our case, if you start your lesson by teaching idioms, then use students' names in the example sentences. Upon seeing their name on the white board or handout, their interest is peaked (a great ECE), and they immediately attend to trying to guess and learn the meaning of the idiom or idioms in question (Randolph, 2013d). Willis (2006) tells us that "a student must care about new information or consider it important for it to go through the limbic system expeditiously, form new synaptic connections, and be stored as a long-term memory" (p. 20). This idea is reinforced by Medina (2009): "The more personal an example, the more richly it becomes encoded and the more readily it is remembered" (p. 155).

Another factor to consider is the timing or delivery of important information. The BEM principle (Jensen, 2008) is something all teachers should be aware of as it is highly relevant to the functioning of students' brains. BEM is the acronym for *beginning, end,* and *middle.* This seems to be the sequence that information is best learned (Jensen, 2008; Sousa, 2011). Our attention peaks when something is introduced and when the sequence of learning is ending. It makes sense as this principle has been built into our evolutionary brain; for thousands of years we learned to pay specific attention to the beginning and end of things, primarily in order to stay alive. "There's a crocodile! Kill it. Okay. We're safe. Let's check, is it dead?" If it was not, our ancestors were in trouble. It also seems that the brain is releasing chemicals in the brain at these two points—the novelty of beginnings creates excitement and the emotional endings elicit neurotransmitter activity in our neural connections.

Finally, we recommend that you teach the general ideas first and then work in the details (Jensen, 2008; Medina, 2009). Reflect for a moment and recall an idea you learned a few years back. Probably, the general notion will come back to you, and then you will remember the details. It's interesting that our brains learn this way and then retrieve it the same way later. In the case of teaching idioms, it's best to start with the general meaning, give examples, and then move onto more specific ideas about the idiom (e.g., its register, sense of formality or informality).

Assuming that we have successfully encoded idioms in learners' minds, how do we effectively keep these stored and, at the same time, assist in retrieving them with the least amount of effort? The answer lies in a method Randolph (2013a) has developed and calls R.E.S.T (repetition, emotions, sensory integration, and teaching). These four components will (1) ensure impressive rates of idiom retention and (2) foster more native-like uses of idioms due to the demands of having to frequently employ the terms in written or spoken work. We summarize the four aspects of R.E.S.T. below.

## Repetition and Spaced-Out Intervals of Review

As we discuss in Chapter 5, repetition is a key element for success in idiom acquisition. Ebbinghaus has told us that we are likely to forget 90% of what we learn today unless we repeat it and review it at spaced-out intervals. So it is vital to review not only the definitions but also the uses every so often in class and use the idioms frequently as well as immediately after teaching them. For optimal learning, students should be given fun and inspiring homework, which requires them to use the learned idioms after class in either written or spoken form.

## Emotions and Personalizing the Material

Emotions, as we saw, are important for encoding, but they are equally important for storage and retrieval. When we teach idioms, we must do so with as much emotion as possible, for when students' brains react to an emotional event or situation, a very significant part of reinforcing memory, the amygdala—described briefly earlier in this chapter—pumps dopamine into their systems. This is important because dopamine is responsible for processing new information and reinforcing their memory. Dopamine also plays a factor in the attention and learning systems of the brain. As we mentioned in the encoding segment, try to incorporate students' names, countries, or some part of their background in the idiom lessons you teach. It will make a significant difference.

## Sensory Integration

Synesthetes are people who see sounds, smell colors, hear tastes, or feel smells. According to Cytowic and Eagleman (2011), the one common quality that all synesthetes share is an excellent ability to retain and recall information. When you think about this integration of senses, it is really a very natural way to learn. Let's take an object like a baseball. When you learned about this object in your native language, you saw the colors of the object, felt its hardness, inhaled its smell of leather, and maybe you even tasted sweat on your tongue from playing with the ball. All of these sensory elements went into the learning of *baseball*. And as Medina (2009) tells us, "Learning abilities are increasingly optimized the more multisensory the environment becomes" (p. 207). If you can use colorful pictures that accurately represent the idioms you teach, bring in the sense of sound and even texture or smell, then students will most likely retain the idioms you teach with uncanny success.

## Teach What You Learn

In Randolph's class syllabi, the following statement is clearly displayed at the top of the first page: "Whatever you learn in here, teach it to others; for learning is teaching and teaching is learning." You can learn something and understand it to a satisfactory degree, but once you can teach it, then your level of understanding and genuine knowing increases significantly. If we can get students to naturally teach or reteach idioms to each other after having learned them, then they will be doing what Craik and Lockhart (1972) called *elaborative rehearsal*. A very nice activity that develops elaborative rehearsal is to simply have students explain to each other the idioms that they learned during the week in a review session. The more fluently and elaborately they can explain the definition and register, and offer one or two examples, the more masterful they will become.

During our short survey of how the brain works and how its functions are related to learning idioms, we reflected on a number of pivotal points to keep in mind as we plan, develop, teach, and critique our lessons. Perhaps the most important idea to be aware of as we teach and continue to learn is to adapt to the moment and let that moment keep us open to the infinite possibilities there are regarding how students learn and how we can successfully teach to the unique universe known as the human brain.

# CHAPTER 4

# How Are Idioms Taught? Methods and Materials

> What is the sound of an idiom being born?
> —*Patrick T. Randolph (after the Zen Koan)*

Even with instruction and good strategies, the task is daunting. What does it mean to know a word? Grasp the general meaning in a familiar context? Provide a definition or a translation equivalent? Identify its component parts or etymology? Use the word to complete a sentence or to create a new sentence? Use it metaphorically? Understand a joke that uses homonyms? (Lightbown & Spada, 2006, p. 100)

Lightbown and Spada (2006) ask these questions in relation to learning any new vocabulary in a second language, but they are just as important, if not more so, when teaching and learning English idioms, and we can also ask ourselves: What does it mean to teach a word? This chapter and the next one address different aspects of this question, focusing first in this chapter on methods and materials for teaching idioms, and next in Chapter 5 on a review of activities and tasks that help learners acquire the various aspects of "knowing a word" in both classroom and extramural contexts. We present findings from both experimental research on idiom learning and classroom-based studies and reviews of pedagogical methods. In particular, we summarize the different best practices and recommendations that TESOL and applied linguistics researchers and teachers have made in regard to teaching idioms, and we offer our thoughts on how we have adapted some of the best practices in our own classrooms. Throughout both chapters, we emphasize an eclectic and postmethod approach to teaching idioms in which teachers draw on the work of theorists, researchers, and other teachers but ultimately make pedagogical choices that fit with their own teaching context and their own understanding of what it means for students to know a word or phrase. Before getting into the specifics of how to organize materials and plan classroom activities for learning idioms, we provide a brief history of ideas and theories of vocabulary learning and teaching as they relate to teaching and learning idioms.

## From Lexicalized Grammar to Grammaticalized Lexis to Lexical Chunks: A Brief History of Vocabulary Teaching

Influenced by structuralist and then innatist theories of language and language acquisition, English language classes prior to the 1990s tended to focus more on implicit strategies and activities for learning vocabulary, and for many teachers vocabulary learning was generally assumed to "take care of itself." For example, Krashen (1989, 2004) famously argued that most successful vocabulary learning is accomplished through extensive reading, without the need to make lists and practice explicit strategies: "Ironically, dumping vocabulary and spelling tests can result in better vocabulary and spelling development. No testing means no time devoted to studying word lists, time that can be devoted to reading and better vocabulary and spelling development" (Krashen, 1989, p. 455). It was not that Krashen and others who follow a more comprehension-based approach did not see the value of vocabulary as essential to proficiency in a language; rather, they argued that the focus should be on comprehending meaningful input and encountering new words incidentally—much like, it was argued, children learn their first language.

Before Krashen and other input-oriented language pedagogues, the widely used audiolingual approach focused even less on vocabulary acquisition. Using this method, audiolingual teachers drilled students on grammatical patterns and phonological structures through the repetition of dialogues in which vocabulary items were introduced to fit into the grammatical slots in the phrases and sentences, limiting any explicit vocabulary instruction. Because grammar and pronunciation were viewed as the primary and underlying structures on which language learning was built, Lewis (1993) calls vocabulary in this approach *lexicalized grammar*. It should be noted, however, that more explicit attention to vocabulary was and is often present in more advanced audiolingual classrooms, and though not explicitly taught, learners do acquire knowledge of idioms and multiword terms through repeated substitution and inversion drills in which only specific terms and replacements are allowed. For example, a teacher may introduce the sentence *I can't put up with X* or *That is a piece of cake* in an intermediate-level dialogue and then practice the idioms by asking a series of questions of students by inverting the statement into a question (i.e., *What can you not put up with?* or *What is a piece of cake for you?*) or by showing a series of photos in which someone is annoyed and asking students, "What can this person not put up with?" In this way, students begin to store the multiword idioms as **lexical chunks** and not individual words. In fact, many of us already do some sort of repetition exercises like this when introducing new vocabulary, evidence of the lasting effect of some audiolingual techniques. Students will also, as discussed in Chapter 3, be creating more memory connections and advancing the items from their short-term to long-term memory.

Vocabulary learning and direct teaching gained more attention in the 1980s through the widespread move in language teaching, at least in the global West, to a communicative approach to learning and teaching. In the communicative approach to language teaching known as communicative language teaching, which grew out of systemic functional linguistics (Halliday, 1973), teachers place an emphasis on language learning as acquiring the necessary language and competencies to communicate meaning in a variety of specific contexts. In a communicative language lesson, attention to vocabulary learning is typically placed at the beginning of the lesson where students learn new terms that will be needed to complete the tasks that are practiced during the lesson. Despite this attention at the beginning of the lesson and the overall focus in the communicative syllabus to acquiring the vocabulary and language resources needed to achieve fluency in different aspects of communicative competence (from strategic to sociocultural), DeCarrico (2001) notes that vocabulary was still "given secondary status, taught mainly as support for functional language use" (p. 286).

Thus, before the turn to more explicit vocabulary teaching in the 1990s, no approach to teaching a language focused attention on how to organize and introduce vocabulary items, nor did one introduce activities that would foster long-term learning and retention of new vocabulary terms. So what changed 20 years ago that brought vocabulary to the attention of TESOL scholars and textbook writers? Boers and Lindstromberg (2008b) argue the key change that brought more attention to vocabulary learning in general, and to idiom learning specifically, was the development of **corpus linguistics** and studies of language that investigated common discourse patterns, collocations, and word patterns through the use of larger and larger digital collections of actual language use:

> The conclusion that a growing number of theorists have drawn from this [corpus linguistic investigations] is that successful L2 [second language] learning is to a very great extent a matter of understanding and remembering collocational tendencies and prefabricated multi-word expressions (i.e. memorized phrases) and that learners ought to be helped to acquire them in large numbers (Nattinger and DeCarrico 1992; Pawley and Syder 1983; Schmitt 2004). The principal rationale for this contention has been that a large mental store of idioms, collocations and other (semi-) fixed phrases increases L2 fluency, especially in unplanned, spontaneous interaction where deployment of rule-like knowledge of syntax and morphology proceeds too slowly (Pawley and Syder 1976 [2000]; Skehan 1998). (p. 7)

In addition to the studies listed above, linguists and vocabulary acquisition specialists cite John Sinclair's work as hugely influential in placing the spotlight on vocabulary learning in general, and collocations and word patterns specifically. In his 1987 article "Collocation: A Progress Report" and his 1991 book *Corpus, Concordance, Collocation*, Sinclair proposed two principles that structure language use: the open choice principle, which states that phrases and sentences are relatively open, only restricted by the grammar of a language; and the idiom choice principle, which states that word choices and combinations are not open but based on "semi-preconstructed phrases that constitute single choices, even though they might appear to be analyzable into segments" (Sinclair, 1987, p. 320). Based on this insight, vocabulary theorists argue that vocabulary learning is just as, if not more, important than learning grammar rules, since a key component of fluency is choosing the correct phrase or string of words for an intended meaning. In other words, grammar is important but in many ways these chunks or language strings or lexis are primary when learning a language, and the basic grammar structures, already encoded into the strings, are secondary (i.e., grammaticalized lexis).

Drawing on this fundamental insight into the place of chunks in language learning, Nattinger and DeCarrico (1992) in *Lexical Phrases and Language Teaching* and Lewis (1993) in *The Lexical Approach* have published specific strategies and activities for language teachers to teach vocabulary as strings of collocations, fixed expressions, and chunks of language. In particular, they emphasize the notion of including idioms as fixed language that is stored together in the brain. This makes sense as neuroscience tells us that, in essence, the brain is simplifying the language, and the brain prefers to keep things simple as opposed to complex (Medina, 2009). Nattinger and DeCarrico as well as Lewis make the argument for basing vocabulary teaching on lexical phrases because of the evidence that this is how we store and retrieve language in our brains, but more important, DeCarrico (2001) writes that lexical chunks "provide learners with an efficient means of interacting with others about self-selected topics" and "for lower level learners the chunks can ease frustration and promote motivation and a sense of fluency" (pp. 296–297).

For the purpose of summarizing key techniques for teaching idioms, it's important to note that key differences exist between Nattinger and DeCarrico's and Lewis's approaches to lexical chunks. Nattinger and DeCarrico group lexical phrases for teaching according to the pragmatic functions—social interactions (e.g., *thanks so much, gotta go*), necessary topics (e.g., *how much is X?, when is X?*), and discourse devices (e.g., *in spite of, in other words*). Lewis (1993), on the other hand, is more broad in his organization of collocations and lexical chunks, and he emphasizes both pragmatic functions as well as a wide-range of lexicogrammatical patterns such as nouns with probable adjective collocates (e.g., *close friend, good friend, intimate friend*, but not *far friend*). Boers and Lindstromberg (2008b) characterize Nattinger and DeCarrico's approach as based more in an English-speaking environment in which a lexical focus could supplement other class content and teaching approaches, but Lewis's well-known lexical approach (indeed his book is titled with *the*) is more encompassing and can be used as the basis for an entire curriculum, particularly in a traditionally defined EFL environment where English is not used or heard often in public or educational contexts.

Despite these differences in application of a lexical approach to teaching vocabulary, this approach to an explicit teaching of vocabulary lists and strategies represents a clear shift from the behaviorist, cognitive, and communicative pedagogies, and these new ideas associated with various lexical approaches to vocabulary instruction inform how many teachers now choose, organize, and teach idioms. In the next sections, we draw on many of the recommendations and activities presented in both Lewis's and Nattinger and DeCarrico's approaches as well as findings from Sinclair and many others who have analyzed large corpora of language usage to better refine what vocabulary we teach and how we organize it. In addition, where relevant, we provide examples of the activities from recent idiom textbooks and dictionaries.

## Materials: Choosing New Idioms for Classroom Instruction

Research into how many words a fluent or native speaker of English knows has varied widely depending on the definition of a *word*. For example, in one of the early counts of words used by native speakers, Seashore and Eckerson (1940) counted word types, and they found that speakers know more than 200,000 words. As Milton (2009) notes, the idea that speakers know so many words mortifies students, but he is able to reassure them when he explains that by counting types, researchers count separate singular nouns from plural nouns and inflected verbs from base verbs; therefore, *child* and *children* would be considered two words, as would *run* and *running*. Milton comforted students by noting that recent research into the lexicon size of a fluent speaker of English counts words according to *word families*, defined by Thornbury (2002) as "the base word plus its inflexions and its most common derivatives" (p. 4). So a word like *understand* includes the following family members: *understands, understanding, understood, misunderstood,* and so on (p. 5). With respect to counting word families, relatively more recent research suggests that educated English speakers know around 20,000 word families (Zechmeister, Chronis, Cull, D'Anna, & Healy, 1995), a number that should reassure some students, but begs the question: How many idioms should a fluent or advanced English language learner know, and which ones?

Perhaps because there are even more difficulties in defining an idiom than defining what a word is, there are no precise counts to the number of idioms a fluent speaker of English knows, or even how may idioms exist in English—the *Oxford Idioms Dictionary for Learners of English* (Parkinson & Francis, 2006) advertises itself as having over 10,000 English idioms. And instead of attempting to determine the amount of words needed for fluency in a particular context, research about learning idioms has focused on building lists of idioms based on four concepts: frequency, usefulness, learnability, and teachability.

Frequency and usefulness are related but dependent on a variety of factors. In terms of frequency, Biber, Johansson, Leech, Conrad, and Finegan (1999), in *Longman Grammar of Spoken and Written English,* reveal that most idioms do not actually appear that frequently; on average, a given idiom appears about only five times per million words. Liu (2008), however, summarizes results from multiple corpus studies to show that despite the infrequent use of a specific idiom, English speakers use on average between three and four idioms every minute, and between 3 and 10 percent of the total words spoken in classroom settings by teachers are idioms. Thus, Liu argues that idioms overall are used frequently and are important to study, and frequency—in terms of specific idioms that occur frequently in multiple contexts—is particularly revealing and useful for students. Liu (2003) did exactly that type of research into three different corpora: (1) a corpus made up of White House news briefings and transcripts of meetings from academic institutions; (2) a corpus of news programs and entertainment shows; and (3) a corpus of academic lectures, advising sessions, and class discussions from a university setting. Liu included phrasal verbs as idioms in his study. As shown in Table 4-1, phrasal verbs are some of the most frequent idioms across all three corpora and according to each corpus.

**Table 4-1. Most Common Idioms Across Different Corpora**

| Corpus | 10 Most Common Terms |
|---|---|
| Across all three corpora | *kind of* (meaning somewhat), *sort of* (meaning somewhat), *of course, in terms of, in fact, deal with, at all, as well, make sure, go through* |
| Professional corpus | *in terms of, deal with, sort of, kind of, in fact, make sure, go on, of course, as well, come up* |
| Media corpus | *kind of, of course, in fact, deal with, at all, sort of, as well, come up, find out, look for* |
| Michigan Corpus of Academic Spoken English (MICASE) | *sort of, kind of, go on, of course, in terms of, in fact, go through, at all, as well, deal with* |

Source: Liu (2003).

In the full list of most common terms cited in the study, there are few pure idioms in which the meaning is entirely opaque. In fact, only *ballpark estimate, the ball is in your court,* and *right off the bat* made the list that compiled all three corpora. This does not mean that pure idioms should not be taught, as they are typically the most difficult to understand and when used may be integral to a conversation or reading passage, but Liu (2003) notes these results are consistent with work by Moon (1998) and Biber et al. (1999) in showing the prevalence of semiliteral idioms. Drawing on this work in corpus linguistics, teachers can use lists like the ones compiled by Liu to design vocabulary units and curriculum which focus on the idioms that will be most useful for students. Of course, which lists are ultimately taught depends on the types of contexts in which students are expected to know and use English (i.e., academic, formal, or informal situations and environments). In Chapter 5, where we describe various effective teaching activities, we demonstrate how teachers can perform their own search into a corpus of language to create a specific list of idioms for students to study.

In addition to frequency and usefulness considerations, Thornbury (2002) notes that some words are more learnable than others. He listed cognates, words that are more or less identical in form and meaning in both a learner's first language and English, as being particularly learnable because they are typically derived from similar origins. For example, the idiom *see the light at the end of the tunnel* in German is *das Licht am Ende des Tunnels sehen,* which is almost an exact word-for-word translation, and the idiom has the same figurative/idiomatic meaning in German as it does in English. A recent blog post on the financial crisis in Portugal comments that "Portugal will Licht am Ende des Tunnels sehen" (i.e., Portugal will see the light; Streck, 2013). This idiom would thus be highly learnable for German learners of English. On the other hand, two idioms that come from the core metaphor *light is knowledge* in English—*see the light* (meaning to come to understand something) and *be in the dark* (meaning to be ignorant or uniformed)—do not translate as easily into German. There is a similar equivalent to *be in the dark* in German: *im Dunkeln sein* or *im Dunkeln tappen* (to grope/walk in the dark), which both mean to be ignorant or uninformed. Learning this idiom and core metaphor would consequently be relatively easy for German learners, but translating *I see the light* directly into German, *Ich sehe das Licht*, would be very awkward and only used by German speakers to imply the light that one sees before dying (i.e., you are about to die when you say *Ich sehe das Licht*). From personal experience, we can tell you that German speakers will get a kick out of you saying that you see the light. Thus, in compiling lists and choosing idioms to focus on in courses, it is important to consider cognates and false friends from the learners' first language. And, as discussed in the previous chapter, the learners' first language may have different core metaphors on which idioms are based, presenting a further complication to the learnability of a word or group of words. Moreover, pay close attention to terms based on different core metaphors in students' first or additional languages.

A final consideration when choosing idioms on which to focus a course or lesson is the notion of teachability. Different than learnability, Thornbury (2002) writes that "words are more easily teachable if they can be demonstrated or illustrated—by the use of pictures or real objects" (p. 35). He goes on to argue that nouns in general are easier to teach than verbs and adverbs, and concrete nouns are more easily taught than abstract nouns. Further, we have found that the most teachable idioms are those for which learners are able to come up with personal examples soon after being exposed to the new idioms.

As discussed in previous chapters, the literal meanings of idioms are often based on concrete nouns and easy to represent in pictures or through physical demonstrations, making most idioms, particularly ones based on core metaphors, teachable and easy to demonstrate (below we return to recent research on presenting idioms with a picture). At the same time, the figurative meaning of an idiom is often not obviously connected to its concrete realization. Thus, some idioms (e.g., those based on core metaphors such as *up in the air, pin him down, fly off the handle, out of my hands*, which are based on the core metaphor *control is contact*) are clearly connected to their physical and literal meanings, and they are more teachable. In contrast, some idioms based on the core metaphors that *people are animals or food* (e.g., *to be bullish, to be a turkey/chicken, to be the big cheese, to chew out someone/something*) are not as clearly linked to their figurative meaning and are typically based on cultural perceptions of the specific animal or food.

In compiling lists of idioms to teach, we need to be particularly careful about how learnable the idioms will be for learners, as well as how we plan to present the idioms and how teachable they will be. Particularly vexing (and at times, we feel, unteachable) are phrasal verbs such as many of the ones listed above. Rest assured, however, we address activities for teaching phrasal verb idioms below.

In describing how to choose idioms to teach from the most frequent, useable, learnable, or teachable idioms, this section has focused on the explicit teaching of vocabulary. The next two sections go into greater depth on ways teachers can explicitly organize and introduce lists of idioms for students. The final part of this chapter details techniques for helping students choose, organize, and learn new idioms from more incidental sources.

## Materials: Organizing New Idioms in Textbooks, Dictionaries, and Class Lists

Following lexicological traditions, idiom dictionary makers typically have chosen not to enter into language acquisition research and debates, and they have opted to simply present idioms in alphabetical order. Many idiom dictionaries have, however, included multiple idioms under the same key word heading. For example, *Collins COBUILD Idioms Dictionary* (2012) is organized alphabetically by groups of idioms that share a "headword," defined as the first noun in the idiom's phrase that does not vary. For example, the headword *hand* occupies over four pages in the dictionary and contains idioms from *bite the hand that feeds you* to *the upper hand*. In addition, the headword *hands* occupies two pages of its own, with idioms such as *wash your hands of something* and *have your hands full*. In addition to the definition of each idiom, the dictionary includes (1) variations in usage of the idiom; (2) examples from a Collins large corpus of spoken and written English; (3) a special marker for key idioms; (4) an explanation of usage, variations, and regional styles; (5) synonyms; and (6) where possible, an explanation of the idiom's origin. For example, the idioms *die like a dog, a dog and pony show, dog-eat-dog,* and *dog-in-the-manger* are organized under the headword *dog* and contain the following information for *a dog and pony show*:

> If you refer to an event as **a dog and pony show**, you mean that it is very showy because it has been organized to impress someone [mainly American]: I'm bombarding him and the other figures with charts, graphs, and figures. The boss responds by dozing off during more of our dog and pony show. NOTE: This expression refers to circus acts involving dogs and horses. (p. 99)

Similarly, the *Oxford Dictionary of English Idioms* (Ayto, 2009) is organized around keywords but with more focus on etymology and examples from past usage. For example, a typical entry would be organized around the key word *stitch*, with the following idioms included under that entry: *a stitch in time* and *in stitches*. Along with the definition of each idiom, the dictionary includes the following information about the idiom *in stitches*, which is defined as "laughing uncontrollably":

> *Stitch*, in the sense of "a sudden localized jabbing pain," such as might be caused by a needle, is recorded in Old English. It is now generally used of a muscle spasm in the side caused especially by exertion. Shakespeare seems to have been the first to describe *stitches* brought on by laughter; in *Twelfth Night* (1601) Maria invites her fellow conspirators to observe the lovelorn Malvolio with the words: "If you . . . will laugh yourselves into stitches, follow me." (p. 285)

In general, the *Collins COBUILD Idioms Dictionary* (2012) is better designed for English language learners as it uses a more layered, conversational approach with many example sentences that teachers can use when defining and explaining new words. The *Oxford Dictionary of English Idioms* (Ayto, 2009) is also useful but is designed for a wider audience, and the focus is more on short definitions and extended descriptions of the history of idiom usage. Thornbury (2002) notes that teachers can draw on the variety of information in dictionary entries by adding shades of meaning through a discussion of the uses of a new vocabulary word (p. 83). For instance, a teacher could potentially discuss the definition of *a dog and pony show* by stating:

> If you refer to an event as *a dog and pony show*, you mean that it is very showy because it has been organized to impress someone. You may feel that an event is *a dog and pony show* if it appears to lack substance and is diverting attention away from more important topics. Some people may call their presentation *a dog and pony show* because they have many attention-grabbing visual aids and activities to keep their audience interested.

Following these dictionary examples, teachers may choose to simply organize lists of idioms for students in alphabetical order by headwords. This approach will work if idioms are being introduced as additional vocabulary or input in relation to the class content. Liu (2008) lists a variety of other more deliberate strategies to introduce new idioms to learners: (1) by grammatical structure, (2) by grammatical function, (3) by motivating concept, (4) by origin or source, (5) by topic on which the idiom is used to comment, (6) by activity in or for which the idiom is often used, (7) by key words (similar to dictionary entireties discussed above), and (8) by semantics (for a more detailed description of these categories, see Liu, 2008, pp. 115–118). These organizational categories provide learners with different structures to help them focus their learning and practice of idioms, and teachers can vary the use of different strategies depending on the specific learning objectives and the topics of different lessons. Indeed, as discussed in the previous chapter, research about memory and learning reveals that when information is presented in an organized framework, the brain can quickly store the new input into its short-term memory (Medina, 2009; Willis, 2006).

At the same time, teachers should be cautious in using just one strategy when presenting lists of idioms for instructional purposes; it's often the case that many idioms with little in common semantically fit into the same category, or, conversely, idioms with very similar meanings are placed in the same category and are difficult for students to differentiate. For example, the textbook *Practice With Idioms* (Feare, 1980) organizes its chapters around sections related to grammatical concepts such as "Intransitive Verbal Idioms" and "Nominal, Adjective, and Adverbial Idioms," and its chapters are further organized around grammatical structures such as "Intransitive Verbs with Particles" and "Nominal Forms: Adjective + Noun Combinations." In these chapters, idioms with little else in common besides grammatical structure (e.g., *to die down* and *to open up*, *last straw* and *eager beaver*) are presented together with idioms that are hard to differentiate (e.g., *to break in* and *to break down*; Feare, 1980). The key point here is that teachers should vary the categories they use to organize lists of idioms for their classes, placing particular attention on pointing out the differences between words. See Table 4-2 for more examples of different types of lists from a variety of textbooks.

The next section deals with methods for presenting new idioms. We further review and evaluate textbooks and dictionaries in detail in Chapter 9, but our brief survey here reveals that the two most popular strategies for organizing idioms in textbooks appear to be (1) by activity in or for which the idiom is often used or (2) by motivating concept/metaphor.

## Materials: Presenting New Idioms in the Classroom

After careful consideration over what new idioms will be taught and how they will be organized, textbook writers and classroom teachers must make the connection to the classroom by deciding how to present the new idioms and with what additional information they will present the idioms. Some of the questions around presentation are also related to how to organize lessons and activities, and we address certain aspects of good learning activities in the next section. Here we review studies and examples in response to key questions textbook authors and teachers must consider when presenting new idioms and vocabulary to students.

### How many new idioms should be presented at one time?

Thornbury (2002) notes that most textbooks present no more than 12 new items per lesson, and our review of idioms textbooks is similar (although some books, such as *The New Idioms in Action* [Reeves, 1985],

**Table 4-2. Examples of Idioms Lists From Textbooks**

| Textbook | Organizing Concept | Sample Chapter | Idioms in the Chapter |
|---|---|---|---|
| *Practice With Idioms* (Feare, 1980) | Grammatical concepts and structures | Chapter 10: Nominal Forms: Pairs of Nouns | *flesh and blood, heart and soul, part and parcel, wear and tear, pins and needles, odds and ends, rank and file, ups and downs, give and take, ins and outs* |
| *The Big Picture* (King, 1999) | Motivating concept | Chapter 1: Ideas Are Balls | *bounce an idea off you, catch (on), ballpark figure, field questions, toss out a suggestion, kick around (kick it upstairs), be on the ball, put a spin on it* |
| *All Clear: Idioms in Context* (Fragiadakis, 1992) | Activity in or for which the idiom is often used | Chapter 9: Pulling an All-Nighter | *pull an all-nighter, burn the midnight oil, cram, in the nick of time, turn/hand in, hand out, get sleep, take/give/make up/correct/ go over a test, be over, type/do something over, take a nap, be under pressure, you can say that again, hit the books, take a test cold* |
| *Attitudes Through Idioms* (T. W. Adams & Kuder, 1994) | Topic on which the idiom is used to comment | Unit 5: Compromise | *be all or nothing, find middle ground, get/have one's own way, give-and-take, go halfway, meet someone halfway, middle of the road, not give an inch, stick to one's guns, strike a happy medium* |
| *The Idiom Book* (Niergarth, 2007) | Topic on which the idiom is used to comment | Lesson 22: Used Car | *pull a fast one, a pig in a poke, on its last legs, on the up and up, within one's means, the real scoop, take one's word for it, at least, in the ball park, comes with the territory* |
| *English Idioms in Use: Advanced* (O'Dell & McCarthy, 2010) | Multiple organizing concepts: topic; type; activity; and key word | Unit 41: Idioms Used in Formal Writing | *first and foremost, on balance, by and large, in the main, on no account, on the one hand, on the other hand, last but not least, in the final analysis, not the whole picture, a case in point, to set the stage, to beg the question, to point the way, to set in motion, to open the door to* |

present as few as 5 idioms per lesson, and *The Big Picture* [King, 1999] presents as many as 15 per lesson). We recommend the same number as *The New Idioms in Action* for a 1-hour lesson. This is manageable in terms of both learnability and teachability. In deciding the number of words to teach per lesson, it is important to ensure that students have opportunities for spaced repetition, which Nation (2001) illustrates as "words might be studied for three minutes now, another three minutes two days later and finally three minutes a week later" (p. 76). We, however, argue that repetition within the hour and spaced interval repetition directly after class is best (Randolph, 2013a). Thornbury highlights additional concerns in selecting the right amount of words for a vocabulary list or lesson: the proficiency level of the learners, the learners' familiarity with the words, the difficulty of the words, the teachability of the words (as discussed above), and whether the words are taught for production (requiring more time) or reception (requiring less time; p. 77).

### How should new idioms first be presented in a textbook: alone in a list, with their definitions, in a dialogue/reading, or through example sentences?

There is not one ideal way to present new idioms for students to learn, but teachers must first examine the goals for students learning the new words as well as the skill focus of the lesson. For example, if the goal of the lesson is purely retrieval of the meaning of the new idioms in order to understand a reading or participate in a class activity in which the new idioms will be used, teachers may opt to simply present the new words with definitions and then practice the words quickly before moving on to the main focus of the lesson. Alternatively, many textbooks provide multiple exercises with the new idioms before providing the meaning, such as providing example sentences or questions about the words. For example, *Idioms in American Life* (Howard, 1987) begins its lessons with a short dialogue containing the new words, requiring students to guess the meanings of the new idioms. Definitions are not listed in the chapter at all but in the book's index. Nation (2001) writes that this extra effort on the part of learners in guessing the meaning can be useful, but it can also take time away from class activities if teachers ask students to guess the meaning of every word. He argues that "simultaneous presentation of a word form and its meaning is best for the first encounter and, thereafter, delayed presentation is best because there is then the possibility of effort leading to successful recall" (p. 79). We find it best to have students guess the meanings of new idioms regardless of the focus of the lesson. The rationale is simple: If students are merely spoon-fed information, they remain one step away from the learning experience. On the other hand, if they are required to guess the meaning, they bridge this gap because they become personally involved in the learning process; they will begin to take emotional stock in their own learning of idioms. And emotion, as we briefly discussed in Chapter 3 and elaborate on in Chapter 10, is a key element in any form of learning. However, in addition to the students' guesses, we advocate making sure to quickly supply the correct definition of the idioms so that they learn the correct meaning if their guesses are a bit off.

Thornbury (2002) offers a middle-ground approach by presenting students with many examples of the new words in context before asking them to guess the new words; thus, students see and, if read aloud, hear the words many times before venturing a guess, adding to the likelihood that the words themselves are retained in students' memory. Thornbury too, however, advocates for quickly reinforcing or offering the correct meaning of the new words after students have guessed at the meaning. We should also note here that many vocabulary experts, including Folse (2004), do not advise presenting idioms with antonyms with beginning learners because this can cause confusion, and we have found it is best to stick to the basic definition of the new idiom quickly after any guessing activity.

### Should new idioms be presented with pictorial depictions or etymological information?

Boers, Eyckmans, and Stengers (2007) point out that many dictionary and textbook authors have been influenced by cognitive linguistics and neuroscientists by adding pictures and etymological information with definitions of idioms. Authors add this information based on two theories of memory as described in Chapter 3: levels of processing theory, which argues that more meaningful analysis of new information (e.g., mapping associations between new words vs. encoding how words sound) leads to better recall; and dual-coding theory, which posits that "the association of verbal information with a mental image is advantageous because it creates an additional pathway for recollecting the verbal information" (Boers, Demecheleer, & Eyckmans, 2004, p. 369). For example, the *Oxford Dictionary of English Idioms* (2009) offers this note when defining the idiom *clean bill of health*: "A bill of health was an official document given to the captain of a ship when leaving a particular port that said that nobody on the ship carried any disease or infection" (p. 62). And the definitions in *The Big Picture* (King, 1999) include sketches of either the figurative or literal meanings of the idioms; for example, the entry for *jump on the bandwagon* begins with a picture of a man jumping onto a wagon full of musicians in a marching band (p. 43), and the definition for *blanket statement* is a blanket covering the word *taxes* in reference to the blanket statement "all taxes are bad" (p. 30).

Recent research has clearly shown that learner retention of idioms is facilitated by what Boers et al. (2004) call *etymological elaboration* and pictorial representations of the idioms, but a few caveats and restrictions are important to consider. First, just as words can be polysemous and lead to confusion and incorrect interpretations, pictures in textbooks may not contain sufficient clues for successful retention or production, or worse, may mislead learners and cause incorrect interpretation and usage. Consider the two examples above; the picture for *jump on the bandwagon* adds a mental image of a wagon full of musicians calling someone to vote for a particular politician, which corresponds closely with both the literal meaning of the idiom and the original source of the idiom from political parades in the 19th century. The picture for *blanket statement* of a blanket covering the word *taxes*, however, does not necessarily correlate with the notion of a statement that "is not justified in its extent," and learners may be able to remember the term but not the exact meaning of the new idiom.

A second caveat about using pictures and etymology is highlighted in recent studies such as Boers, Lindstromberg, Littlemore, Stengers, and Eychkmans (2008); Boers, Píriz, Stengers, and Eyckmans (2009); and Szczepaniak and Lew (2011). These studies reveal that pictures which are truly close to the literal readings of the target idiomatic forms do indeed aid with the retention of meaning, particularly with learners who already show an inclination toward a visual cognitive learning style. Boers et al. (2009) go on to conclude, however, that "there seems little reason to believe that the pictures will also stimulate retention of the precise linguistic form that is used to denote those concepts" (p. 378). In other words, pictures aid in retention of meaning that can be used when someone else uses the idioms, but learners who are introduced to idioms with pictures have not shown significant increases in their abilities to use the new idioms in spoken or written tests. In fact, when the meaning of new words is provided only verbally, Boers et al. (2009) argue learners will likely remember only the picture, not the meaning of the words.

Further, Boers et al. (2007), Boers (2001), Kövecses and Szabó (1996), and other researchers have shown that etymological elaboration in the form of providing students with information on the literal usage and origin of the idioms they are about to learn improves both retention of meaning and production of new idioms, but Szczepaniak and Lew (2011) point out that "the mere presence of etymological notes in dictionary entries cannot guarantee deep processing of their content" (p. 342). In fact, they write that "superficial reading of such notes may divert learners' attention from the actual meaning or result in actual and etymological meanings being mixed up" (p. 342). Thus, in summarizing the research into the use of etymological meanings when presenting new idioms, it is clear that teachers should provide opportunities for learners to guess at the origin of idioms and how their literal and figurative meanings are related and perhaps have changed over the years. But teachers must also provide guidance toward the correct motivating links between literal and figurative meanings and offer explicit instruction about the etymology of the idioms in order to focus learners on the actual use of a given expression.

Finally, it is also important to note that pictorial depictions and etymological information are not the only ways to stimulate learners to make correlations between new idioms. Traditional dictionary definitions contain information on synonyms and antonyms that can be useful in defining new idioms. For example, *The New Idioms in Action* (Reeves, 1985) offers "equivalents" and "contrasts" when providing definitions; for example, the definition for the term *get behind* lists the equivalents "fall behind [and] be behind" and the contrast "keep up" (p. 28).

***Is it useful to present new idioms with information from corpus
studies such as concordance examples, frequency of use, or other
data-driven information?***

As illustrated above, many vocabulary teachers and theorists have
gained insight into vocabulary teaching and learning through analysis
of large corpora of written and spoken texts, and many corpus linguists
argue that this information should be presented directly to students
when learning new words. Nation (2001) posits that presenting this
information in classroom activities will give learners the chance to
"meet vocabulary in real contexts" and "construct generalizations and
note patterns and exceptions" between new words (p. 111). Balunda
(2009) writes that there are basically two key ways teachers can use
corpus information in classrooms: (1) direct access to a corpus and
concordancing software or (2) activities, definitions, and other curriculum containing "the raw data, or concordance output, from a corpus"
(p. 9). For example, the Touchstone series by Cambridge offers the following information in the teacher's edition about the new vocabulary
item *at least.*

> The expression *at least* is in the top 500 words and expressions in
> conversation, and it accounts for over 90 percent of the uses of the
> word least. About 25 percent of the uses of *at least* are in the meaning
> taught in the lesson. The expression usually comes at the beginning
> of the sentence rather than the end. (McCarthy, McCarten, & Sandi-
> ford, 2006, p. xxx)

If the textbook you use is not based in corpus studies and does not
provide this type of information, there are numerous online corpora
available for gaining information to present to students. For example,
when presenting a new idiom such as *a red herring*, along with the definition and etymology, teachers could present the usage information in
Figure 4-1, which is from *The Corpus of Contemporary American English*
(*COCA*; Davies, n.d.)

After presenting this information, teachers could ask: Does
this idiom appear to be used in more formal or informal contexts?
Is it more spoken or written? In some cases, it will be clear that a
certain idiom has become less often used or more restricted to a
certain context.

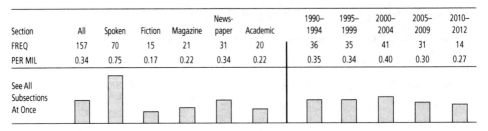

| Section | All | Spoken | Fiction | Magazine | News-paper | Academic | 1990–1994 | 1995–1999 | 2000–2004 | 2005–2009 | 2010–2012 |
|---|---|---|---|---|---|---|---|---|---|---|---|
| FREQ | 157 | 70 | 15 | 21 | 31 | 20 | 36 | 35 | 41 | 31 | 14 |
| PER MIL | 0.34 | 0.75 | 0.17 | 0.22 | 0.34 | 0.22 | 0.35 | 0.34 | 0.40 | 0.30 | 0.27 |

See All Subsections At Once

*Figure 4-1. Usage Table from* COCA *for* a Red Herring

Further, teachers can develop concordance examples from existing corpora. For example, the following list for presenting *a red herring* is adapted from examples produced through a basic search in the *COCA*:

1. Your argument is **a red herring.** You're not talking about what's going on.

2. He calls the issue **a red herring** to divert attention.

3. Capital punishment is **a red herring,** distracting us from the real work.

4. Is that **a red herring** or is that interesting to you?

In this way, students begin to see what types of things are called red herrings—an argument, an issue, and so on—and they also begin to connect the term to its synonyms and collocated words—diverting attention, distracting, not interesting.

### Should new idioms be translated into learners' native language?

Most textbooks present definitions for new vocabulary and idioms only in English, and most widely available idiom dictionaries for learners are entirely in English. Many research studies have found positive effects, however, when teachers or textbooks provide simple translations or allow students the chance to translate new idioms as part of the introduction activities when encountering new idioms (Elley, 1989; Laufer & Shmueli, 1997). Unless you have strictly set up the classroom to follow the direct method of instruction or create a total immersion classroom, most teachers and vocabulary experts agree that translation is allowable as part of the learning process, and it can be an economical way to quickly explain a new idiom. Of course, the drawback is that students may become over-reliant on using a language other than

English in the classroom, and the use of translation may preclude the higher order thinking and correlations that can be made when using etymology or corpus-based data to present definitions. Thornbury (2002) notes that translation may be most effective for explaining incidental vocabulary that students ask about during a lesson. Moreover, we have found that it helps students connect better to the material, especially beginning or intermediate learners.

The textbook *The Big Picture* (King, 1999) offers somewhat of a middle ground by introducing some chapters with questions about the underlying concepts of the new words in the students' native languages. For example, when introducing idioms that share the underlying concept *ideas are sharp instruments,*

> in your native language, how do you describe a person with good ideas, an intelligent person? Do you use adjectives like sharp or quick? And how do you describe a person whose ideas are foolish? Translate these descriptions and share them in groups of three or four. (p. 17)

In this way, students begin to see where connections between English and other languages can be made. Furthermore, they can begin to analyze how often idioms produce false cognates that will lead to misunderstandings if they translate directly between their first language and English.

### What are the best ways to explain new idioms and incidental idioms when students encounter them for the first time?

When presenting formal lists of new idioms or when students bring up incidental idioms in class, teachers often attempt to explain the new terms with additional information and illustrations with simple definitions as presented in dictionaries and textbooks. This helps learners see how the word is used, compare it to other words, and begin to practice its pronunciation. In fact, we often take notes next to new idioms to remind ourselves of key points we want to make about them. Some useful information to give students in addition to the meanings includes pronunciation tips, information on register (i.e., formality) and typical context for use, allowable substitution and grammatical variances (e.g., you can *chicken out of something* or *be a chicken*, but you cannot *\*chicken into something*).

Liu (2008) separates three common strategies teachers use when explaining idioms for the first time: definition, elaboration, and paraphrasing (p. 162). Consider the following explanations we have given for new idioms in our own classrooms (the idioms were taken from Steve Jobs's famous commencement speech at Stanford in 2005)[1]:

> *priceless* (definition): If something is priceless it is extremely valuable, worth more than money. For Jobs, curiosity was priceless in helping him succeed.
>
> *connecting the dots* (elaboration): Jobs says that the first story was about connecting the dots. When you were a kid, did you ever have those drawings that were just a pattern of dots on the page, and you had to draw the lines between the dots, and in the end a picture appeared? These kinds of drawings were popular in the past. So you did like this (place dots with chalk on the board and then draw lines to reveal a basic picture of a fish). In this way, you connected the dots and everything made sense, became clear.
>
> *kept me going* (paraphrasing): Jobs notes that what kept him going throughout his entire career—in other words, what made him get up in the morning and gave him energy to keep working through the problems—was the fact that he always loved what he did. And if he didn't love what he was doing he certainly would not have kept going.

Liu (2008) notes that when providing the definition, it is useful to use a signal phrase such as *this means* or *what we mean is* in order to draw attention to the meaning. In this way, our classroom example using Steve Jobs's speech may not have been as effective as it could have been. Regardless, in providing explanations in class for both prepared lists and incidental idioms that come up spontaneously in class, all researchers on vocabulary instruction agree that explanations need to be clear, simple, and brief, and "particularly in the first meetings with a word, any explanation should not be complicated or elaborate" (Nation, 2001, p. 90).

------

[1] http://news.stanford.edu/news/2005/june15/jobs-061505.html

## Pedagogical Perspective:
## Choosing and Developing Materials

In deciding what information to present with new idioms, one clear point is made by all vocabulary experts: It is important to link the form of the new idiom with its meaning early and repeatedly. Activities to prime learners in order to categorize and compare definitions based on corpus data or other additional information can help introduce new words but are most effective after the definitions of the new idioms have been provided. In focusing on providing students with as much relevant information as possible to help them learn new vocabulary items that we, as teachers, provide for them, it is important not to forget the effectiveness of learning new idioms and vocabulary through incidental exposure, particularly through extensive reading. The technique of extensive reading, as described above and associated with Stephen Krashen's work on comprehension-based methodology, should not be discounted as a valuable way to increase students' knowledge and use of idioms. As described in some of the activities in the next chapter and more extensively in some of the lesson plans presented in Chapter 8, it is very important to motivate students to look for new words in both their academic and personal reading. Numerous studies have shown the impact that extensive reading has on the development of vocabulary learning in all learners, including English language learners (Martin-Chang & Gould, 2008; Stanovich & Cunningham, 1993). And in addition to new idioms provided by textbooks and dictionaries, teachers should encourage students to create their own lists of new idioms from their own experiences.

# CHAPTER 5

# How Are Idioms Taught? Classroom Strategies and Activities

*Education is all a matter of building bridges.*
—*Ralph Ellison*

Without delving deeply into the extensive literature on individual differences in language learning, it is important to note at the outset of this chapter that when designing classroom activities, teachers must consider key attributes in which learners differ in their approach to classroom activities, including differences in personality (C. Cooper, 2002), aptitude (Gardner, 1983; Skehan, 2002), motivation (Dörnyei, 2001, 2003), learning styles (Kolb, 1984; Riding, 2002), and investment in their learning context (Norton, 2000). An overriding theme in all of this work is the need to both recognize these differences and build opportunities and experiences into classroom activities that will connect with most, if not all learners. Thus, in this chapter we summarize effective classroom activities and strategies, and where appropriate, we reference the above concepts and how to build attention to individual differences into classroom activities. Also, note that following this chapter, in Part 2 of the book, in particular Chapter 8, we present classroom lesson plans in more depth.

## Cognition and Brain-Based Activities

As we discussed in Chapter 3, insights from cognitive linguistics and brain-based research about language learning can be directly applied in the classroom to create enjoyable and successful activities for students (Boers, 2001; Boers & Lindstromberg, 2008b; Croft & Cruse, 2004; Kövecses, 2002; Kövecses & Szabo, 1996). In particular, Boers and Lindstromberg (2008b) argue that cognitive linguistics-inspired teaching helps students

> attain a more profound understanding of the target language, better remember more words and phrases . . . , appreciate the link between language and culture, and become more confident (once they realize that—because language is not entirely arbitrary—pathways for insightful learning are available as alternatives to blind memorization). (p. 27)

One of the most widely researched topics in cognitive linguistics is the description and analysis of the underlying metaphors and concepts that motivate idiomatic language and idioms, and many researchers have proposed activities that help students understand these underlying metaphors. For example, we have often used a simple activity from Boers and Lindstromberg (2008a) in which students place a list of idioms in the appropriate source domain ovals of a Venn diagram, as shown in Figure 5-1.

The diagram can be drawn on a chalkboard or on a poster, and, in groups, students place note cards with the individual idioms written on them, such as *a loose cannon* or *gain ground*, in the appropriate spaces. The teacher can then ask different groups to explain their choices and even use the new idioms in example sentences. For less proficient students, this activity can be done as a whole class with individual students placing the cards in the appropriate place on the diagrams after the class has agreed where to place the terms. Or the teacher could make the activity into a total physical response–based lesson and have the students physically mime the source domain(s) where the students would place the idioms when going over the new idioms. We have also added miming to group quizzes and competitions when reviewing new idioms.

In addition, we have used an activity called *alphabetical alliteration* by Boers and Lindstromberg (2005) to illustrate the motivating

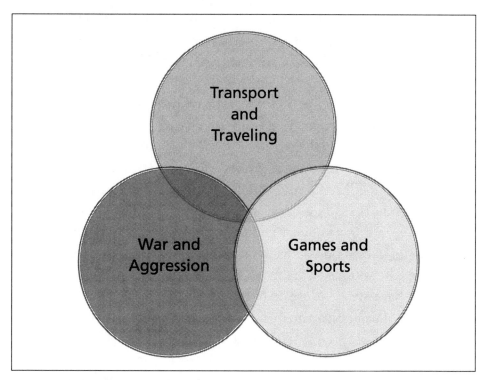

*Figure 5-1. Diagram of Overlapping Source Domains*
Source: Boers & Lindstromberg (2008a, p. 378).

concept of idioms as well as help students memorize the forms of new idioms by activating multiple levels of processing through the alliteration or rhyming of the new phrases. In this activity, we give students a page in which one side contains a list of idioms in alphabetical order. All of the idioms have some alliterative or rhyming quality (e.g., *bend over backwards* for the B entry, *fit as a fiddle* for the F entry). We then have either pictures or some visual representation of the idioms on the back of the paper, or we have students draw a picture/representation. The pictures are labeled according to the alphabet, just as the idioms are. For example, *bend over backwards* is represented with a stick figure of a person bending over next to the B entry. After going over the pictures and the idioms, we have students quiz each other first on what the visual representation of the idiom is while one student looks at the idiom and the other has the visual hint. Then, switching roles, students quiz each other while one student looks at the visual representation of the idiom and tries to guess the idiom. After this practice and quizzing is completed, we often like to play a game of Pictionary as a class. Here, two teams compete to guess the new idioms as quickly as possible, as one student draws a visual representation of the idioms. Depending on the level of the students, we also add new idioms to the game that are based on similar metaphors as the ones just studied.

These activities can be adapted in many ways to draw attention to the motivating concepts of new idioms as well as provide multiple levels of processing and dual-coding of the new idioms, including (1) play/sing songs with the new idioms (for an additional task, take out the key idioms from a song and have students fill in the blanks), (2) replace a short reading passage with idioms that have some sort of rhyming or alliterative quality and then create a gap activity or some other memorization quiz in which students quiz each other and give hints about the sounds of the new idioms (Boers & Lindstromberg, 2008a), (3) have students create note cards with the motivating concept on the back of each card and use these cards to study and play memory games, and (4) have students translate a song or poem that uses one or more of the idioms from your class. Or for lower proficiency levels, provide a translation and discuss the similarities and differences in the motivating concepts.

As a final summary of activities for learning idioms based on cognition and brain-based activities, we find it useful to consider Howard Gardner's (1983) theory of **multiple intelligences (MI)** when planning activities for learning idioms based on activating our students' cognitive abilities. As briefly discussed in Chapter 3, Gardner originally proposed seven intelligences in which learners reveal distinct abilities: linguistic, musical, logical-mathematical, spatial, bodily-kinesthetic, intrapersonal sense of self, and interpersonal. There are likely many more intelligences, and recent research in neuroscience questions the discreetness of any of these categories, but they are useful, nonetheless, in organizing different types of activities for learning idioms. T. C. Cooper (1998) has organized activities for learning idioms based on the different intelligences, and, as illustrated in Table 5-1, many of his suggested activities are similar to activities offered in this chapter and throughout our book.

In recent years, Gardner has revised his model, combining intrapersonal and interpersonal into a single intelligence and adding other intelligences, such as naturalistic intelligence—the ability and empathy

# Table 5-1. Summary of Suggested Activities for Teaching Idioms Based on Multiple Intelligences

| Intelligence | Core Components | Key Teaching Suggestion |
|---|---|---|
| Linguistic | Sensitivity to the sounds, structure, meanings, and functions of words and language | Discuss idioms and figurative speech |
| Logical-Mathematical | Sensitivity to, and capacity to discern, logical or numerical patterns; ability to handle long chains of reasoning | Sort idioms into thematic categories |
| Spatial | Capacity to think in visual images and to recreate, transform, or modify images | Illustrate idioms to show the contrast between figurative and literal meanings |
| Bodily-Kinesthetic | Ability to control one's body movements and to handle objects skillfully | Act out the meaning of idioms |
| Musical | Ability to produce and appreciate rhythm, pitch, melody, and timbre | Engage students in idiom jazz chants |
| Interpersonal | Capacity to understand and respond to the moods, temperaments, motivations, and desires of other people | Define the social situations for the use of various idioms |
| Intrapersonal | Ability to assess one's own emotional life and to have knowledge of one's own strengths and weaknesses | Have students create a dictionary of their favorite personal idioms and explain how the expressions give insights into understanding themselves |

Source: Cooper (1998, p. 260).

for categorization of natural things. His theory has received criticism for a general lack of empirical evidence proving the existence and effects of MI and the loose definition of intelligence as something closer to talents than actual intelligence and IQ as defined by psychologists (Waterhouse, 2006). These criticisms of MI, just as any criticisms of other theories described in this book, are important qualifications for practicing teachers, but we still argue that we have found the categories of MI to be very helpful as an organizing method for planning activities for learning idioms.

## Conversation Analysis Activities

Similar to research in cognitive linguistics, conversation analysts have revealed aspects of language that are not arbitrary, but rather follow certain patterns and rules. In particular, we have drawn on work in conversational analysis to create exercises that help students practice using new idioms, look for idioms in everyday speech, and understand the pragmatic role idioms play in conversation. In particular, exercises based on work by Drew and Holt (1998, 2005) and McCarthy (1998) allow students to see how idioms function as conversational pivots and provide speakers with space to evaluate and change topics in conversation. In beginning our lessons inspired by conversation analysis of idioms, we usually present the following conversational formula:

1 → Speaker A: Figurative summary

2 → Speaker B: Agreement (or other expression of contiguity)

3 → Speaker A: Agreement/confirmation

4 → Speaker A/B: Introduces next topic (Drew & Holt, 1998, p. 506)

We explain that often an idiom is used at a specific point in a conversation, perhaps not consciously, to summarize a story and introduce a new topic in a stepwise fashion.

Next, we offer the following examples, adapted from Drew and Holt (2005) and McCarthy (1998), as categories to use in analyzing idioms as conversational pivots.

*To evaluate an event in a story*

S1: And I said, what would you like to do this afternoon. And she says, I'd like to go play bingo. . . . Now, bingo was never ever *my cup of tea*, but I says, OK, Mary. Where do you want to go play bingo?

*To self-summarize the end of a story*

S1: Still that's the way it happened for you.

S2: That's right.

S1: The *big break*, wasn't it? And now you are a successful small business owner.

*To other-summarize the end of a story and introduce a new topic*

(S1 is telling her mother about an acquaintance that has recently died.)

S1: He was a buyer for the only horse hair factory left in England.

S2: Good gracious.

S1: And he was their buyer.

S2: Hmm . . .

S1: So he had *a good innings*, didn't he?

S2: Yes.

S1: Anyway, we had a very good evening on Saturday.

We emphasize that the third example illustrates what conversation analysts describe as *other attentive* commentary that is geared toward what Jefferson (1984) calls *topical rupture*, which is often an attempt to move away from a troubling or sad story.

After more examples, some taken from TV show dialogues or online videos, we give students the following assignment:

1. Find a 2- to 4-minute recording of a natural conversation or dialogue from a TV show in which idioms are used. Try to find a recording that also has a written transcript to analyze. (Tip: Use the closed caption button for YouTube videos.) The conversation can be from a movie as long as it's a spoken interaction and idioms are used in the conversation. (This should not be hard because idioms are used often in spoken interactions.)

2. Write down or underline on the transcript all of the idioms that are used. Write out the definition of the idioms in your own words.

3. Write down or underline the sentences/utterances spoken before and after the idiom (use above as an example).

4. Analyze the pragmatic reason/function that each idiom serves in that conversation. Use the functions listed above or create your own analysis.

5. Bring examples from your conversations to the next class. Bring a copy to turn in.

We also mention that for adventurous students and budding applied linguists, they may wish to record a conversation among their friends to analyze. Overall, this activity is for more advanced students, but we have used the above categories and presented example conversations with good results in intermediate-level classes as well. We feel that presenting information such as these explanations of the conversational function of idioms allows students to see some of the patterns in language use. Moreover, it appeals to logical/mathematical learners (Gardner, 1983) and it leads to reflective observation, an important aspect of the learning and critical thinking cycle as described by Kolb (1984).

Finally, if the above conversation-based activities are too challenging for beginning learners, or if there is not enough time in a class to assign students to find and analyze the idioms in an authentic dialogue or transcript, at times we have also simply followed up on our initial introduction of the conversation features of the new idioms with a series of questions based on specific narrative contexts and asked learners to pick the best idioms for a particular context, followed by a discussion about why they have chosen those idioms. McCarthy (1998, p. 147) provides the following example of this type of task:

A friend tells you a story about how she discovered that a colleague she has worked with for ten years went to the same school as her thirty years ago, even though they had never realized this before. What could you say at the end of her story? Which of these idioms would be suitable and why?

  a. "Oh well, that's life."
  b. "It's a small world, isn't it."
  c. "I bet you were on cloud nine when you heard."
  d. "You live and learn, don't you."
  e. "Well, would you believe it!

## Corpus-Based Activities

As discussed in Chapter 4, many textbooks and teachers use information from a variety of online corpora and corpus studies to add information when presenting definitions and word lists of new idioms. The following are some popular and comprehensive corpora (both print and online)[1]:

- Corpus of Contemporary American English (COCA):
  http://corpus.byu.edu/coca
- Michigan Corpus of Academic Spoken English (MICASE):
  http://quod.lib.umich.edu/m/micase
- British National Corpus (BNC):
  http://corpus.byu.edu/bnc
- TIME Magazine Corpus (TIME):
  http://corpus.byu.edu/time
- Scottish Corpus of Texts and Speech (SCOTS):
  http://www.scottishcorpus.ac.uk
- Vienna-Oxford International Corpus of English (VOICE):
  http://www.univie.ac.at/voice
- International Corpus of English (ICE):
  http://ice-corpora.net/ice

Further, teachers can ask students to do a variety of activities in which they find and analyze information themselves by searching one or more of the online corpora. For example, drawing on examples in Sinclair (2003) and Balunda (2009), we created the following activity for students to complete before we discuss a list of new idioms.

1. Examine the collocation patterns below that contain the word *bluff*. Categorize or separate the example according to its part of speech (noun, adjective, verb, adverb, preposition, gerund/infinitive/participle, etc.).
   - to bluff
   - to call a bluff
   - to call his bluff

---

[1] Reppen (2011) offers a more comprehensive list and analysis of online corpora for language teaching.

2. Categorize or separate each part of speech according to its meaning.

3. How many meanings for the word did you find?

4. Look at the language data again according to its part of speech. This time locate any recurring patterns in the data that you think are idiomatic phrases or collocations.

5. Create one original sentence for each meaning of the word.

This is another activity that is geared toward more advanced language learners, but even advanced learners should be introduced to what a corpus is and how to read the concordance lines. And one example activity should be done together as a whole class before asking students to work on their own.

Based on work by Shaw (2011), the following is another effective corpus activity that can be adapted to various learner proficiency levels. In this activity, learners are introduced to the idea of collocation, "the statistical tendency of words to co-occur" (Hunston, 2002, p. 12). We begin by providing examples of collocations such as the following:

- Our research does *indicate* that the public believes that the mission will ultimately succeed.

- He used it to *indicate* that we're going to be tough.

- That would seem to *indicate* that there wasn't a big risk.

- But, overall, there's nothing to *indicate* that we are being harmed.

- I want you to *indicate* with your applause who you believe. (Shaw, 2011, p. 81)

We ask students to try to guess the meaning of the word by substituting a synonym for *indicate*. Next, we ask them to look at a list of collocations from the above sentences: *that, results, research, studies, data, study, finding, respondents, evidence,* and *significant*. Finally, we ask students: "What do these words describe?" and "What does this tell you about how to use the word *indicate*?"

Having established the types of insights that collocations offer, we move on to examples of idioms such as the following:

- So we stood and chanted in unison the formula we had learned *by heart* and repeated over and over for a year.

- By now you probably can recite *by heart* the late 80s management litany.

- He knew every Beach Club member's name *by heart* and the names of all the children.

- . . . as if reciting something he has learned *by heart* and means to repeat exactly as he heard it.

Following the same procedure as above, we ask students to come up with synonyms and then present them with the following collocations: *recite, know, repeat, formula, song, poem,* and *names*. And we ask them to come up with examples of other things that are learned "by heart."

More advanced classes can be shown how to use the collocation resources in corpora such as COCA and then complete searches for collocations on their own, even presenting their findings to the class in short research presentations. Corbett (2010) details this type of activity using the BNC. After presenting introductory information about what idioms are and how to use a corpus to search for information about idioms, Corbett presents students with an example idiom, *kettle of fish*, and the results of a basic search of usage patterns, including the 37 examples from the BNC, a selection of which are shown below (p. 208):

| | |
|---|---|
| it'd be a different | **kettle of fish** altogether. |
| oh that'll be a different | **kettle of fish** wouldn't it? |
| Well that's a different sort of | **kettle of fish** when you think about it. |
| And hay harvesting was a different | **kettle of fish** altogether. |
| It was a real | **kettle of fish** and no mistake. |
| You're a very different | **kettle of fish** from Flora. |

Based on these results, students can see/learn that the term occurs primarily in fiction and never appears in academic contexts. After asking students to come up with more examples and contexts in which using this idiom would be appropriate, Corbett (2010) presents the results of the search for collocations using the List function on the display page and searching for all adjectives that appear before the idioms by typing *[j\*] kettle of fish* in the Word(s) box, as displayed below:

DIFFERENT KETTLE OF FISH (n=32)

FINE KETTLE OF FISH (n=2)

REAL KETTLE OF FISH (n=1)

This search reveals the ubiquity of the collocation pair *different* and *kettle of fish*. Based on the above search processes, teachers can next give students new idioms to plug into the corpus; Corbett (2010) provides students with more idioms related to the topic of food, such as *cool as a cucumber* and *piece of cake*. Teachers can ask students to first make educated guesses on aspects of the idiom's frequency, register, context(s), and collocations, and then confirm their hypotheses through data searches.

Similar to the conversation analysis activities described above, creating activities in which students hypothesize, search, and analyze the results of online corpora connects with students' analytic, linguistic, and mathematical abilities and validates the computer and online skills many students possess. And in addition to improved knowledge, memory, and use of new idioms in our classes, using online corpora and comparing usages across contexts can lead to interesting and important classroom discussions on register, language varieties, and World Englishes, particularly when activities are based on corpora listed above, such as ICE and VOICE. As Reppen (2010) notes, "As corpora and corpus tools become more available, and as teachers become better trained and more comfortable with corpus resources . . . the ways in which corpora will be used for language learning will continue to expand" (p. 45).

## Digital Media Activities

Similar to key differences between comprehension-based teaching methods and more output and lexical approaches, research and teaching related to learning vocabulary within **computer-assisted language learning (CALL)** can be divided between activities that see "vocabulary as a skill to be taught explicitly" and "vocabulary as something that is to be acquired peripherally while the student is engaged in an authentic task" (Levy & Stockwell, 2006, pp. 187–188). In the latter approach, vocabulary may come up as part of the task, and students may even use digital media to look up words or discuss the meanings and usage of idioms with partners, but the focus of the lesson is not on acquiring vocabulary but rather on completing a task. We detail here some effective activities that adopt the former approach to explicitly teach learners new idioms.

A simple CALL addition to any lesson or activity involving a written text is to provide hyperlinks to additional content for any vocabulary words that you want students to focus on. Laufer and Hill (2000) show that students had higher recollection of target words that were linked to definitions, translations, and audio recordings of the new terms. Yeh and Wang (2003) further reveal the use of hyperlinks to provide videos and pictures about the new words, offering a further level of processing to aid in retention and aligning with the learning styles of visual learners. Of course, this activity requires teachers to have a digital copy of the reading in order to create the hyperlinks, and students must have computer and Internet access to see the links. See the website Elllo (www.elllo.org) for examples of texts that contain hyperlinks to chosen vocabulary along with additional information and short quizzes and activities that students can use on their own to practice new words. Idioms are not highlighted on this website, but many of the new words in the texts are idioms.

An online search for example uses of key idioms is another easy and effective activity that allows students to see where and how idioms in the class vocabulary list are used. For example, pairs of students could be given idioms and asked to search online for at least three examples on the website of a specific newspaper or news source (e.g., www.nytimes.com, www.bbc.com/news). Various websites will work, but it is much easier for students if the sites have a built-in search tool as many news sites have. In reporting their findings, we often ask students to respond to the following questions:

1. Does the idiom have the same meaning in all of the examples? Explain.

2. Does the idiom appear to be more formal or informal? Explain.

3. Are there any similarities in the topics that the idioms are used to discuss? Or does the idiom appear to be unrestricted in its usage? Explain.

As suggested by Mack and Ojalvo (2010) as a follow-up to this activity, we sometimes read the article "Shanghai Is Trying to Untangle the Mangled English of Chinglish" (Jacobs, 2010) with advanced university students. We then discuss the difficulties of translation in any language, particularly when it comes to idioms. Of course, a discussion of the subtleties of translation and "native" speaker norms are most effective with advanced students. However, performing basic searches for use of new idioms on particular sites is an easy task for intermediate to high-proficiency students. Moreover, any discussion and whole-class presentations of findings will appeal to verbal learners, and Jacobs's (2010) article about Chinglish brings up many questions about identity and motivation for using and learning English in foreign contexts (Dörnyei, 2001, 2003; Norton, 2000).

Different from the discussion of the previous activities that primarily draw on linguistic, logical, and comprehension abilities, Wong and Looi (2010) present an innovative activity that connects an inter-/intrapersonal focus with visual and spatial experimentation. In their research, they aimed to incorporate the ubiquitous use of smartphones and tablet computers by middle school, high school, and university students—a subset of CALL that is referred to as mobile-assisted language learning (MALL). In their study, Wong and Looi present the following idea in a lesson on learning idioms.

First, after briefly going over the meanings and pronunciations of the new words, the teacher shows short animations that depict idioms to a middle school class. The animations are mobile-optimized, often comical in nature, and available 24/7 for students to view through a class website. After an additional lesson to ensure that students have a good understanding of the new idioms, the teacher asks the students to find examples of the idioms in their daily lives and then take photos or make videos of the context or activity that represents the idioms. Students then make sentences using the idioms to describe the visual material and post them on a class wiki. The wiki is organized to have one page for each idiom covered in the class. As students post their photos, videos, and explanations on the idiom pages, other students in the class can compare and edit the information and post follow-up pictures and descriptions of the idiom, creating a detailed definition of the idiom with a large amount of student-created content pertaining to the same idiom. As they post new information and content, students are encouraged to perform peer reviews on the wiki by commenting on, correcting, or improving their peers' sentences. Finally, after a specified amount of time, the class convenes as a whole group to discuss the idiom pages and vote on items such as best page or best image. This activity is particularly useful and enjoyable with high school and university learners and appeals to the computer skills of many students and their use of smartphones to take pictures and create videos. For less proficient students, more specific tasks and roles can be given, and students can be divided into groups to work on only one specific idiom page.

This is just one activity using wikis or other student-centered online content that can be adapted, revised, and continually discussed, but it is particularly effective and useful for vocabulary and idiom teachers because it prevents classroom activities from having an "end" when the teacher evaluates and grades the project. Instead, the wiki allows students to continue to create experiences and memories with the new idioms and class content, even after the lesson is over. In some of our colleagues' classrooms, the teachers have asked students to revisit blogs and wikis later in the semester or school year and publish the content as learner dictionaries or online vocabulary tutorials.

One caveat: Wong and Looi (2010) note that there was a large disparity in student contribution during their pilot study, with one student posting 141 photo and sentence examples—37% of the entire wiki postings in the class of 40 students. Teachers will have to create some structure and monitor closely the contributions in order to ensure that posting and contributing online is equal for all students.

Another effective digital activity outside of the classroom that multiple researchers have demonstrated to be effective in learning vocabulary is videogaming (Gee, 2003, 2006; Piirainen-Marsh & Tainio, 2009; Sundqvist & Sylvén, 2012). Many learners from all proficiency levels enter the English classroom with experience playing computer and video games in English, and multiple studies have shown increases in student recognition and production of new vocabulary as the result of game playing (Reinders, 2012). As an early proponent of incorporating digital game playing and language learning, Gee (2012) writes:

> But the main thing games can do for language learning is to "situate meaning." Games associate words with images, actions, goals and dialogue, not just with definitions or other words. Learners come to see how words attach to the world's contexts or situations that they are about and help to create or manipulate. If learners can only "cash out" words for words, they have a purely verbal understanding of talk and texts. This may be good for test passing but it is not good for deep understanding. If they can "cash out" words for images, experiences, actions, goals and dialogue—for a virtual theatre of motivated action in their minds—then they have deep understanding and real learning. (p. xiv)

Of course, few teachers have the ability or time to develop entirely new video games for students to play, but a start would be to connect classroom discussions and pedagogy to games that students already use. As Sundqvist and Sylvén (2012) write, "such discussions would most likely increase intrinsic motivation and promote learner autonomy" (p. 203). Teachers could create modules based on the different levels in which students practice using chosen idioms that have been presented to the whole class while they are playing the games. As they play, they are encouraged or required to use English with their partners and keep a language use log or diary about their experiences playing the games and when the different idioms are used.

Also, in an attempt to connect to the extramural online habits of students, we have developed a presentation activity in which students use and report to the class on the merits of a particular vocabulary website that has sections devoted to idiom learning. The instructions are as follows:

> Research one of the websites from the list below (to be assigned in class). Be prepared to give a brief oral report (no more than 5 minutes) to a group of students about your website. In your report, you should do the following:
> - Give a general overview (overall description).
> - Explain how English language learners could use the website to help them learn new words and phrases.

- Give at least one specific example of how the website works (test it out for us!).
- Give your own evaluation (i.e., Is it very useful? Moderately useful? Not at all helpful?).

We particularly like this activity because it helps students practice learning vocabulary and idioms on their own and challenges them to make their own decisions and analyses about the types of learning activities that they enjoy and learn from the most. We change the websites each year depending on what sites are active and what new sites have been created. See Chapter 9 for a full report on websites and online learning tools for idioms that can be used with this activity.

## Idioms in Action Activities

Similar to the digital and corpus-based activities, we have created a few activities that are effective in getting students to immediately see the high-frequency use of idioms and/or phrasal verbs outside the classroom and to simultaneously get the students to use them. These are simple activities that are primarily geared toward English language learners in an English-speaking environment, and they can be used with a variety of proficiency levels from high-beginner to advanced. We call these activities Idioms in Action tasks.

For the first activity, students study a set number of idioms in class (five to six is an ideal number). After they have gone over the definitions, examples, register, and syntax, assign on-campus interviews as homework. Ask them to interview three to four local, English-speaking students about the recently learned idioms or phrasal verbs. They can ask questions such as the following:

1. Have you ever heard of the idiom/phrasal verb _____?
2. Do you use it?
3. How often do you personally use _____?
4. Do you think it is a useful expression? Why or why not?
5. If you don't use it, what do you use instead?

Then ask students to gather their results and either write a summary of what they learned or present on the results for an in-class presentation.

The benefits of this activity are fourfold: (1) ELLs will be able to practice their speaking and listening skills with the idioms as their target, (2) the idioms and phrasal verbs will gain credence in the minds of students as they see their use by native speakers, (3) ELLs will learn new vocabulary by talking to the respondents, and (4) students will reinforce the use of the idioms in a focused and natural conversation. This, in itself, will help them participate in the R and T of the R.E.S.T method discussed in Chapter 3.

A second Idioms in Action activity is to get students to attend a lecture or presentation on campus. It is recommended that they ask for permission to record the lecture. This will allow them to review the lecture or parts of it a second or even third time. While listening to the lecture, have students write down any interesting idioms or phrasal verbs that they hear. In addition, have them write down the points covered in the lecture and see if they can hypothesize why the idioms/phrasal verbs were used in the way they were. Have students offer synonyms that could have been used in place of the idioms. Why did the lecturer use certain idioms or phrasal verbs as opposed to the single-word equivalents to convey his or her point? For homework, have students write a summary of the idioms used, hypothesize why they were used, and then present on the findings the next day in class.

Because these types of activities require students to actively explore and engage with speakers and language in their surroundings, they can be adapted to teach more than idioms. We have used similar interview and observation tasks as the basis for classes from oral presentations to academic writing (McPherron & Randolph, 2013).

## Dictionary Activities

Miller (2012) writes that there are three main types of English dictionaries for learners: monolingual (purely in English), bilingual (in English and in the speaker's first language), and bilingualized (includes translations but gives definitions in English). She lists the following monolingual dictionaries as the most commonly used by English language learners around the world:

- Longman Dictionary of Contemporary English: www.ldoceonline.com

- Macmillan English Dictionary for Advanced Learners: www.macmillandictionary.com
- Oxford Advanced Learner's Dictionary: www.oxfordadvancedlearnersdictionary.com
- Cambridge Advanced Learner's Dictionary: http://dictionary.cambridge.org
- Collins Cobuild Advanced Dictionary: www.mycobuild.com/free-search.aspx
- Merriam-Webster's Learner's Dictionary: www.learnersdictionary.com

Miller (2006, 2012) argues that dictionaries are often underused as teaching resources, and teachers are not often aware of the variety of collocational, pronunciation, idiomatic, and etymological information available in dictionaries. Miller (2012), Thornbury (2002), and many others argue that monolingual dictionaries in particular can be used productively to develop vocabulary acquisition activities and overall awareness of the lexical and syntactic patterns of English, in addition to the basic definitions of new words and idioms. For example, teachers can create activities that compare pronunciation and spelling in British versus American dictionaries; instruct students to determine the grammatical part of speech and collocated prepositions of new idioms; find and write new example sentences; differentiate between synonyms, antonyms, homonyms, and polysemes; and, in general, determine the types of information in different dictionaries for better self-study. It should be noted that although this is a nice activity for advanced ELLs, English-only or monolingual dictionaries are difficult for beginning or even intermediate learners. With these ELLs, bilingual dictionaries are most efficient and inspiring.

Toward the objective of determining the types of information in different dictionaries, we created a simple activity in which we bring in a stack of learner dictionaries or use a classroom with computer and Internet access.

Directions: In your pairs or groups, use the dictionaries I've brought to class (and your own if you wish) to discover what else you can add to your understanding of the words below. Your task is to add more information to the Answers.com dictionary entries. You can add words, phrases, sentences, or helpful tips. Look especially for information about collocations, style, connotations, related phrasal verbs, and grammatical patterns.

Sample dictionary entry: *pull one's leg*

1.  Play a joke on, tease, as in "Are you serious about moving back in or are you pulling my leg?" This term is thought to allude to tripping someone by so holding a stick or other object that one of his legs is pulled back. [Late 1800s]

An additional activity could be to ask students to evaluate dictionaries based on the following categories provided by Nation (2001) for evaluating features of learner dictionaries:

*   There should be ways of finding the appropriate word.

*   The dictionary should provide information about constraints on use of the word.

*   The dictionary should provide plenty of understandable example sentences as models for use.

*   The dictionary should contain easily understood information about the grammar and collocations of the word.

*   The dictionary should show the spelling of inflected and derived forms.

*   The dictionary should show how the word is pronounced.

Nation (2001) cautions that teachers should limit their expectations of dictionary activities because students need to meet new idioms and vocabulary in a variety of contexts and experiences for actual acquisition and production. With this caveat, however, we argue that these dictionary activities help students not only analyze new idioms in depth, but also think critically about the materials that they use. Further, this knowledge of dictionary preference will directly help students when creating personalized vocabulary notebooks of new idioms and words to study as well as word cards, two practices highly recommended by vocabulary experts in applied linguistics.

# Pedagogical Perspective: Meeting Student Needs

> It may not be enough to present, practice and produce words (or even words in sentences) when we are dealing with the kinds of lexical features we have argued to be central to conversational language. A language-awareness approach may be more effective and appropriate at the outset, and encouraging the "learner-as-researcher" may be the best long-term strategy for empowering the learner to become a natural user of the target spoken vocabulary. (McCarthy, 1998, pp. 127–128)

In promoting a learner-as-researcher approach to vocabulary teaching—in which teachers highlight how vocabulary such as idioms function in conversation—but also stressing the ultimate goal of acquisition and use of new words, McCarthy (1998) steps outside the use-versus-analyze debate that Celce-Murcia (2013) describes as a pendulum that has swung back and forth in language teaching approaches since the 19th century. Similarly, instead of taking a strong stance on any of the many debates on teaching vocabulary—be it the debate over implicit versus explicit teaching or questions over the effectiveness of digital media versus traditional "chalk and talk" lectures—this chapter has focused on teaching activities and approaches that adapt to a variety of proficiency levels and uses. We also agree with McCarthy in his general suggestion to encourage students to be aware of the ways language functions and to be open to exploring the uses and meanings of new words, in particular idioms, in addition to putting in the needed memory and retention work. In fact, we encourage vocabulary teachers to incorporate language awareness activities, such as the corpus and conversation analysis tasks introduced above, at the beginning of lessons on idioms. We have found that these activities both introduce the meanings of the new words and activate the critical thinking and self-learning that are central to many education policies and reforms (Bellanca, Fogarty, & Pete, 2012).

By the same token, as we ourselves are often fascinated by the use of idioms, we want students to explore and research idiom usage on their own. However, we must be sensitive to the multiple demands on students; sometimes memorization and recognition of new vocabulary such as idioms is the final student objective. This point was illustrated for McPherron during his first year of teaching in China. Similar to many foreign teachers at his university, he was not familiar with the College English Test (CET) that almost all Chinese university students take to demonstrate their English proficiency, and instead of focusing on the vocabulary listed in special practice books for the CET, he would begin every class with a student mini-presentation on a new word that they had "found" from outside the class. The university administrators had not told him about the CET, except to inform him that the goal of English language education at this university was to become more communicative and bring in creative and critical thinking activities, moving away from the rote memorization of vocabulary and grammar rules typically tested by the CET. At the beginning of his classes, however, McPherron realized that all of the students were silently reading the CET vocabulary books, quietly practicing the words and definitions by themselves. When class would start, they would put their CET books away and engage in the class activities. Similarly, in the early mornings, he would often see and hear students reading aloud from the CET practice books, often in a nearby park, even shouting the new words to themselves as advocated by Li Yang and the Crazy English curriculum (Osnos, 2008). Randolph found himself in a similar situation in the Japanese public junior high school system. Weekly, he would bring new idioms related to formal and informal, academic and nonacademic situations for students to learn. Although they learned these and took great interest in them, the idioms were not used on the schools' tests, and later many idioms were forgotten as the students geared up for their high school entrance exams. Thus, a key question became: How much should we emphasize production, exploration, and language awareness in our classes if the students were primarily interested in memorizing as many words from the CET word lists and preparing for prefectural tests without any concern for idioms?

We have had similar experiences and discussions about using student-as-researcher activities in our classrooms when students have such a variety of motivations and needs (McPherron & Randolph, 2013). The answer we have always found is balance in terms of not focusing only on recognition and memorization tasks and not assuming all students have the same interest and receive the same benefits from interactive tasks and creative explorations. In designing our lessons around such different learner characteristics, we are inspired by much of the work on postmethodology, whose advocates, such as Kumaravadivelu (2003, 2006), describe teaching macro strategies such as "foster language awareness" but also "ensure social relevance." In the same way, we encourage teachers to adapt the activities in this chapter as well as the lessons in the next section of the book to meet the needs of students.

PART 2

# Teaching Idioms to English Language Learners Around the World

# CHAPTER 6

# Teacher Perspectives on Teaching English Idioms

To know that you do not know is the best.

—*Lao Tzu*

Outside of comments and examples from our own teaching experiences, mostly at the end of the chapters, the first section of this book dealt primarily with summaries of experimental, classroom, and theoretical research on teaching and learning idioms. In the second section of the book, we now deal more explicitly with views from the classroom, including (1) surveys of teachers and students about learning and teaching idioms and (2) reviews of a variety of materials for teaching idioms. And perhaps most practical for teachers, in Chapter 8 we present lessons for teaching idioms from contributors around the world. We start this second section of the book, however, by presenting and analyzing the results of a survey we conducted with 103 teacher participants about their experiences and practices in teaching idioms. We begin this chapter with a brief summary of the methods we drew on in conducting the survey, then present the key findings from the survey through a series of tables, charts, graphs, and a discussion section. We end this chapter, as we end Chapters 7 and 8, with a note on implications for future research on teaching and learning idioms. We include this note to connect the teacher, student, and classroom per-

117

spectives presented in these chapters to research projects and themes from the first section of the book.

## Our Survey and Data Collection Methods

There have been few resources that collect and analyze actual classroom practices of teachers of ELLs addressing idiom learning. Much of the work addressing teaching and learning idioms is based on questions about idioms and cognition (Boers & Lindstromberg, 2005, 2008a, 2008b), idioms as metaphors (Kövecses, 2002), or idioms in discourse (Reppen, 2010, 2011). Outside of classroom reports and lesson plans that address vocabulary more broadly, no study has included data from the experiences of language teachers and learners about how they perceive, teach, and learn idioms. In particular, no study has surveyed teachers and learners in a variety of teaching contexts around the world. In addition to many years of teaching at secondary and university levels in our native United States, we have extensive experience teaching in countries such as China, Romania, Turkey, Japan, and Ecuador, and we have both taught language teachers from more than 50 countries in MA-TESOL and teacher education programs. Thus, we drew on our network of contacts around the world to find diverse participants, for both the teacher survey reported here and the student survey reported in Chapter 7. See Figures 6-1, 6-2, and 6-3 for a breakdown of the backgrounds and teaching contexts of the 103 survey participants.

Following survey tips and instructions in Heigham and Croker (2009), Dörnyei (2007), and Richards (2003), we created a survey with 13 questions that used both five-point Likert scale items (in which respondents rank their responses to statements on a scale of 1 to 5) and short open-ended questions (in which respondents provide responses based on their experiences). Participants were instructed to respond in the language that they felt most comfortable using, although most responded to the short-answer questions in English. Due to the diversity of the participants and their proficiency in English, we decided not to translate the questions into any other language.

We created and distributed the survey through SurveyMonkey. Based on our connections with teachers and researchers around the world, we found participants for the survey primarily through a

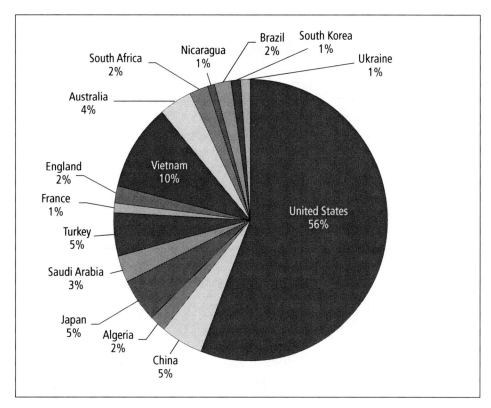

*Figure 6-1. Countries Where Survey Participants Teach*

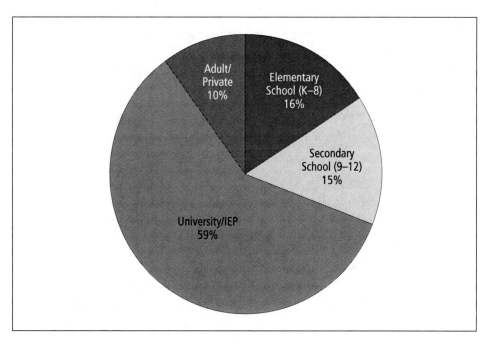

*Figure 6-2. Levels at Which Survey Participants Teach*

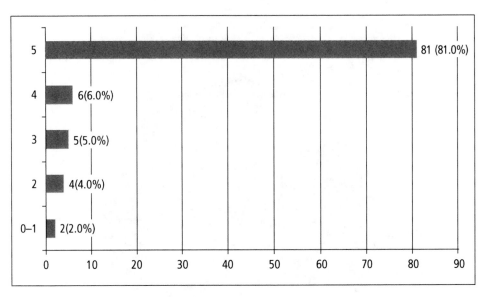

*Figure 6-3. Survey Participants' Years of Experience*

snowball sampling approach (described in Richards, 2003) in which we emailed the survey link to colleagues and asked them to forward it to other English language teachers whom they worked with. We also placed calls for participants in the newsletters and online journals of TESOL affiliates in Arkansas, California, Illinois, Michigan, and Florida. All respondents were anonymous. As seen in Figure 6-1, respondents represent every continent, except Antarctica, and although the majority of the respondents teach in university settings, we were able to represent teachers from private intensive English programs and elementary and secondary schools. Further, the teachers self-reported a variety of classroom topics and subjects, including 40% reading classes, 45% writing classes, 33% speaking classes, and 20% some sort of integrated skills classes, and as detailed in Figure 6-3, most of the teachers reported having more than 5 years of teaching experience.

We chose an online survey tool primarily because it allowed us to quickly distribute the survey around the world while maintaining security features, such as a password-protected login and limits on the number of surveys that could be taken from one computer. Paolo, Bonaminio, Gibson, Partridge, and Kallail (2000) note that respondents provide longer open-ended responses to e-mail than to other types of surveys, and responses to online surveys tend to be more candid than responses to mail or phone surveys (Bachman, Elfrink, & Vazzana, 1999).

We based the survey questions on key aspects of teaching idioms similar to those surveyed in the first section of this book: What are the best materials for teaching idioms? What are the most useful definitions for teaching idioms? What are the best ways to categorize idioms? For many of the questions, we drew on topics and definitions as outlined by Liu (2008) because his book has been one of the most widely used to guide teachers on teaching idioms, and we wanted to gain the perspective of practicing teachers on the definitions, materials, and activities that he summarizes in his chapters. In addition, we asked closed and open-ended questions about how much time participants can focus on idioms in their classes and what problems or difficulties they face in addressing idioms in their classes. Before distributing the survey to a wider audience, we piloted it with 10 teachers in Michigan, New York, Illinois, and China. We asked the participants in the pilot test about the clarity, quality, and importance of the questions as well as ease of understanding the directions. Based on the feedback from the pilot test, we combined two open-ended questions into question 11 and added question 12 about idioms that are particularly difficult to learn (see a list of idioms partially based on question 12 in Appendix B and the full survey in Appendix C). We feel that by incorporating responses from the pilot survey, we ensured the content validity and relevance of the results of the survey.

As you read the report and analysis of the survey results, it is important to note that we designed the survey only to provide descriptive statistics and themes about teacher perspectives, and we did not perform any inferential statistic measurements. Through the surveys of teachers and students, we obtained a general, wide-angle view of key themes and issues that teachers share across teaching contexts; more in-depth examinations of variables and correlations could be tested in future surveys. In this way, we feel that the survey sheds light on the topics discussed in previous chapters and provides a link to our discussion of materials and lessons in Chapters 8 and 9.

## Survey Results: What Do Teachers Say About Teaching Idioms in Their Classrooms?

When putting together the teacher survey, two of the first things we wanted to know were simply how often teachers address idioms and idiom learning in their classes and what might be some of the reasons that they find it difficult to bring idioms into their curriculum. In response to the first question, we asked directly on the survey: "How often do you teach your students about idioms and/or idiomatic language in the classes that you teach?" And we received the responses shown in Figure 6-4.

Although response 2 elicited the largest number of responses, if we add 4 and 5 together and 1 and 2 together, 43.9% of participating teachers address idioms at least once a week, compared to 37.5% of teachers who rarely or never address idioms. Thus, participants report addressing idioms in their classroom fairly regularly, and many teachers who responded that they rarely teach idioms were not opposed to teaching idioms and did not feel that it was a frivolous topic; rather, these teachers responded to the request for comments with responses such as "I teach idioms as they become relevant to the content I am teaching" and "I address idioms as they come up, but I do not systematically teach them."

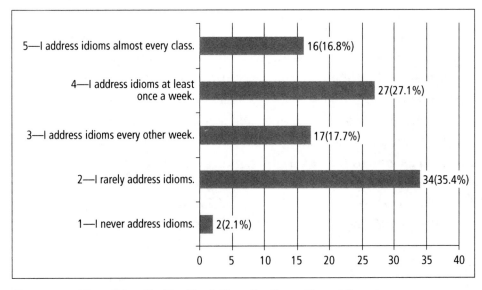

*Figure 6-4. How Often Do You Teach Your Students About Idioms?*

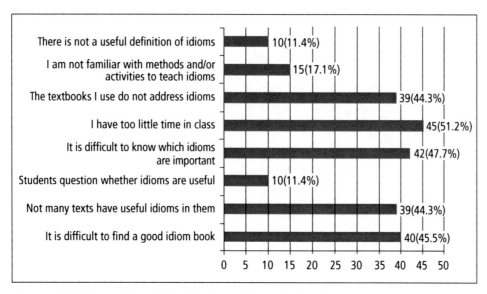

*Figure 6-5. Factors That Make Teaching Idioms Difficult*

In terms of the difficulties teachers report in addressing idioms, Figure 6-5 shows that time and materials are the largest factors, not student or teacher interest (see Appendix C for full text of response choices).

It is interesting to note that "Students question whether idioms are useful to their overall English language learning" received the fewest responses (11.4%), and few teachers feel that they are not familiar with methods on how to address idioms (17.1%) or how to define them (11.4%). At the same time, many teachers note that the textbooks they use do not address idiom learning (44.3%), and they have difficulty choosing which idioms are important for students (47.7%). Perhaps not surprisingly, most teachers simply report that they do not have enough time to cover the core class topics and supplement them with attention to idioms (51.2%). However, just as in response to the previous question on how often they address idioms, respondents wrote that even if they have experienced difficulties, including textbooks that focus more on grammar and tests that are based on academic word choice and not necessarily spoken idioms, teachers feel that idioms are important to address. One participant noted, "Because professors will use common, colloquial language to explain more complicated, scientific ideas, it is important for ELL students to learn idioms. They are not fluff—they are the way real people express themselves."

In addition to discovering more about how often the survey participants address idioms and what difficulties they have incorporating idioms into class activities, we asked questions about three key topics surveyed in Chapters 2, 4, and 5: What are the most useful definitions of idioms? What are the best ways to categorize idioms? What are the most useful classroom activities for teaching idioms? The possible response choices for best ways to categorize idioms and most useful classroom activities were based on lists complied from Liu (2008). Figures 6-6, 6-7, and 6-8 detail overall responses to these questions (see Appendix C for full text of response choices).

In terms of most useful definitions (Figure 6-6), teachers did not clearly view one definition as not useful or not useful at all, but when categories 4 and 5 are combined, three definitions were viewed as either very useful or extremely useful by the majority of the 103 participants:

- Idioms include full sentences and sayings such as *It's a small world* or *Don't put all of your eggs in one basket*. (55.1%)

- Idioms are set expressions (i.e., if one word is substituted or the word order is altered, the phrase's meaning may change or become meaningless). (54.6%)

- Idioms change meaning when translated word for word into another language. (53.4%)

These definitions are preferred to the other three definitions listed—idioms as figurative, idioms as noncompositional, and idioms as breaking the rules of syntax and semantics, definitions that are much more common in textbooks and dictionaries. In fact, the highest ranked category for each of these definitions was somewhat useful.

Analyzing the results of how teachers prefer to categorize idioms (Figure 6-7), teachers view one category, *By degree of literalness*, as not very useful, with the majority (54.3%) ranking this category as either not useful at all or not very useful. Alternatively, the majority of teachers ranked the following two categories as 4 or 5:

- By activity for which the idiom is used, for example, dating (*go steady, hit it off*). (70.6%)

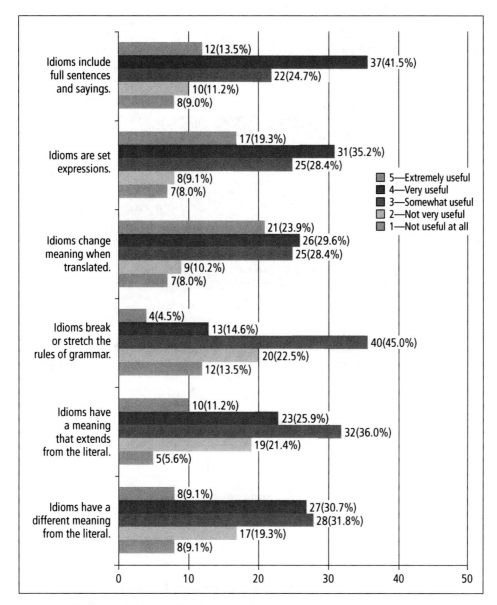

Figure 6-6. Most Useful Definitions of Idioms

- By origin or source, for example, from sports (*hit a home run*), from body parts (*hold their feet to the fire*), from food (*dough, go nuts*). (51.8%)

No other category (Figure 6-7) received strong endorsement from the participating teachers, with the remaining categories receiving somewhat useful as their highest ranking. Teachers clearly prefer to categorize idioms according to the activity in which the idioms are used.

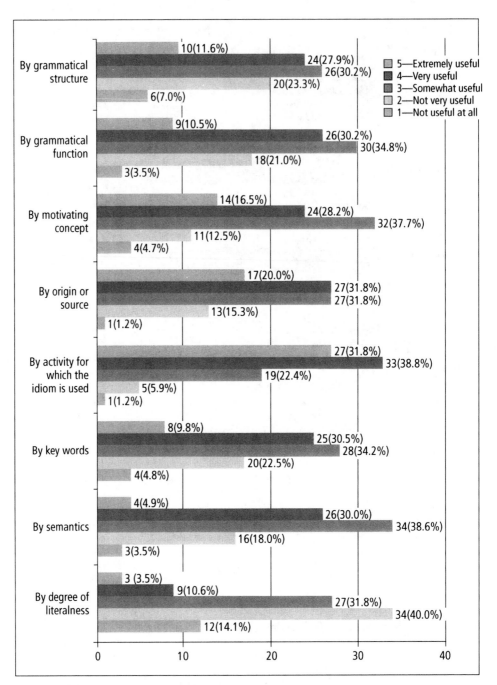

By grammatical structure
- 10(11.6%)
- 24(27.9%)
- 26(30.2%)
- 20(23.3%)
- 6(7.0%)

By grammatical function
- 9(10.5%)
- 26(30.2%)
- 30(34.8%)
- 18(21.0%)
- 3(3.5%)

By motivating concept
- 14(16.5%)
- 24(28.2%)
- 32(37.7%)
- 11(12.5%)
- 4(4.7%)

By origin or source
- 17(20.0%)
- 27(31.8%)
- 27(31.8%)
- 13(15.3%)
- 1(1.2%)

By activity for which the idiom is used
- 27(31.8%)
- 33(38.8%)
- 19(22.4%)
- 5(5.9%)
- 1(1.2%)

By key words
- 8(9.8%)
- 25(30.5%)
- 28(34.2%)
- 20(22.5%)
- 4(4.8%)

By semantics
- 4(4.9%)
- 26(30.0%)
- 34(38.6%)
- 16(18.0%)
- 3(3.5%)

By degree of literalness
- 3 (3.5%)
- 9(10.6%)
- 27(31.8%)
- 34(40.0%)
- 12(14.1%)

Legend:
- 5—Extremely useful
- 4—Very useful
- 3—Somewhat useful
- 2—Not very useful
- 1—Not useful at all

*Figure 6-7. Most Useful Ways to Categorize Idioms*

This relates to many of the comments about addressing idioms only when they come up in class or in a specific context or text that the class is focused on. This preference is reflected in many of the textbooks that organize idioms according to specific activities, and it has even been attested to in the general vocabulary literature. As summarized in Chapter 5 and by Folse (2004), numerous studies have revealed the inefficacy of presenting new vocabulary as semantic sets, such as *clothing* or *hobbies*, and the preference of the teachers in our survey to organize idioms as activities/thematic units such as *cooking something* or *a trip to the mall* is clearly in line with these research results and vocabulary teachers. At the same time, although attested to in the literature by Kövecses (2002) and the basis for several textbooks, including *The Big Picture* (King, 1999) and *Idioms Organiser* (Wright, 2002), grouping new idioms according to motivating concept or origin is viewed only as somewhat useful by participating teachers.

In terms of most useful activities for teachers (Figure 6-8), the participants did not clearly rate any activity as not useful at all. In fact, participants ranked many activities as very useful or extremely useful, including the following scores in which the majority of respondents answered with a 4 or 5.

- Making up example sentences using idioms (69.4%)
- Guessing the meaning of the idioms from context (65.9%)
- Reading and identifying idioms in a passage (62.1%)
- Guessing the meaning of the idioms using pragmatics, conceptual knowledge, and imagination (57.2%)
- Keeping a list of idioms from reading outside of class (55.3%)
- Writing and performing skits using idioms (52.4%)
- Playing idiom games such as Pictionary or charades (53.6%)

The top four activities are all fairly well-known activities that are found in many vocabulary textbooks and often taught as strategies for L1 activities, and it follows that teachers use these activities and find them effective. It is important to note, however, that strategies or activities that are based on guessing the meaning from context or guessing the meaning of the idioms using pragmatics, conceptual knowledge, and imagination can actually detract from learning and remembering a new word if the correct meaning is not supplied by a teacher or textbook soon after a guess is made. As Folse (2004) writes, a learner must have a very large vocabulary in English to use only context clues in order to learn and remember a new word, and Nation (2001) emphasizes that the correct meaning must be encoded in a learner's memory soon after noticing the new word. Guessing activities are good for

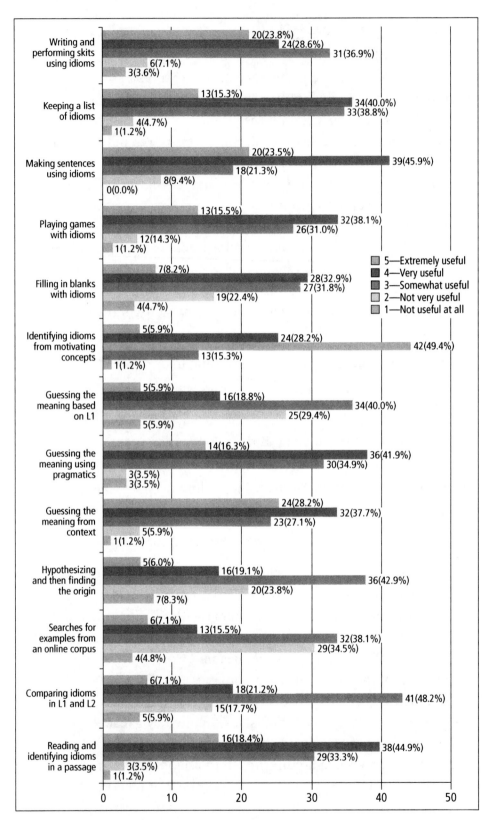

*Figure 6-8. Most Useful Activities for Teaching Idioms*

creating motivation but not sufficient for promoting learning—there must be a balance between the two.

Further, and similar to the question on categorizing idioms, the teacher respondents did not find as highly effective some activities that are highly recommended by vocabulary researchers. In particular, more than 30% of respondents ranked the following activities as either 1 (*not useful at all*) or 2 (*not very useful*):

- Conducting searches for idiom examples from an online corpus (39.3%)

- Guessing the meaning of the idioms based on knowledge of L1 idioms (35.3%)

- Hypothesizing and then finding the origin of the idioms (32.1%)

As explained in Chapters 4 and 5, we still find the above activities useful, but these results point out that perhaps few teachers have learned about activities such as using corpus searches or how to use idioms dictionaries to draw on etymology when learning idioms. Indeed, in response to a question about what materials teachers commonly use, idiom dictionaries were the lowest ranked (31.8%) in comparison with similar results for all other materials (see Figure 6-9).

Thus, from the preferred list of activities and materials, it is clear that the teachers in our survey relied mostly on more traditional vocabulary learning activities such as keeping word lists and making sentences, and the effectiveness of using alternative activities such as corpus searches and etymological background information need more research and discussion at teaching conferences and in teacher education programs if they are to become more widespread.

Finally, we end this section with further notes on the comments teachers included in their open-ended responses. From the above figures, it is clear that many teachers enjoy teaching students about idioms when they come up in class, but many teachers have little time to cover idioms in class. Further, teachers commented that they do not focus on many idioms in lower level classes because idioms are complex and can be overwhelming for learners.

Beginners and intermediate ELLs can easily become overwhelmed by the use of too many idioms. Textbooks that focus on idioms usu-

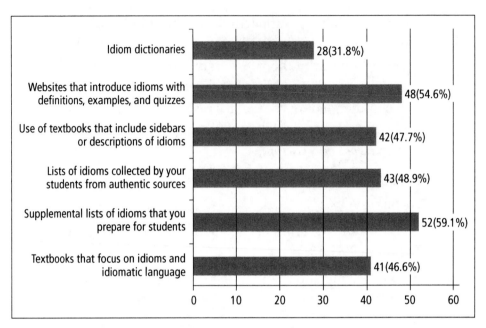

*Figure 6-9. Common Materials Used for Learning Idioms*

ally feature a long list of idioms in each chapter. The exercises often center around defining the idiom; however, idiom texts frequently lack activities in which students use the idioms in a meaningful way. (Response to question 5)

Some of the previously listed activities are very time-consuming. In low-level classes, dealing with one idiomatic expression can consume a large percentage of class time. (Response to question 12)

In addition to adapting idiom exercises to lower proficiency levels, many respondents noted that teachers need to adapt material to modern usage as many idiom textbooks and online materials become dated very quickly.

Although it has never been a huge focus in my classes, my students always enjoy learning the ones that people often use. It's important to edit anything you find in books or online, because often many of them are very old. (Response to question 12)

Another issue with idioms is that there are new ones forming every day and old ones disappear. (Response to question 12)

In addition to these comments, many teachers noted that idiom-only textbooks are an expense they do not want to ask students to spend, and as Figure 6-9 reveals, the teachers prefer to create lists and materials on their own as supplemental to the main course content.

One of our final questions on the survey asked teachers to provide idioms that students find particularly difficult. Teachers listed numerous idioms, but the following appeared more than once in response to our open-ended request:

- *Where there is a will there is a way*
- *in your face* (and other idioms involving body parts)
- *take a shower* (and other phrasal verbs/idioms with *take*)
- *run for president* (and other phrasal verbs/idioms with *run*)
- *raining cats and dogs*
- *alarm going off* (and other prepositional/phrasal verbs with *of*)
- *make up* (and other phrasal verbs with *up*)

Based on these responses and our own summary of useful and difficult idioms online and in textbooks, we provide our own lists of idioms for instruction in Appendix B.

## Discussion

### Implications for Classroom Teaching and Learning of Idioms

> The last category [idioms, especially the "picturesque kind"] is usually seen as the icing on the cake for learners who can already "say what they mean." It has also frequently been easy to criticize the actual language taught in these categories [idioms, collocations, and other fixed expressions] as dated, not what people really say, inappropriate for non-native users, ethnocentric, and for a host of other, often valid, reasons. It is time for us to revise our view of Fixed Expressions in the light of evidence from modern corpora based on what David Brazil has aptly termed "used language." (Lewis, 2002, p. 10)

Lewis (2002) was responding to criticism of his lexical approach, but from the results of our survey presented above, a strong majority of practicing teachers now see the importance of teaching idioms and fixed expressions as central to learning a new language such as English. This newfound acceptance and interest in teaching idioms is probably due in part to approaches to vocabulary teaching such as Lewis's lexical approach as well as the many textbooks and studies based on conversation analysis and corpus studies of "actual usage," as mentioned in the first part of this book. Despite the awareness and interest in teaching idioms in English language classrooms, teachers continue to have difficulties deciding on when, where, and how to incorporate idioms into their syllabi. Based on the results presented above coupled with insights from recent research on vocabulary learning, we offer the following implications for incorporating idioms into English language classes.

*The most popular way to present new idioms is to organize them around specific activities or through finding them in reading/listening passages.* Many textbooks as surveyed in Chapter 4 and reviewed in Chapter 9 organize learning idioms around specific activities or an authentic text in which many idioms are used, not semantic sets or grammatical categories that can feel forced and have been shown to actually confuse learners (Folse, 2004). Teachers agree with organizing idioms in this way, most likely because adding idioms to core class content through reading an article or watching a video is the way many teachers address idioms in their classes. At the same time, this supplemental approach to introducing idioms may not be systematic and, instead, somewhat haphazard in what idioms teachers end up addressing. If you supplement your course with readings that introduce new idioms, we recommend editing any material to be based on or adapted from an original source in order to have control over what specific idioms are introduced and to ensure that the idioms are the most useful for students in your class. At the same time, one of the best ways to increase student interest in learning idioms is simply to count the number of idioms and amount of idiomatic language present in any particular text, allowing students to understand that everyone from the president of the United States to talk show hosts to athletes draws on idioms when speaking and writing. As a further example, as referenced in Chapter 4, when teaching courses at Stanford University in the heart of Silicon Valley, McPherron had students analyze the famous graduation speech Steve Jobs delivered to the class of 2004.[1]

From the speech, students picked out 15 idioms to study as a class (although there were probably over 100). This simple activity generated interest in learning idioms, and it reinforced the point that idioms are used everywhere and by everyone.

*Teachers are skeptical of activities based on corpus, discourse, and conversation studies.* Looking at the many ELL textbooks produced by top publishers and the multiple studies on language acquisition based in corpus and discourse analysis, this may come as a surprise. It appears that there is somewhat of a gap between what many researchers and theorists are advocating as sound pedagogy and the interest in using these new materials by practicing teachers. Perhaps one of the key problems, particularly in using online corpora as activities or to generate materials for classes, is simply that most if not all of the online corpora that we have looked at are difficult to use quickly and easily. And many teachers simply do not have the time or motivation to spend hours playing around on a website to develop a lesson plan. Similarly, online corpora such as the Corpus of Contemporary American English are very interesting to explain and demonstrate to students; students in our classes have enjoyed the assignments we have built around these corpora, but we have yet to hear about any former students who have used an online corpus in order to study English on their own outside of our classes. However, we feel that these tools are very new, and we should continue to experiment with activities to see how corpus tools and other discourse and conversation analysis methods can be used effectively with students. Basically, more materials need to be produced that are user-friendly.

*More idiom textbooks and materials are needed that address the specific needs of learners and are targeted at a specific population.* We realize that the realities of the English language textbook industry encourage authors and publishers to write more generalist books that could be used in a variety of courses, and there is little incentive to write books for a very narrow population of learners. In addition, there are so many different cohorts of students—from Brazilian high school students interested in learning the idioms used by teenagers in the United States to Saudi Arabian professionals interested in appropriate idioms

---

[1] http://news.stanford.edu/news/2005/june15/jobs-061505.html

for business meetings to international graduate students interested in the idioms of their specific field—that it is probably impossible to expect textbooks suitable for every population.

We see at least three ways to address the lack of materials that would be suitable to your particular teaching context. First, we can continue, as is apparent from our survey, to create lists and activities on our own. As we review in Chapter 9, there are many websites that list idioms according to a variety of categories, and many of the better websites are based on discourse, conversation, and corpus analysis of the idioms used in authentic materials. In addition, many websites offer free materials that teachers can adapt to their specific needs. Next, there are some textbooks that focus on the needs of specific groups, and you could find a text such as *Idioms at Work* (McLay, 1998) or *A Year in the Life of an ESL Student: Idioms You Can't Live Without* (Francis, 2010) that have the specific idioms that would be most useful for students. A third option that may be both practical and economical for students is to use a general speaking/listing or reading/writing textbook that draws on idioms and idiomatic language but is still general enough to be used in your courses in order to teach grammar, writing, or any other content or skills addressed by your curriculum. For example, the earlier editions of the book series *All Clear* that we review in Chapter 9 focus on learning and using idioms, but the current edition, though retaining a focus on idioms, has become more of an all-purpose speaking and listening text at multiple proficiency levels. The *Touchstone* textbook series by Cambridge is also a general purpose multiskills book, but it is based on idioms and "everyday language." Regardless of what choice of textbook or online materials you use, at this point—as with most aspects of teaching—it's up to you as the classroom teacher to make any material work.

### Implications for Future Research on Teaching and Learning Idioms

From the results of the survey, it is clear that more action research and ethnographic studies are needed to fully understand how teachers address idioms in their classroom and their preferences for organizing and presenting idioms as well as choosing materials. As mentioned above, there may be a perception against the effectiveness of using corpus-, conversation-, and discourse-based materials, but this may simply be a matter of lack of experience with these materials and a lack of time or incentive to investigate them. Further, much of the research into vocabulary learning and teaching appears to be too theoretical or at least driven by the researcher's particular perspective on best practices, and much of this research comes across as alienating, at worst, or not relevant to the working lives of many teachers, at best. Further, although experimental studies into vocabulary learning are very useful and very much a central method for investigating how our brains process and store new language such as idioms, much of the writing about the results of these studies views students as "subjects" and essentially "computers" who need the right kind of input in the right form. More research needs to be done by teachers in their classroom, analyzing how they have applied some of the studies we reviewed earlier and how they have managed to teach students new idioms. This type of research not only views the "pure" benefits or drawbacks of a particular activity for learning idioms, but also takes into consideration all of the influences and factors for why teachers and students may or may not find a lesson effective, including out-of-class pressures from school administrators and parents.

# CHAPTER 7

# Student Perspectives on Teaching English Idioms

A school should be a place where teachers learn.
—*Mortimer J. Adler*

Now that we have presented data and analysis from our survey of English language teachers around the world, we turn to examining the results of a similar survey we conducted in 2013 with English language learners around the world. Similar to our survey of teachers, our goal with this survey was to gain a perspective and understanding from students about key aspects of learning idioms. On this survey our guiding questions were as follows: How important are idioms to English language learners? What activities are the most useful for learners when studying idioms? How often do their teachers and classes address idioms? In addition, we simply wanted to learn more about how students perceive their own learning of idioms. As summarized in Chapters 2 and 3, there are numerous experimental and theoretical studies of first and second language idiom learning that test aspects of learning and remembering idioms. This spans from questions about the primacy and effects of literal versus nonliteral processing of idioms (Cacciari & Tabossi, 1988; Cieślicka, 2006; Gibbs, 1980), to the role of identical idioms in the first and second language (Irujo, 1986), to the different strategies used by nonnative speakers of English while interpreting idioms in a think-aloud experiment (T. C. Cooper, 1999; Pimenova, 2011). We, however, did not want to impose or test a specific theory or model on student perspectives. Instead, our goal with the student survey was to learn as much as possible about what students think about learning idioms, both inside and outside the classroom, in their own words and not in a testing or experimental context.

This chapter follows a pattern similar to that of Chapter 6. First, we provide information on how we conducted the survey and who took it. We then present key results from the survey in the form of graphs and tables, and we end the chapter with two discussion sections, one on implications for teaching and one on implications for future research on teaching and learning idioms.

## Our Survey and Data Collection Methods

As with the survey of teachers, we distributed the survey using Survey-Monkey. Our response goal was also similar in that we attempted to find students from a variety of language backgrounds who had learned or were learning English in diverse contexts and at a variety of proficiency levels. Figures 7-1, 7-2, and 7-3 depict the general backgrounds of survey participants. As we both work at the university level, we distributed the survey through a snowball approach (Richards, 2003) by first sending the survey to our own students, who were graduate and undergraduate students at universities in Michigan and New York City. Then we sent the survey to our colleagues in secondary and university institutions in Vietnam, China, and Japan. We asked these colleagues (many of them former students of ours) to distribute the survey among their colleagues' classrooms as well. In total, 47 students took the survey. All student participants were anonymous.

Similar to the teacher survey, the student survey consisted of 13 questions that used both 5-point Likert scale items and short open-ended questions. Participants responded in the language that they felt most comfortable using, although they mostly responded in English. We asked students at the beginning of the survey to define, in their own words, what an idiom was and to provide examples. After they reported their definitions, we provided the following definitions and example for their use on the rest of the survey:

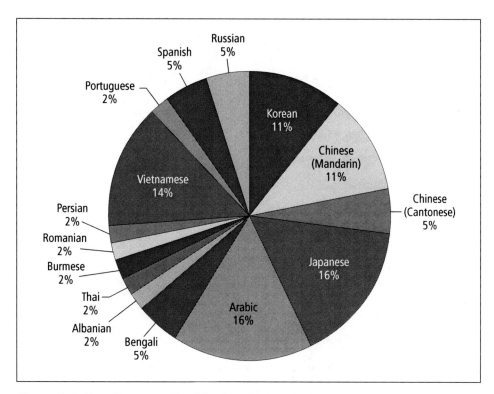

*Figure 7-1. First Language(s) of Student Survey Participants*

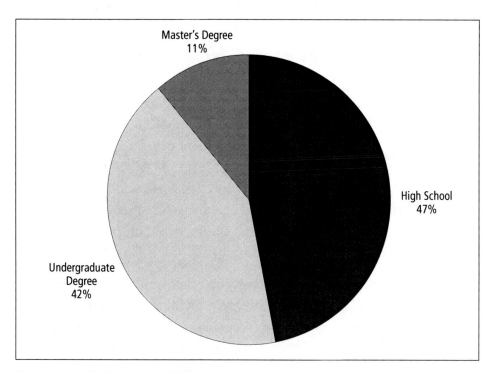

*Figure 7-2. Highest Level of Education of Student Survey Participants*

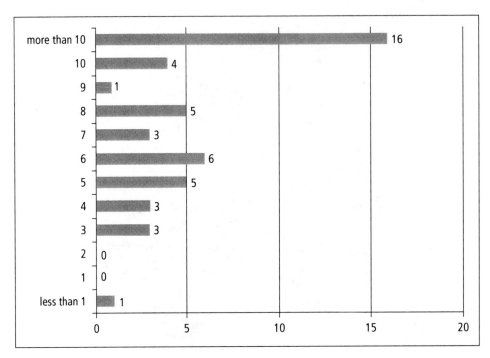

*Figure 7-3. Years of English Study of Student Survey Participants*

- Idioms are words or combinations of words that have a meaning that is different from or extends the literal meaning of the individual word or words.

- Idioms break or stretch the rules of grammar and word order to a certain degree.

- Idioms change meaning when translated word for word into another language. For example, if I say, "I put my foot in my mouth the other day at Nancy's house. I asked who was going to marry John," what does it mean? If you do not know that "put your foot in your mouth" means saying something accidentally which upsets or embarrasses someone, it is difficult to know exactly what the sentence means. It has a nonliteral or idiomatic meaning.

Also similar to the teacher survey, we asked students to rank activities from Liu (2008) from extremely useful to not useful at all in order to compare with the teacher responses, and we asked students to list idioms that they felt were particularly difficult to learn. Unlike the teacher survey, however, we felt students might have difficulty coming up with the idioms on their own, so we added question 10 which asks about the difficulty of specific idioms:

> How difficult do you feel the following idioms are to learn? Please use the scale provided: 1 (*not very difficult*) to 5 (*extremely difficult*). Note that the definition of each idiom is in the parentheses that follow the idiom.

For this question, we provided idioms that fit multiple categories, from semantically opaque (*a red herring*) to full proverbs/sayings (*every cloud has a silver lining*). We also piloted this survey with a small group of participants to edit any unclear questions. Based on the pilot survey, we narrowed down the list of idioms we provided in question 10 and added question 11 (How important is it for you to learn and use idioms?), which really was the key question we wanted to ask students. We provide the entire student survey in Appendix D, and the list of difficult and useful idioms in Appendix B. This list in Appendix B is a compilation of idioms from the student and teacher surveys as well as from our own classrooms and from our review of idiom materials and studies.

## Survey Results: What Do Students Say About Learning Idioms Inside and Outside Classrooms?

Drawing on our key research questions, one of the first questions on the student survey asked straightforwardly: "How important is it for you to learn and use idioms?" We received the responses as shown in Figure 7-4 ($n = 47$).

From the majority of respondents who claimed that learning and using idioms is important or very important (72.2%), it was clear that students perceive idioms as central to their learning English. The fact that only 2.8% responded that idioms were not important at all or not important is a further indication that students generally value learning about and using idioms. These results connect with the fact that only 10.1% of the teachers on their survey responded that "Students question whether idioms are useful to their overall English language learning" when asked about difficulties when teaching idioms.

Further, in response to the request to explain their response, many students made comments that centered on the usefulness of idioms in

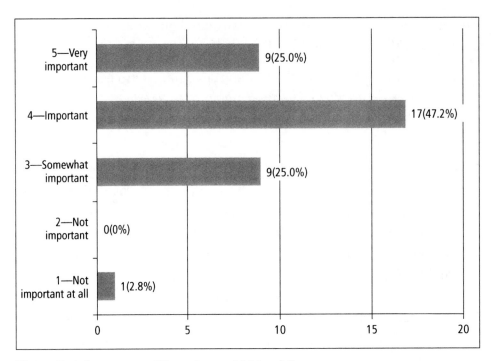

*Figure 7-4. Importance of Learning and Using Idioms*

daily conversation, in particular, with so-called native speakers, such as "Idioms always come up in daily life," "Idioms build major part of language and they will be used in daily conversations," and "because we live in the U.S, and the native speaker use it." Some students noted that idioms are not used only when speaking and that they are useful for writing as well, in comments such as "I want to use English fluently, so I think I have to include some idioms in my writings or speaking" and "It might be a good fact when a reader look the use of them and therefore my writings taken as a seriously writing, thus opportunities will increase with no doubt." In addition to most students' seeing the value of learning idioms, some students voiced frustration about learning idioms, particularly regarding what idioms were useful. As one student wrote, "I have already known many words, but sometimes I think I don't know idioms which is very useful. I only know that I can use in my tests. So, I want to know useful idioms." Further, some students separated knowing idioms and using them, as evidenced by this comment: "It is important to understand people's talking but I won't use them because I don't use idioms in my own language." Although this student was mistaken in thinking that her or his first language does not have idioms, the student does draw attention to the fact that some students may understand that idioms are necessary to learn and understand, but they may not want to use them often, particularly idioms associated with informal, spoken conversations. As noted in Chapter 1, this fear of using idioms has come up repeatedly in our classes, and as further noted in Chapter 6, we need to reinforce for students the ubiquity of idioms in formal and informal language use.

Figure 7-5 details student responses to our adapted list of activities for learning idioms (see Appendix D for full text of response choices).

Similar to the teacher responses to this question, students did not clearly rate any activity as not useful at all or not very useful, and respondents ranked many activities as very useful or extremely useful, including the following scores in which a majority of respondents responded with a 4 (*very useful*) or 5 (*extremely useful*).

- Making up example sentences using idioms (76.3%)
- Writing and performing skits using idioms (63.1%)
- Guessing and then finding out the origin of the idioms (62.1%)
- Playing idiom games such as Pictionary or charades (56.7%)
- Identifying and guessing the meaning of idioms in a reading passage (52.6%)
- Taking quizzes (either online or in class) (55.2%)
- Keeping a list of idioms from readings from outside of class (50.0%)

It is interesting to note that this list (albeit adapted for the student survey) includes all of the highly rated activities in the teacher survey, with "Taking quizzes" the only activity that did not show up in the teacher survey. In fact, in both surveys, teachers and students ranked "Making up example sentences using idioms" as the most useful activity.

Also like the teacher survey, similar activities were ranked as not very useful in comparison to others, with the following activities receiving the most responses of not very useful at all or not very useful.

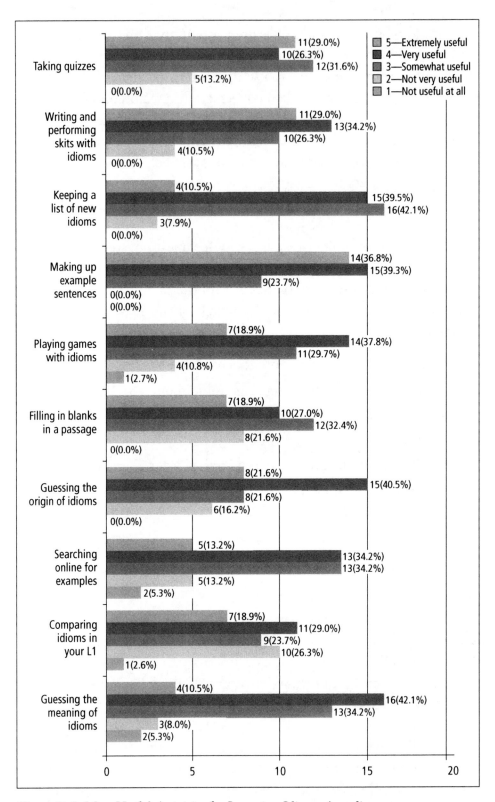

Figure 7-5. Most Useful Activities for Learning Idioms According to Student Participants

- Comparing idioms in English with your first language (28.9%)
- Filling in the blank words in a passage with the correct idioms (21.6%)
- Conducting searches for idiom examples from online sources (18.5%)

Similar to teacher respondents, students in our survey were not as interested in using online materials such as corpora to search for idioms, and they strongly felt that comparing idioms in English to other languages is not very useful, despite the fact that these are highly regarded activities in many textbooks and vocabulary instruction manuals. In addition, at least some students did not appear interested in filling in blanks in reading passages, a very popular activity in many textbooks and an easy way for teachers to create materials themselves from authentic texts.

Similar to the reported data for the first two key questions on the student survey, we posed the third key question ("How often do teachers and classes address idioms?") as a way to compare teacher and student responses on the surveys. Figure 7-6 shows the percentages of the 47 responses to this question.

The response to this item is similar to the teacher survey in that students indicated that idioms are addressed in class sometimes, but

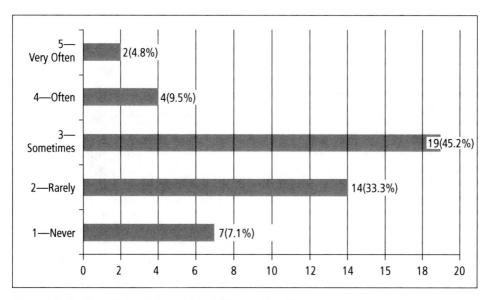

*Figure 7-6. How Often Idioms Are Addressed in Class*

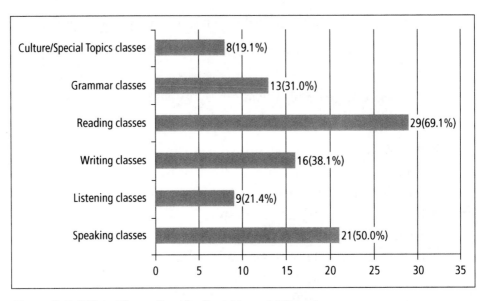

*Figure 7-7. What Classes Specifically Addressed Idioms?*

most students did not feel that teachers bring them up often or very often. In response to the invitation to explain their responses, students described similar situations to the teachers in that idioms were addressed when they came up ("We did not discuss or being taught about them directly, but from time to time a teacher says an idiom and provide us with its meaning") or when they were relevant to exams ("In my high school days, I studied English for the entrance examination of university. So my English teacher sometimes tought me idioms which frequently appeared in the examination").

Perhaps more revealing than how often teachers addressed idioms from students' perspective are the classes in which they were specifically addressed and what materials were most often used. Figures 7-7 and 7-8 reveal student responses to these questions (see Appendix D for full text of response choices).

Similar to the teacher responses, students reported that they most often use lists of idioms generated by their teachers, and they rarely use websites, student-prepared lists, or idiom dictionaries. Twenty-five percent of the students used a textbook focused specifically on idioms. However, the most common seemed to be texts which merely give idioms in random examples. We mentioned two of those in Chapter 6: the *All Clear* and *Touchstone* series. An intriguing result that we didn't expect was that students ranked reading classes more often than other

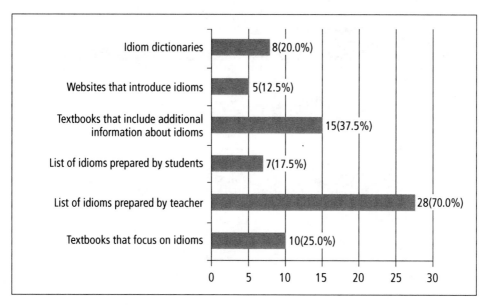

*Figure 7-8. What Materials Were Used for Teaching Idioms?*

courses in which idioms were specifically addressed, even higher than speaking classes. This may be due to the number of incidental idioms that would come up when reading authentic materials or the fact that many reading classes also focus heavily on vocabulary learning. Regardless, both students and teachers appeared to value idioms as central parts of learning English, and both groups agreed on many of the activities that are most useful; however, there was still ambivalence toward using online materials and search activities as well as a general perception of a lack of good textbooks that address idioms.

An additional topic that we included on the student survey asked for opinions on the difficulty of certain idioms, and we invited participants to list any further idioms that they felt were difficult. We listed a range of idioms that fit the various categories for defining idioms as summarized in Chapter 2, from transparent to opaque, from fixed to semi-fixed, from sayings/proverbs to phrasal verbs. Figure 7-9 provides the results in terms of the degree of difficulty or learnability of each idiom.

Few of the idioms were clearly considered very difficult or difficult by students, with 51.3% of the survey respondents ranking *red herring* with only a 1 or 2. Participants chose somewhat difficult as the top ranking for seven of the idioms: *red herring* (37.8%), *the dog days*

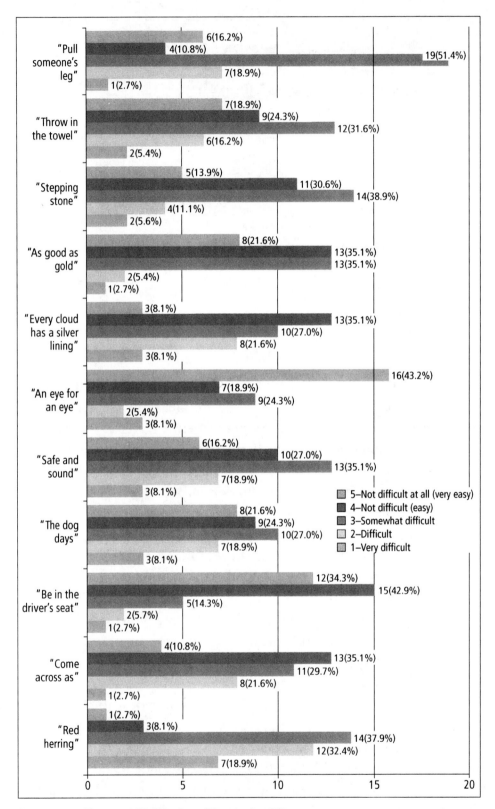

Figure 7-9. Degree of Difficulty of Particular Idioms

(27.0%), *safe and sound* (35.1%), *as good as gold* (35.1%), *stepping stone* (38.9%), *throw in the towel* (35.1%), and *pull someone's leg* (51.4). Three idioms were ranked highest as not difficult: *come across as* (35.1%), *be in the driver's seat* (42.9%), and *every cloud has a silver lining* (35.1%). One idiom ranked highest as not difficult at all: *an eye for an eye* (43.2%). And one idiom ranked equally as somewhat difficult and not difficult: *good as gold* (35.1% in each category). These results confirm Grant and Bauer's (2004) contention that the most difficult idioms to learn, and thus what we should focus in teaching, are the "pure" idioms such as *red herring*. In addition, the fact that students ranked the more transparent and decomposable idioms such as *be in the driver's seat* and *an eye for an eye* as easier is supported in the literature on student processing of idioms (Cieślicka, 2006). Finally, many of the idioms that students listed as difficult in response to the open-ended request were also less transparent and nondecomposable: *out of the blue, break a leg, a change of pace, the bottom line, to put something off, to ring a bell, to save your breath,* and *raining cats and dogs.*

A final topic we included on the student survey to prime students about what they knew already concerning idioms was the open-ended question "In your own words, how would you describe what an idiom is? What are some examples?" Thirty-five survey respondents answered this question, and answers varied, but responses mostly included one of two aspects of idioms: nonliteral meaning and informal language. For example, many students included a description and example of literalness, such as "Idioms are phrases which use common words with uncommon meaning and they are popular among people" or "An idiom is a phrase with an implicit meaning, used informally or colloquially more often than not. Some examples are—Pain in the neck; kick the bucket." Few students used the word *literal,* but through terms such as *implicit* and *different meaning,* students taking our survey clearly picked up on the nonliteralness of idioms. They also tended to provide decomposable idioms and informal phrases as examples. Perhaps this was because of the idiom lists they were presented with in their classes, but as teachers we should be careful to point out more than informal idioms that are clearly figurative; instead, students, as mentioned numerous times above, should also learn the idioms and figurative language that are central aspects of language use.

## Discussion

### Implications for Classroom Teaching and Learning of Idioms

The introduction to the *Collins COBUILD Idioms Workbook* (2002) offers the following justification for using idioms:

> Idioms exist in all languages. They form an important part of everyone's vocabulary and are used in both formal and informal language, but are much more common in informal, spoken English. They should not, however, be confused with slang, which is very often inappropriate in certain social situations. We use idioms:
>
> - To be amusing or witty
> - To play with words
> - To be different
> - To put other people at ease, even in the most formal situations
> - To express something which other words do not quite express
> - To communicate more clearly and more visually (p. 4)

Based on the student responses to our survey, we note that there is clearly a desire to study idioms and understand them; however, students appear to need further clarification about when and how to use idioms, in addition to grasping their ubiquity. In making the case for not just studying idioms but also using them, the above points are a great starting point, and in addition to making these points, we pull out additional key points and themes here that we can take from the survey results in relation to teaching and learning idioms.

*Teachers and students agree that more interactive games, skits, and interactive play are effective activities for learning idioms.* It may not be surprising that students and teachers enjoy interactive games and activities that require students to move, talk spontaneously, and act. In Chapter 3, we reviewed how the brain learns and what it needs, including activity and movement that "feed" the brain and get neural connections firing—those microscopic workhorses of memory. What is surprising, however, is how few textbooks and language learning materials for learning vocabulary and idioms include interactive activities and movement. However, there is no need to despair, as many of the lesson plans in Chapter 8 illustrate some great ideas for getting students moving in their classrooms. We are not advocating turning all English language learning into drama workshops or classrooms into recreation rooms, and we understand that students in different cultures will approach interactive games and movement in the classroom in different ways. Further, due to physical challenges, not all students are able to interact in these activities in the same way. However, we argue that teachers should make the effort to include some aspect of creative play in all lessons, in which students are doing more than filling in the blanks of a worksheet with the correct idioms.

*Reading and speaking classes are where idioms are most often addressed, but we should continue to create activities to show where idioms are used in all contexts and in all classes.* This is one of our main points throughout the book and one of the reasons that the above argument for why we use idioms is so important to make with students. Because of students like the one who responded to our survey stating that his or her first language did not have idioms, teachers need to reinforce the ubiquity of idioms not just in speaking and reading classes when the topic perhaps comes up more often, but also in classes such as Academic Writing or Working in the United States. It is true that idioms may be difficult to introduce in a beginning-level class—at least the more difficult and figurative idioms—but a great deal of beginning-level classes are built around fixed phrases such as "How are you?" And we argue that you can build into class activities student awareness that English, just like other languages, has its own idiomatic and at times figurative way of phrasing everything from how heavy the rain is falling to simple greetings. Similarly, as described in the Caveats section following each lesson in Chapter 8, many of the lesson plans can be adapted for a more beginner-type class.

*Students find the nondecomposable idioms the most difficult to learn. More attention should be placed on these idioms when creating lists and materials.* One benefit of thinking through the various aspects of idiom definitions is that teachers can begin to see the reasons why idioms are difficult for students to understand and use, particularly the more figurative and nondecomposable idioms. It's clear from various studies and the responses to our survey that students have difficulty with new idioms that are less transparent and more figurative, and teachers should pay more attention to these idioms in warm-up activities and application exercises. As Grant and Bauer (2004) argue, these idioms are so difficult because there are little to no patterns to understand them outside of the sentence and usage context. We divided our list of idioms in Appendix B according to degree of figurativeness, and we encourage students to make lists of idioms in the same manner, or at least to note in some way on their lists the differences in compositionality of the idioms. Drawing attention to the types of idioms that students are learning can reinforce the patterns of the more transparent idioms and help students make mental notes of the more difficult idioms that they will need to memorize on their own.

## Implications for Future Research on Teaching and Learning Idioms

The student survey reported here is primarily a general survey of opinions and attitudes about learning and using idioms, and similar to the teacher survey, more ethnographic and classroom-based action research is needed to gain further perspectives on how students and teachers address idiom learning in the classroom. Due to the discourse and corpus studies summarized in previous chapters, we have developed a better understanding of how idioms are used and when, but we need more complex understandings of how teachers and students use activities such as the digital media activities presented in Chapter 5. In fact, we would welcome an entire volume consisting of the results of action research on idiom lessons from classrooms around the world and at different proficiency levels.

# CHAPTER 8

# Example Lessons for Teaching Idioms From Around the World

We must make learning fun.

*—Plato*

From the beginning of our discussions on writing a book on teaching and learning idioms for TESOL Press, we realized that we wanted this book to be as hands-on as possible but still based in the academic literature on vocabulary and idiom learning, and one of the first ideas we had was to devote an entire chapter to lesson plans. We decided that, in addition to our own ideas, it would be more interesting and helpful if we could find contributors from around the world of TESOL to contribute lesson plans and materials that have been successful in their classrooms. We consequently put out a call for contributors through the TESOL website and other local English language teaching professional newsletters and webpages, and the response was inspiring; we did not realize how many teachers were addressing idioms and idiomatic aspects of vocabulary learning. This chapter represents the 12 best lessons from those who sent us submissions for inclusion in this book, plus an additional "baker's dozen" lesson from Randolph. The lessons are not arranged in any particular order, but in addition to being great activities that are "Monday-morning ready," all of them connect to both the research findings presented in Part 1 of the book and our survey results presented in Chapters 6 and 7. We have also included a note at the end of this chapter that makes some of those connections and suggestions for future research more explicit.

As a final note of introduction, the lessons presented here are the work of the contributors listed at the beginning of each lesson. We have carefully made needed changes for clarity and edited all of the entries to fit a format similar to lessons published in the TESOL New Ways series. Specifically, for each entry you will find the following:

- Title
- Contributor's name and contact information
- Levels, context, and type(s) of learner
- Aims
- Class time, out-of-class time (if applicable), and preparation time
- Resources needed
- Rationale
- Procedure/tasks
- Caveats and options
- References and further reading (if applicable)
- Appendix (if applicable)
- Short bio on the author

We have provided email addresses and a short background statement on each contributor, and we invite you to contact the contributors directly with questions about the lessons or just to send a note about how you used the lesson. In combination with the next chapter, which focuses on reviewing textbooks, online resources, and dictionaries, we hope that these lessons provide you with ideas that you can use "as is." You should, of course, feel free to adapt, edit, and create new lessons and materials based on the plethora of effective and creative teaching ideas found in all of the following lesson plans.

## Lesson 1: Meaning From Guessing, Ownership From Play

Contributed by Michael Gilmore (gilmore@siu.edu)

| | |
|---|---|
| Levels/context | High beginner/low-intermediate, adult (could be adjusted for various settings) |
| Aims | — Understand that an idiomatic expression is a phrase with a unique meaning completely different from its literal meaning<br>— Be able to recognize and understand four idioms |
| Class time | 60 minutes |
| Preparation time | 20–30 minutes |
| Resources | Handout defining *idiom* and providing four idioms + definitions + example sentences, two rolls of tape, four sets of colored pencils or markers, four poster boards or large pieces of paper, four large printed sentences using the idiomatic expressions being taught (cut up word by word) |

### Rationale

This activity is meant to be an introduction to idioms. It focuses on a small number of idioms, gets students engaged, and encourages them to be creative. After working in small groups to develop their interpretation of a single idiom, the class as a whole learns what idioms are and sees that their interpretations may be literally correct without showing the actual intended meaning. Students then correctly order a teacher-provided sample sentence and attach it to a picture. The visuals that they create help them remember the idioms. The sample sentences they put in order help them remember the idioms' true meanings. Students also benefit from the collaboration and negotiation that come into play during the group work.

## Procedure

1. Divide the class into four groups. Provide each group with poster board and colored pencils.

2. Give each group one idiom without context. Instruct students to create whatever image comes to mind when they read their particular idiom.

3. Collect drawings and put them on the board or classroom walls.

4. Distribute idioms handout with definitions and example sentences for all four idioms. (Example idioms for this lesson: *I'm all ears.* / *You're dead meat!* / *He is under the weather today.* / *This quiz is a piece of cake.*) Discuss as a class. Students' drawings will most likely show the literal meanings for the phrases and might be very comical. These can then be used to contrast the literal/actual meanings.

5. With students still in their groups, distribute a cut-up sentence to each group.

6. Instruct students to order their sentence, and as they finish, ask them to tape it to the corresponding poster board.

## Caveats and Options

1. The number of idioms taught could be adjusted depending on class size.

2. The number of cut-up sentences could be increased to two or three if time allows.

3. More advanced students could generate their own example sentences and write them on the poster boards.

## Contributor

Michael Gilmore is a lecturer at the Center for English as a Second Language at Southern Illinois University, Carbondale.

# Lesson 2: Digging Out the Origins of Idioms

Contributed by Feifei Han (feifei.han@sydney.edu.au)

| Levels/context | Intermediate or above |
|---|---|
| Aims | — Find out how an idiom comes together<br>— Develop idiomatic awareness<br>— Practice retelling skills in English |
| Class time | 30 minutes |
| Preparation time | 15–30 minutes |
| Resources | Some English idioms, stories on which these idioms are based, two small paper or cardboard boxes |

## Rationale

Learning idioms often requires memorizing multiword units. The rote learning approach, however, often leads to boredom for learners. Most idioms come to exist as they are because there is a history behind them. For instance, the idiom *to cry wolf* comes from the story *The Boy Who Cried Wolf*. Knowing these stories behind idioms can be a fun way to learn idioms. Through reading these stories, students have a better chance of internalizing the idioms as genuinely as possible. This leaves learners with a stronger memory trace for the idioms they are about to learn. According to the depth of processing theory (Craik & Lockhart, 1972; Craik & Tulving, 1975), if a lexical item is processed deeply, it is more likely to be retrieved from memory at a later time. This activity creates an opportunity for students to learn about the stories behind the idioms through using the media of idioms. It also increases learners' idiomatic knowledge by teaching them how idioms come together due to historical factors and how these prefabricated units are fixed. Third, this activity helps students practice the art of retelling stories.

## Procedure

1. Divide the class into two groups. Each student in group A picks an idiom from box A, and each student in group B picks a story from box B.

2. Give students in each group 10 minutes to read the stories and prepare to retell them. Ask students in group A to go around the classroom to find the story behind the idioms they picked.

3. When a student from group A approaches a student from group B, the student in group B should retell the story he or she selected. Group B students should retell the stories and not just reread them.

4. Repeat Step 3 until all students in group A find the stories behind their idioms.

5. Then ask each student in group A to go to the front of the classroom, write the idioms from the story on the board (without seeing them on paper, if possible), and retell the story to the whole class.

## Caveats and Options

1. If time allows, you can prepare extra idioms and stories, and ask students in groups A and B to exchange their roles.

2. This activity can be done as a role-play activity rather than a retelling. Divide the class into groups, and assign each group an idiom and a story. After reading the story, students act it out. Ask each group to perform in front of the classroom, and ask the rest of the students to guess the idiom on which the story is based.

## References and Further Reading

Craik, F., & Lockhart, R. (1972). Levels of processing: A framework for memory research. *Journal of Verbal Learning and Verbal Behaviour, 11*, 671–684.

Craik, F., & Tulving, E. (1975). Depth of processing and the retention of words in episodic memory. *Journal of Experimental Psychology: General, 104*, 268–294.

**Contributor**

Feifei Han has taught English to Chinese tertiary students. She is currently a PhD candidate in TESOL at the University of Sydney.

# Lesson 3: Comparing Idioms in L1 and L2

Contributed by Nadezda Pimenova (npimenova@bsu.edu)

| | |
|---|---|
| Levels/context | Intermediate intensive English program |
| Aims | — Increase awareness of idioms<br>— Develop cross-cultural and cross-linguistic comparison skills |
| Class time | 10–15 minutes |
| Preparation time | 15–20 minutes (for students) |
| Resources | Any American idiom dictionary (hard copies or online) |

## Rationale

*Second language (L2) learners pay attention to the constituents of idiomatic expressions.* According to Abel's (2003) data, when native German speakers encountered an unknown idiom in English, "the majority answered that they consider the literal meaning of the constituents and then try to put together the idiomatic meaning of the whole phrase" (p. 349). The results of Bortfeld's (2003) study prove that speakers of three different languages (English, Latvian, and Mandarin) "were able to interpret unfamiliar (e.g., other languages') idioms depending largely on the degree to which they were analyzable" (p. 217).

*L2 learners use the first language (L1) to understand L2 idioms, but should be aware of interlingual transfer.* The results of Irujo's (1986) study with Spanish-speaking students learning English prove that L2 learners "whose first language is related to the second can use their knowledge of idioms in their first language to comprehend and produce idioms in the second" (p. 298). Even if the L1 is not closely related to the L2 (e.g., Russian and English), language learners still search for similar expressions in their L1 to understand unfamiliar idioms (Pimenova, 2011). However, it is important to make L2 students aware of interlingual transfer of idioms. Sometimes it is positive and sometimes negative. Boers and Demecheleer (2001) suggest alerting L2 learners to the risk of "being mistaken for the equivalent of a resembling expression in L1" (p. 260).

## Procedure
### *Homework*
1. Have students find three similar or identical American English idioms that have the same structure, word components, and meanings as in their native language.

2. Have students find three American idioms that are different than in their native language (idioms that have the same constituents but different meanings or idioms that have the same meanings but different constituents).

3. Tell them to write a story using these six idioms.

### *In class*
Match students in pairs (preferably representing different L1s) to talk about the idioms they chose (identical and different) and explain their meanings.

## Caveats and Options
1. If time permits, ask students to share their stories, too. In pairs, they read idiom stories to each other. Alternatively, partners can exchange their stories and read them silently. Then each student finds all six idioms that his or her partner used in the text.

2. If six idioms are too many, ask students to find four idioms (two identical and two different). When explaining the homework task, give an example of each kind of idiom.

## References and Further Reading
Abel, B. (2003). English idioms in the first language and second language lexicon: A dual representation approach. *Second Language Research*, *19*, 329–358.

Boers, F., & Demecheleer, M. (2001). Measuring the impact of cross-cultural differences on learners' comprehension of imageable idioms. *ELT Journal*, *55*, 255–262.

Bortfeld, H. (2003). Comprehending idioms cross-linguistically. *Experimental Psychology, 50*, 217–230.

Irujo, S. (1986). Don't put your leg in your mouth: Transfer in the acquisition of idioms in a second language. *TESOL Quarterly, 20*, 287–304.

Pimenova, N. (2011). *Idiom comprehension strategies used by English and Russian language learners in a think-aloud study* (Unpublished doctoral dissertation). Purdue University, West Lafayette, IN.

### Contributor

Nadezda Pimenova is an assistant professor of ESL in the Intensive English Institute at Ball State University, in Muncie, Indiana.

### Appendix: Student Worksheet

| | Identical or Similar Idioms | Dissimilar Idioms |
|---|---|---|
| American English Idiom<br>L1 Idiom<br>Definition<br>Source | 1. | 1. |
| American English Idiom<br>L1 Idiom<br>Definition<br>Source | 2. | 2. |
| American English Idiom<br>L1 Idiom<br>Definition<br>Source | 3. | 3. |

# Lesson 4: Play With Idioms

Contributed by Chanchal Singh and Sohani Gandhioke
(chanchals82@yahoo.co.uk, ssohani1809@yahoo.co.uk)

| Levels/context | Intermediate to advanced |
| --- | --- |
| Aims | — Develop cross-cultural communication and understanding |
| Class time | 20–30 minutes for each activity |
| Preparation time | 10–15 minutes teacher preparation for Activities 1 and 2 (students' out-of-class preparation for activity 3 will vary) |
| Resources | PowerPoint presentation, charts used to write parts of the idioms |

## Rationale

The idea behind this lesson is that idioms are acquired and not learned. Drawing on this theory, students are asked to compare and contrast some basic or regularly used idioms in their L1 to the ones used in the foreign language. Interestingly enough, students are not usually intimidated, but rather accept the use and application of idioms with an open mind. The purpose of the activities is to help students acquire the use of idiomatic phrases in day-to-day speech and learn to understand expressions used by native speakers of English. Such activities used in ELL classrooms can go a long way toward encouraging ardent learners to use experiential and pedagogical methodologies in order to augment their language skills. The association with their L1 makes them understand the existence of idioms in their own language and helps them accept this aspect of English that they need to acquire in order to aid cross-cultural communication.

## Procedure

1. *Activity 1: Complete the Idiom.* First, have students study a set number of idioms. Then write down these idioms, breaking

them down into parts on a few pieces of paper. Arrange students into teams of four or six, depending on the number of students in the class. Then jumble one complete idiom to give to each team. All the teams get a jumbled idiom and all start the activity together. Students have to arrange the idiom in the right order. The team that correctly assembles a complete idiom first wins a point. The activity can go on with more idioms added to prolong the learning process.

2. *Activity 2: Guess the Idiom.* This time, jumble the meanings of the idioms and then have student teams arrange their individual jumbles and guess the correct idiom with reference to the meaning they arranged. Once again, the first team to achieve success is the winning team. The game can go on until you achieve your purpose of the activity.

3. *Activity 3: Play With Idioms.* Here, *play* means making a short play or skit which uses the idioms. The teams prepare and present short skits to clearly bring out the meaning of their idioms without using the actual idioms. The other teams then have to guess the idioms. If the other teams guess successfully, the presenting team wins for having made the story so lucid and explicit. There is a penalty for wrong guesses. The facilitator, for variety and fun, can make twists in the rules of the game.

## Contributors

Chanchal Singh has been delivering voice, accent, and speech training for the last 32 years and currently works at the English Language Center at Shantou University, in China.

Sohani Gandhioke is an experienced academician delivering voice, accent, and speech training and currently works at the English Language Center at Shantou University, in China.

# Lesson 5: Slogans for Success

Contributed by Hillary Gardner (hillary.gardner@mail.cuny.edu)

| | |
|---|---|
| Levels/context | Low- to high-intermediate learners in an adult education/college/career preparation course |
| Aims | — Develop awareness of how idioms/proverbs are used in times of trouble to express encouragement or motivation for future success<br>— Create a personal essay featuring a slogan for success |
| Class time | 60–90 minutes |
| Preparation time | 30–60 minutes |
| Resources | "Slogans for Success" handout or discussion strips (see appendix), sample of student essays featuring slogans for success (optional: any source of sayings from famous writers or other cultures related to the theme of overcoming difficulty and achieving success) |

## Rationale

Scholarship applications and even job applications require students to write a personal essay in which they must tell a compelling story of their lives. In times of trouble, people often turn to sayings for motivation. While native speakers are taught to avoid common sayings as cliché, nonnative speakers of English can learn more about idioms in English by examining them in relation to their own slogans for success.

## Procedure

1. Introduce the concept of slogans for success. Write the following questions on the board and have students briefly discuss them with a partner:

- Do you have a motto or saying to help you through hard times? If so, what is it?

- Did someone in your life regularly give you a piece of advice in the form of a saying?

- Are there common sayings or slogans from your culture that you've heard people use in times of trouble?

2. Have students share sample answers with the whole class and compile a short list to return to in the writing portion of the lesson.

3. Prepare Slogans for Success handout, one for each student (see Appendix).

4. Have students work in pairs to discuss and define each saying. As an alternative, have them match each saying to a list of definitions you have prepared and posted on the board.

5. Ask students to write about one of their own slogans using the following prompts:

- What is one of your slogans for success?

- What is the source of the slogan? Who said it? Where did you first hear it?

- What problem did it help you resolve? How is your life different because of this slogan?

- What is one of your goals for the future, and how will your slogan help you achieve it?

**Caveats and Options**

1. Make the handout into discussion strips, enough so that each pair or small group has one strip to define and discuss. Have each group pick a saying at random from the set of cut-up strips and prepare a short explanation by writing a definition, drawing an illustration, writing a skit, or writing a short song or poem using the saying.

2. Have students continue to look for examples of slogans for success in personal essays, magazine articles, or newspaper articles.

3. Choose a sample student essay for students to read and reflect on the author's slogan for success (see suggested titles from *Literacy Review* below) using the following prompts:

- What is the writer's slogan for success?
- Who is the source of the slogan?
- What problem or difficulty causes the writer to remember this slogan?
- How does the slogan change the writer? What is different now?

## References and Further Reading

Personal essays by adult learners published in the *Literacy Review* are available online at http://www.gallatin.nyu.edu/academics/under graduate/writing/literacyproject.html

## *Example essays and slogans*

Deng, Z .P. (2009). Lost and found. *Literacy Review*, 7, 78.

Slogan: "If you try to do it one time, then you will know how to do it forever."

Domukhovsky, N. (2009). The life-changing sport. *Literacy Review*, 7, 111–112.

Slogan: "Talent and hard work are equally important."

Sanchez, R. (2009). I didn't miss my class. *Literacy Review*, 7, 140–141.

Slogan: "You are an immigrant but you are not disabled."

Thein, K. M. (2009). All my dreams were gone. *Literacy Review*, 7, 92.

Slogan: "Don't ever go against anger with anger."

## Contributor

Hillary Gardner is an ESOL Professional Development Coordinator for The City University of New York Adult Literacy Programs.

## Appendix: Slogans for Success Handout

Do you agree or disagree with the following idioms? Why or why not? What does this saying mean to you?

"Don't count your chickens before they hatch."

"The grass is always greener on the other side."

"The early bird gets the worm."

"Don't cry over spilt milk."

"If you can't be with the one you love, love the one you're with."

"Let sleeping dogs lie."

"A stitch in time saves nine."

"Laughter is the best medicine."

"Time heals all wounds."

"Save the best for last."

"When life gives you lemons, make lemonade."

"Don't make a mountain out of a molehill."

"What doesn't kill you makes you stronger."

# Lesson 6: You're the Expert!

Contributed by Regina Dahlgren Ardini (wordgarden@optimum.net)

| Levels/context | Intermediate to advanced (high school or higher education) |
| --- | --- |
| Aims | — Identify idioms overheard in conversation<br>— Discover new idioms related to overheard idioms<br>— Learn idioms by teaching them to classmates |
| Class time | 20–30 minutes for each activity |
| Preparation time | None |
| Resources | Prior to activity: theme cards, sign-up sheet. During activity: students' choice but, typically, computer, projector, board, markers, sometimes other props for dramatic readings or skits |

## Rationale

This activity is learner driven and follows classes in which the instructor has explained idioms and taught two to three lessons of idioms to model the activity. Students enjoy being the experts and teaching their classmates, and they enjoy learning idioms this way, particularly with examples that are relevant to them.

## Procedure

1. Create theme cards—cards containing a theme or category of idioms and an example, such as *Time: once in a blue moon* or *Food: piece of cake*. There should be one card per presentation group.
2. Create a sign-up sheet that lists presentation dates.
3. Determine student groups, or have students choose their own partners. Depending on class size or course duration, students can also present individually.

4. Groups choose a theme (on their own or from one of the theme cards) and sign up for a presentation date. Encourage students to identify idioms they hear in conversations outside of class and identify a theme related to those idioms.

5. Students research their idioms and prepare their presentation, which can take the form of a PowerPoint, Prezi, skit, dramatic reading, video, or some combination of methods. The presentation has three parts: list of idioms, brief definition of each idiom, and example of each idiom's use. Idioms can be found in a dictionary or, even better—and to be encouraged—by listening to conversations, lectures, or other input by native speakers of English. Examples must be original and relevant to the audience—that is, not copied from a dictionary. Be sure to indicate the number of idioms they should present and the amount of time they have to present.

6. Students present their idioms to the class and answer questions from their audience. You are there to clarify usage and help with pronunciation—and sometimes offer alternative idioms.

## Caveats and Options

1. Students' choice of idioms must be monitored. They often find idioms from other English-speaking countries that may cause confusion or that are out of date. Requesting that students meet with you as they are finalizing their list of idioms solves this confusion.

2. This activity is also a way to practice oral presentations. With my advanced classes, I have required the audience to give anonymous written feedback via a simple three-question form. I also use a simple rubric to assess presentation techniques and give critical feedback.

3. This activity can also be used to practice writing skills, and students can publish their presentations on a course management system (e.g., Moodle, Blackboard). Part of

the rubric can then include correct grammar and sentence structure in general or of particular forms.

## Contributor

Regina Ardini is assistant professor of liberal arts at the Culinary Institute of America, where she teaches college writing for English language learners, supports international students in a variety of ways, and is developing the ESL program.

## Lesson 7: Sounds Like . . . Idiom!

Contributed by Emily Green (emigreen83@gmail.com)

| Levels/context | Intermediate; review activity; secondary school ELL support setting |
|---|---|
| Aims | — Expand knowledge of English idiomatic expressions<br>— Develop cross-cultural communication skills<br>— Foster collaborative skills<br>— Convey meaning through use of gestures and body language |
| Class time | 15 minutes |
| Preparation time | 5 minutes |
| Resources | Prior to activity: theme cards, sign-up sheet. During activity: students' choice but, typically, computer, projector, board, markers; sometimes other props for dramatic readings or skits |

### Rationale

This activity provides an enjoyable and engaging review of idiomatic expressions previously taught. Students may be more willing to participate because oral communication is between two people rather than an entire class. Students draw on cross-cultural communication skills as they first work with partners to create silent performances and then attempt to convey meaning without speaking to the entire class. In order to be successful in this activity, partners need to work together and respect each other's contributions. The use of movement in this activity proves particularly effective with kinesthetic learners.

### Procedure

1. Place students in pairs.
2. Distribute one idiomatic expression card to each pair of students.

3. Explain to students that they need to work in pairs to silently act out the meaning of the idiomatic expression written on the card provided.

4. Reveal the challenge: Each pair will perform for the class. Members of the class will try to guess the idiomatic expression from a provided list of expressions.

## Caveats and Options

1. Pairs of students can trade idiomatic expression cards for multiple rounds of silent performances.

2. More advanced students can find and research idiomatic expressions, choosing a favorite to perform silently for the class.

3. For large classes, students can work in small groups rather than in pairs. For more advanced students, this is also an option to increase collaboration and communication.

4. For less advanced students, shorten the list of idiomatic expressions.

## Contributor

Emily Green is an ELL and English teacher as well as a freelance writer who lives with her family in Toledo, Ohio.

## Appendix: Sampling of Idiomatic Expressions

*To smell a rat*: To sense unfair actions or foul play

*A bookworm*: Someone who reads a lot

*As easy as pie*: Very easy

*To be all ears*: To listen eagerly

*To read between the lines*: To pay attention to what is implied

*The pot calling the kettle black*: To criticize others for a fault you possess

*On pins and needles*: Anxious or tense

*Mind your Ps and Qs*: Be on your best behavior

*A couch potato*: Someone who spends too much time watching TV

*Cut it out!*: Stop doing something that is annoying

*To break up with someone*: To end a relationship
*A bee in my bonnet*: A problem on my mind
*An arm and a leg*: A huge amount of money
*A bull in a china shop*: Knocking everything over
*Keep a straight face*: Look serious

## Lesson 8: Figurative Language in Idioms

Contributed by Veronica Csorvasi (veracs@sbcglobal.net)

| Levels/context | Advanced |
|---|---|
| Aims | — Understand and use idioms as figurative language |
| Class time | 45–50 minutes |
| Preparation time | 10–15 minutes |
| Resources | Internet access, chart paper |

### Rationale

A prerequisite of this activity is for students to already understand and be able to use figurative language. A step further would be for students to understand and use idioms that contain figurative language (similes, metaphors). Students work in groups of three to guess the meanings of the idioms. After the correct meanings have been given, students write a narrative using these idioms. The narratives are posted and students do a gallery walk to read all the stories.

### Procedure

1. Have students work in groups of three.

2. Give each trio a three-column chart with five or six idioms that contain figurative language (see appendix). The idioms will be in the first column.

3. In their groups, students discuss the possible meanings of the idioms and write their guesses in the second column. Each group has to agree on the meanings of the idioms.

4. As a whole class, go over the students' guesses. If the guesses are correct, have students write them in the third column.

5. Give students the right meanings of the idioms if they did not guess them.

6. In their groups, have students write a short narrative on chart paper using the idioms on their chart.

7. Display the charts and have students do a gallery walk to read all the stories.

## Caveats and Options

1. You can scaffold the activity by having students illustrate the idioms before they guess their meanings.

2. To make the activity more challenging, give students idioms that are close in meaning or related to the same theme (e.g., fear, happiness, danger). Have students write a story in which they use the idioms toward a more nuanced narrative.

3. As students do the gallery walk and read the stories, they can also evaluate each story by using the star system (5 stars for the best).

## Contributor

Veronica Csorvasi currently works as an ESOL adjunct faculty member at Richland Community College, in Dallas, Texas.

## Appendix: Idioms Handout

| Idiom | Our Guess | What It Means |
|---|---|---|
| Butterflies in one's stomach | | nervous, fearful |
| Heart in one's mouth | | nervous |
| Jump out of one's skin | | be extremely frightened |
| Mad as a wet hen | | furious |
| On pins and needles | | very nervous |
| Push the panic button | | become terrified, overreact |

# Lesson 9: Idiom Hunt in the Community

Contributed by Michelle Lam (mlam@teachbeyond.org)

| Levels/context | Intermediate to advanced students living in an ESL environment |
|---|---|
| Aims | — To develop listening skills<br>— To develop learner autonomy<br>— To make connections between "real life" and the "classroom" |
| Class time | 15–30 minutes / out-of-class time 30 minutes |
| Preparation time | None |
| Resources | None |

## Rationale

Listening skills are one of the most difficult kinds of language skills to teach. Teaching listening strategies can help, but having a task that engages learners with real-world language is critical in making the connection between real life and their classroom experience. By having a specific task related to listening, learners are encouraged to engage with the English-speaking world around them in a nonthreatening way.

## Procedure

1. Discuss with students where they hear English speakers talking (on the bus, at the coffee shop, etc.).

2. Have students choose a time when they will intentionally listen in on the people around them. Students will jot down any unfamiliar phrases they hear, making note of common idioms.

3. In the next class, students share their phrases and brainstorm together what the idioms might mean.

## Caveats and Options

1. If students feel uncomfortable listening in on other people's conversations, they can use radio, TV, movies, or other media. This has the added benefit of allowing students to stop and playback the segment as often as needed.

2. An adaptation for very low-level learners could be to use movies or TV with English subtitles.

3. You can encourage students to build this practice into their regular lives. If they can turn time (such as when riding the bus) into learning time, it is an excellent way to become lifelong learners. Facilitate this habit-forming activity by being available to answer questions about unfamiliar idioms or phrases. You can also build this activity into the classroom routine (starting every week with a few new overheard idioms, for example).

## Contributor

Michelle Lam is the director of teacher training and development for Lucas Detech International Education, in Tuy Hoa, Vietnam.

# Lesson 10: Common Idioms in the News

Contributed by Michelle Jackson (mmjackson2@utep.edu)

| Levels/context | Advanced (university) |
|---|---|
| Aims | — Increase knowledge of high-frequency idioms<br>— Infer the meanings of idioms from contextual cues<br>— Use idioms in a short writing task<br>— Strengthen oral communication skills and group cooperation |
| Class time | 45–60 minutes (15–20 minutes per student) |
| Preparation time | 5 minutes |
| Resources | Short list of idioms selected from a list of frequently used idioms in spoken American English |

## Rationale

Advanced English language learners have likely already been exposed to idioms and understand how they function. To enhance their acquisition, these students need opportunities to infer the meaning of new idioms from contextual cues (Joe, 1995). They also need practice using idioms in writing, which has been shown to increase retention (Hulstijin & Laufer, 2001). As some of the most commonly used idioms are not found in standardized ELL textbooks (Liu, 2003), this lesson focuses on some of the most frequently used idioms in American English (Liu, 2003) and situates learning within the context of authentic material (Percy, 2013). This activity allows students to learn the meanings of idioms by reading authentic material and then producing idioms from the reading in their own writing.

## Procedure

1. As homework, assign one idiom to each student (see the appendix). The students' task is to become experts on their assigned idiom by the next class period by doing the following:

   - Search the Internet for a short text that contains the idiom. For example, typing "go over" and "NPR" in a search engine will provide a list of articles containing the idiom.

   - Read the selected text and prepare answers to the following questions:
     — Where was this text published?
     — Who is the audience for this text?
     — What is the author's thesis?

   - Be able to explain what the idiom means within the article's context.

   - Write one original sentence about the topic of the article. The sentence must contain the assigned idiom.

   - Bring two copies of the text to class with the idiom highlighted.

2. Divide the class into groups of three. Each student takes turns teaching his or her assigned idiom to the group. As a group, students do the following:

   - Read the text containing the idiom. Confirm that all members of the group understand the main ideas of the article.

   - Use contextual cues in the article to deduce the meaning of the idiom. The expert student can help guide the other students and offer explanations as necessary.

   - Discuss the sentence prepared by the expert to ensure that they understand the meaning of the idiom and how it is used.

   - As a group, create one original sentence about the topic of the article. The sentence must contain the assigned idiom.

3. As groups finish, have each group present their best sentence to the class.

## Caveats and Options

It helps to remind students that when they search for the idiom, they might find it in a different tense (e.g., *went over, was going over, had gone over*). This can yield more search results. Some website suggestions are provided in the References and Further Reading.

## References and Further Reading

www.theatlantic.com

www.bbc.com

www.npr.org

www.nytimes.com

Hulstijn, J. H., & Laufer, B. (2001). Some empirical evidence for the involvement load hypothesis in vocabulary acquisition. *Language Learning, 51*, 539–558.

Joe, A. (1995). Text-based tasks and incidental vocabulary learning. *Second Language Research, 11*, 149–158.

Liu, D. (2003). The most frequently used spoken American English idioms: A corpus analysis and its implications. *TESOL Quarterly, 37*(4), 671–700.

Percy, B. (2013). The realm of realia: The use of authentic materialism in the English language classroom. *Global Education Review, 1*(3), 14–18.

## Contributor

Michelle Jackson is the program manager of the English Language Institute at the University of Texas at El Paso.

## Appendix: Short List of Idioms From Liu's (2003) Corpus Research

| bring up | find out | look for | take on |
| --- | --- | --- | --- |
| carry out | get through | point out | take place |
| come up with | give up | set up | work out |
| deal with | go over | show up | |

# Lesson 11: Find the Missing Half: Matching Idiom Pairs

Contributed by Jean L. Arnold (jeanworld@hotmail.com)

| | |
|---|---|
| Levels/context | Intermediate and higher |
| Aims | — Learn more idioms by guessing the other halves of idioms |
| Class time | 5+ minutes |
| Preparation time | 5–20 minutes |
| Resources | Strips of paper with half of an idiom written on them (optional: basket or container out of which to draw the strips) |

## Procedure

1. If you have covered specific idioms and want to review them, type or write the idioms on a piece of paper and cut the sentence in half at a logical breaking point (e.g. *When the cat's away / the mice will play, Don't look a gift horse / in the mouth*).

2. Lists of idioms can also be found online; choose idioms that best suit students' level, needs, and interests.

3. Create a list (see appendix), leaving a space between the two halves of the idioms to make it easier to cut all the idioms in half all at once. For example:

   | | |
   |---|---|
   | When the cat's away | the mice will play. |
   | Don't look a gift horse | in the mouth. |

4. Cut the strips horizontally and make sure you have a pair of scissors in class. Keep the pairs of idioms together until you see how many students you have in class, then choose enough matched pairs for each student to get one slip of paper. Snip the idioms into halves, mix the papers up, and have students choose one slip of paper at random.

5. Instruct students to read their half of the idiom and then mingle with their classmates until pairs think they have a

match. They should sit together and discuss what the idiom might mean, or think of examples of when this idiom would be used.

6. Mingle with the class to make sure the matches are correct, encouraging students to look for clues to be sure the strips are a match (e.g., only one of the strips should begin with a capital letter or end with a punctuation mark; there should be some semantic similarity between the two halves).

7. When all students have found their match and had a chance to discuss their idiom in pairs, and once the class has quieted, take turns letting each pair say their idiom and describe the meaning and/or when it would be used. Be sure to immediately check the correctness of each idiom's meaning.

## Caveats and Options

1. Groups can discuss whether there is a similar idiom in students' native language(s).

2. As homework, have students research idioms online and find others that are interesting. Let them report about these the next day.

3. For extra credit, ask for a volunteer to create this activity with another group of idioms that weren't previously used.

4. This activity can also be geared to specific grammatical forms, such as various forms of conditionals. For example,

| | |
|---|---|
| When the cat's away | the mice will play. |
| When the going gets tough | the tough get going. |
| When life gives you lemons | make lemonade. |
| If the shoe fits | wear it. |

## Contributor
Jean L. Arnold is a full-time lecturer in the English as a Second Language Program at the University of Nebraska at Lincoln.

## Appendix: Idiom Matching Activity

Ask students to select from these idioms that relate to animals or other critters to create your own idiom-matching activity.

| | |
|---|---|
| A bird in the hand | is worth two in the bush. |
| Birds of a feather | flock together. |
| Don't bite the hand | that feeds you. |
| Don't cast your pearls | before swine. |
| You'll catch more flies | with honey than with vinegar. |
| The chickens have come home | to roost. |
| Don't count your chickens | before they hatch. |
| Don't look a gift horse | in the mouth. |
| The early bird | catches the worm. |
| He's like a fish | out of water. |
| Get down off your | high horse! |
| Wait a minute! Hold | your horses! |
| You're in the | dog house now! |
| Kill two birds | with one stone. |
| Knee-high | to a grasshopper. |
| Let the cat | out of the bag. |
| Let sleeping dogs | lie. |
| Lock the barn door | after the horse is out. |
| Live high | off the hog. |
| Mad as | a wet hen. |
| Make a mountain | out of a molehill. |
| Make a silk purse | out of a sow's ear. |
| There's more than one way | to skin a cat. |
| Open a can | of worms. |
| To play cat | and mouse. |
| Pull a rabbit | out of a hat. |
| Quiet as | a mouse. |
| It's raining cats | and dogs. |
| It's as scarce | as hen's teeth. |
| She's sick as | a dog. |

| | |
|---|---|
| I smell | a rat. |
| He's a snake | in the grass. |
| Stir up | a hornet's nest. |
| The straw that broke | the camel's back. |
| Take the bull | by the horns. |
| Throw a monkey wrench | into the works. |
| 'Til the cows | come home. |
| What's good for the goose | is good for the gander. |
| When the cat's away, | the mice will play. |
| He's a wolf | in sheep's clothing. |
| He went on a wild goose | chase. |
| You can lead a horse to water | but you can't make him drink. |
| You can't teach an old dog | new tricks. |

## Lesson 12: Anger Idioms

Contributed by Sam Weekes (samjweekes@gmail.com)

| | |
|---|---|
| Levels/context | Upper intermediate; university students and adults |
| Aims | — Develop ability to recognize idioms<br>— Infer the meaning of four idioms using literal and contextual clues<br>— Use the idioms appropriately to discuss experiences of being angry |
| Class time | 60 minutes |
| Preparation time | 10–15 minutes |
| Resources | Student worksheet, answer key |

### Rationale

This lesson aims to introduce four idioms related to anger and guide students in interpreting and using them appropriately. Understanding an idiom involves a pragmatic act of recognizing that something does not make sense and reinterpreting it into something that does makes sense (Grant & Bauer, 2004). This is easier to achieve when idioms are presented in a context (T. C. Cooper, 1998) and are transparent, that is, their literal and metaphorical meanings are connected (T. C. Cooper, 1998; Irujo, 1986). Therefore, the idioms in this lesson were chosen because there is a connection between the metaphorical concepts (blood boiling, letting off steam, keeping cool, and seeing red) and physical reactions associated with being angry (a rise in body temperature and reddening of the skin). These physical reactions are explored in Step 1. In Step 2, students generate a definition of *idiom* which is used in Step 3 to identify idioms in four short sentences. In Step 4, students notice themes and literal and metaphorical connections in the idioms. In Step 5, they use these along with contextual clues from the sentences to infer the meaning of each idiom. In addition to understanding idioms, learners also need to use them appropriately.

Generally, idioms can be learned as fixed expressions; however, verbs and pronouns still need to be changed accordingly (Irujo, 1986). The sentence stems in Step 6 provide a structure to support students by using the idioms in discourse. In Step 7, through question formation, students manipulate grammatical features of the idioms; for example, *keep my cool* can also be *keep your cool*. Finally, in Step 8, the teacher can monitor students' use of the idioms as they participate in a mingle activity.

**Procedure**

1. On the board, write *angry*. Ask students what physical feelings/reactions they experience when they are angry. Elicit that our body temperature rises, we feel hot, we go red, we shake, and so on.

2. Explain that the lesson focuses on anger idioms. Elicit a definition of *idiom*, for example, "an expression that cannot be understood by the meaning of the separate words, but has a separate meaning of its own" (Merriam-Webster, 2014).

3. Hand out the first part of the worksheet (see appendix). Students read the sentences and use their definition from Step 2 to identify one idiom in each sentence.

4. Ask if students notice any themes in the idioms. Elicit the idea that the idioms relate to the theme of hot and cool. Draw their attention to the connection between this theme and the physical reactions to anger they discussed.

5. Have students speculate about the meaning of each idiom. Remind them to think about the connection of anger and heat, and to use the contextual clues in the sentences.

6. Hand out the second part of the worksheet. Ask students to complete each sentence with information about their own experiences.

7. Write the first sentence stem (*makes my blood boil*) on the board. Elicit a question that could be asked about this sentence, for example, "What makes your blood boil?" Draw students' attention to the change from *my* to *your*. Elicit

grammatical changes that might occur in the other idioms (changes in possessive adjectives and verb tense). Students work in pairs to write one question for each sentence.

8.  Students ask and answer the questions in a mingle activity.

9.  Monitor students' use of the idioms.

## Caveats and Options

1.  In Step 5, for less able learners, provide meanings to match to the idioms.

2.  As a follow-up, ask students to find more English idioms related to hot and cool.

## References and Further Reading

Cooper, T. C. (1998). Teaching Idioms. *Foreign Language Annals, 31,* 255–266. doi:10.1111/j.1944-9720.1998.tb00572.x

Grant, L., & Bauer, L. (2004). Criteria for redefining idioms: Are we barking up the wrong tree? *Applied Linguistics, 25*(1), 38–61. doi:10.1093/applin/25.1.38

Irujo, S. (1986). A piece of cake: Learning and teaching idioms. *ELT Journal, 40,* 236–242. doi:10.1093/elt/40.3.236

Merriam-Webster. (2014). *Idiom.* Retrieved from http://www.learners dictionary.com/search/idiom

Sinclair, J. M., & Moon, R. E. (1995). *Collins COBUILD dictionary of idioms.* London, England: Collins.

## Contributor

Samantha Weekes is a materials writer and teacher trainer for the Burma Education Partnership in Thailand.

**Appendix: Anger Idioms Student Worksheet**

Part 1. Read the text in each bubble. Identify and <u>underline</u> one idiom in each bubble.

> I really care about the environment. If I see people dropping litter on the street, it makes my blood boil!

> I almost lost my temper at work today. My boss made a mistake and blamed it on me! But I managed to keep my cool.

> I have a short temper. When people annoy me, I just see red and usually start shouting.

> Ah! I feel so angry! I need to let off steam.

Discuss the meaning of each idiom. Write your ideas in the table.

| Idiom | Meaning |
|---|---|
|  |  |
|  |  |
|  |  |
|  |  |

Part 2. Complete the sentences with information about your own experiences.

1. _____ makes my blood boil!

2. I find it difficult to keep my cool when _____ because _____.

3. _____ I saw red!

4. If I need to let off steam I _____.

**Answer key**

I really care about the environment. If I see people dropping litter on the street, it <u>makes my blood boil</u>!

I almost lost my temper at work today. My boss made a mistake and blamed it on me! But I managed to <u>keep my cool.</u>

I have a short temper. When people annoy me, I just <u>see red</u> and usually start shouting.

Ah! I feel so angry! I need to <u>let off steam</u>.

| Idiom | Meaning |
|---|---|
| (to) makes one's blood boil | to make you very angry |
| (to) keep one's cool | to control your temper and keep calm |
| (to) see red | to suddenly get very angry |
| (to) let off steam | to do or say something that helps you get rid of your anger |

*Definitions taken from *Collins COBUILD Dictionary of Idioms* (1995).

**Possible questions.**

What makes your blood boil?

When do you find it difficult to keep your cool?

Can you tell me about a time you saw red?

What do you do if you need to let off steam?

# Bonus Lesson Plan:
# Let's Get Physical—Idiom Use and Exercise

Contributed by Patrick T. Randolph (patricktrandolph@gmail.com)

| | |
|---|---|
| Levels/context | Intermediate to advanced, secondary to higher education |
| Aims | — Review idioms in a fun and competitive environment<br>— Use movement and exercise to enhance learning and retention of idioms<br>— Learn how to use idioms<br>— Learn about error correction |
| Class time | 40 minutes |
| Preparation time | 10 minutes |
| Resources | Prior to activity: large flash cards. During the activity: white board, colored markers, student notebooks, pens/pencils |

## Rationale

This lesson presupposes that students have already studied the target idioms in a lesson earlier in the week or month. As discussed in Chapter 3, exercise during class helps students focus better on the lesson and learn the material at a deeper level. This activity gets students up and moving while simultaneously keeping them focused on the task at hand. As discussed in Chapters 3 and 4, review is an essential tool for transferring any kind of information from short- to long-term memory. The pace of this activity allows students to review the terms multiple times by seeing them, hearing them, reading them, and writing them in the context of a meaningful sentence. And finally, this activity attempts to develop students' awareness of written errors through both self-correction and correction of others' errors.

## Procedure

*Part 1*

1. Organize the class into groups of three, and have students place their notebooks and pens/pencils in front of them.

2. Take a moment to get students focused and attentive.

3. Hold up a large flash card with a concise definition written on it (e.g., "feel extremely happy").

4. Students see this and raise their hand to answer (e.g., "be in seventh heaven").

5. The fastest hand in the air gets the first chance to answer, the second hand gets the second chance to answer, and so on.

6. The student who answers correctly first gets one point for his or her group.

7. However, if the answer given is not 100% correct and another group corrects it, then that group gets one point. For example,

   The teacher shows the card for "feel extremely happy."

   Student from Group 1: "be in a heaven."

   Student from Group 3: Actually it's "be in seventh heaven."

8. After all the idioms and their definitions have been presented, write the idioms on the board and ask the class for their definitions as a quick review.

9. Students write the idioms and their definitions in their notebooks.

*Part 2*

10. Keep the same groups, and give each group a white board marker or piece of chalk, depending on your classroom "technology."

11. Write the group names on the board (in this example there are five, but you may have a different number), write the word "Points" along the left-hand side, and draw lines to separate each group:

| | Group 1 | Group 2 | Group 3 | Group 4 | Group 5 |
|---|---|---|---|---|---|
| Points: | | | | | |

12. Next, take a moment to get students focused and ready to do Part 2.

13. Say one of the idioms presented in Part 1 out loud. One student from each group runs to that group's place on the board and writes an example sentence using the idiom. If an idiom such as *be in seventh heaven* is used, then they should explain why they are happy and not just the fact that they are happy. For instance, the sentence should have a justification such as this: "Mariam and Nelma are in seventh heaven because they got As on their exams."

14. The fastest team done gets one point. However, their answer must be correct. If the fastest team's answer/example is not correct, and another team recognizes it and orally corrects it, then that team gets two points. For example,

> Group 1's written work: "My teacher was in seventh heaven, his daughter was born."

> Group 2's correction: Correction on Group 1's sentence. It should be "My teacher was in seventh heaven after his daughter was born."

15. The team with the most points wins. Note: It's fun to keep the same groups for a few weeks and have multiple competitions. That way they develop a sense of camaraderie, and the competitive energy increases, as does the learning of idioms.

16. After finishing Part 2, do a review of the idioms with their definitions and examples.

**Caveats and Options**

Depending on the time you have and the level of the class, you could either use both of these activities (Parts 1 and 2) or simply focus on one per lesson.

## Appendix: Sampling of Idioms and Their Definitions

*come up with*: create, produce, invent, think up

*bend over backwards*: try hard to help someone

*feel like a million dollars*: feel very healthy and happy, feel great

*find out*: learn about something, gain knowledge, ascertain something by way of inquiry

*have a ball*: have a fun time

*hinge on*: depend on, be contingent on

*look up to*: show respect, admire someone

*shed light on*: make clear by explanation, clarify

*spread oneself too thin*: become too involved in too many activities

*think outside the box*: think freely, not bound by limiting ideas

## Contributor

Patrick T. Randolph, coauthor of this book, teaches at Western Michigan University. He lives with his family in Kalamazoo, Michigan.

## Discussion

### Implications for Future Research on Teaching and Learning Idioms

This collection of lesson plans, we believe, is a solid reflection of the ideas discussed in Chapter 3 in terms of how students' brains and minds best learn idioms, and it supports a vast number of the pedagogical ideas covered in Chapters 4 and 5, and the survey results presented in Chapters 6 and 7.

As highlighted in many of the lesson plans, physical exercise plays a significant role in many of the activities. As discussed in detail in Chapter 3, the importance of exercise cannot be overstated. Another important factor that is prevalent is the idea of personal involvement and ownership in the activities. Any time we as teachers can inspire students to get personally involved and take stock in the material, the better they will learn it and develop deeper connections in the brain. A third and very crucial element in these lesson plans is the idea of critical and creative thinking. This factor is present in all 13 lesson plans. Without actually calling it critical or creative thinking, we are getting students to do it naturally by asking them to think about idioms, respond to their uses and meanings, and implement them as best they can in and out of the classroom.

True to our initial pledge and purpose for this text, we offered these plans as working ideas which instructors can use, develop, and alter to fit the needs and interests of students. Perhaps what is necessary now is for more classroom teacher–based research to be done to see which activities help students learn idioms or at least help them become aware of idiom meaning and usage. We urge our fellow instructors to keep the ball rolling by paying close attention to what works in the classroom and discuss with others what we need to do more of in order to facilitate idiom understanding and keep instructors from being tongue-tied in the process.

# CHAPTER 9

# Overview and Critiques of Resources for Teaching and Learning Idioms

"Only the glistening key of silence can open our door of dialogue."

—*Scott J. Brooks (American Poet)*

In addition to ready-to-use lesson plans, we want our readers to be familiar with a vast array of very useful idiom textbooks, websites, and other resource materials, so this chapter offers practical suggestions for teachers looking for materials to use in their classrooms. Here we summarize many useful textbooks, online resources, and dictionaries, and we specifically offer critiques of the best and most useful textbooks and websites for teaching idioms or for learning idioms on your own.

The chapter is set up in the following way: (1) textbook reviews, (2) website reviews, (3) a list of recommended dictionaries, workbooks and other reference materials. Each textbook and website review contains an Overview and Content portion, ideas for Teacher Uses, ideas for Student Uses, a Critique, and a Rating. Our rating uses the following system: 1—poor (not worth a look); 2—average (worth looking through for some ideas); 3—good (a few good lesson plans and activities here); 4—very good (you will want to use this in class multiple times); and 5—excellent (you could actually build your class around this material).

We hope that these resources provide additional inspiration, energy, and excitement as you reflect on and plan your next lesson on idioms. We would like to point out that, as websites are continually being updated and improved, it is a good idea to check them regularly for additional content, examples, and explanations. Also, as you will notice, the publication dates of the textbooks, dictionaries, and additional resources vary from more recent to older texts. We have searched and analyzed the catalogs of a variety of publishers and talked with many practicing teachers as well as drawn on our own teaching experiences to find the books that we feel are the most useful to review here. In the case of some of the older books, we included them because they are classics or very popular in our field, and we attempted to review the latest edition of the dictionaries. But as you will notice, some of the materials we review here are rather dated and in need of new editions. And, in general, as noted in the teacher survey, there are simply not many high-quality textbooks that have been published in recent years. Perhaps this lack of relevant textbooks should inspire someone to put together a new idiom textbook that draws on some of the topics and themes we have discussed in this book.

## Part 1: Textbook Reviews

**Dixon, Robert. *Essential Idioms in English: Phrasal Verbs and Collocations*, 5th ed.**
White Plains, NY: Pearson Longman. 2004. Pp. xi, 276.
ISBN: 0-13-141176-4.

*Rating:* 3.5

*Overview and Content*
This popular book is now in its 5th edition. Dixon organizes lists of new idioms into lessons according to sections labeled "Beginning," "Intermediate," and "Advanced." The 5th edition adds more recently used idioms and removes outdated ones. Most useful for teachers and students, this edition includes collocations in each section.

*Teacher Uses*
This book has been a solid supplemental text or resource for teachers for many years because it is clearly organized and offers straightfor-

ward definitions, example sentences, and brief quizzes and exercises for each lesson. Each section also contains a review with further exercises that can be easily used as quizzes and classroom activities.

## Student Uses
Advanced students will be able to use this book easily as a resource for new idioms and self-learning. Answers to all exercises are located in the appendix, and, as with previous editions, translations of all of the idioms into French, Spanish, and Portuguese are listed in the appendix.

## Critique
Although the book is easily used as a supplemental resource for teachers, it is limited as a source of creative exercises and offers little additional explanation of new idioms or strategies for practicing idioms. Outside of the proficiency-level organization, the individual chapters have no clear context, further highlighting the need for use in a classroom with teacher guidance.

**Feare, Ronald.** *Everyday Idioms for Reference and Practice.*
White Plains, NY: Pearson Longman. 1997. Pp. vi, 168 (book 1), Pp. viii, 168 (book 2). ISBN: 978-0201834086 (book 1), 978-0201441819 (book 2).

*Rating:* 4

## Overview and Content
*Everyday Idioms* is a two-part series for intermediate and advanced learners, focusing on American idioms. Feare has collected more than 1,200 idioms in the two books from many media and dictionary sources. Many of the idioms are from students at San Diego State University. The books each contain 50 units organized around a variety of topics, from government and politics to expressing oneself. In addition to definitions and example sentences (with usage notes), each unit contains practice exercises, including open-ended activities such as creating plays.

## Teacher Uses
Teachers may be able use these books as the main text in a vocabulary/ idioms class because both books cover so many idioms and offer exercises after each unit. At the same time, the units are short, and teachers will want to supplement the text with outside activities.

*Student Uses*
Similar to *Essential Idioms in English*, these textbooks are best used in a classroom setting for intermediate learners. More advanced learners can use the books' extensive lists of idioms and examples as the basis for self-study, but many of the suggested activities involve a partner.

*Critique*
The book series contains a plethora of information on idioms and is a great starting point for teachers. The unclear reasoning behind the organization of the unit and the repetition of dialogue and role-play activities in nearly every chapter limit the usefulness of the series.

**Fragiadakis, Helen. *All Clear: Listening and Speaking.***
Boston, MA: Heinle Cengage Learning. Pp. xvi, 240 (book 1, 2nd ed., 2008); pp. xvi, 224 (book 2, 3rd ed., 2007); pp. xvi, 224 (book 3, 2nd ed., 2008). ISBN: 978-1413017038 (Book 1), 978-1413017045 (Book 2), 978-1413017052 (Book 3).

*Rating:* 4.5

*Overview and Content*
Based on the lexical approach, this comprehensive three-part speaking and listening series is an expansion from the 1st edition of *All Clear*, which focused only on idioms. Book 1—Beginner to Book 3—Advanced now use idioms as springboards for listening and speaking activities. All of the lessons are organized around a particular activity such as "pulling an all-nighter" or a debate topic such as "violence in the media," and they begin with warm-up activities and listening to a dialogue before providing definitions and a variety of activities.

*Teacher Uses*
Depending on the length of the course, these textbooks could easily form the basis of an entire class or mini-course. From activities focusing on error correction to culture and language on the Internet, each lesson has enough activities to take up an entire week of class time.

*Student Uses*
Each book has an answer key, and there is plenty of additional information for self-study, such as pronunciation tips, but many exercises are designed for classroom and partner use.

*Critique*

These books offer teachers a way to teach general speaking and listening skills while drawing on idioms from everyday speech. There are many warm-up activities when learning the definitions that teachers must move quickly through in order to emphasize the correct meaning.

**King, Kevin. *The Big Picture: Idioms as Metaphors.***
Boston, MA: Heinle Cengage Learning. 1999. Pp. xiv, 194.
ISBN: 978-0395917121.

*Rating:* 4

*Overview and Content*

This textbook draws on cognitive linguistics and metaphor theory to organize 209 idioms around eight target domains such as ideas, knowledge, and money. Each idiom is illustrated and given a metaphorical explanation along with example sentences and a dictionary definition. All chapters begin with a warm-up that introduces the metaphor and asks students to compare the underlying metaphors in English to their first language. Exercises range from sentence completion to making presentations using idioms.

*Teacher Uses*

The limited number of idioms and the focus on underlying metaphors make this book particularly useful as a secondary textbook for teachers to use in vocabulary and speaking classes.

*Student Uses*

Advanced learners will find the pictures and detailed explanations of the underlying metaphors useful for self-study, but beginners or students not interested in how language works may find that the emphasis on metaphors takes away from practicing the new idioms.

*Critique*

The book offers an innovative and intellectual approach to organizing idioms that can be motivating for students. But some of the illustrations may distract learners, and the activities are repetitive with the same fill-in-the-blank, conversation sentences, and presentation activities offered in every chapter.

**O'Dell, Felicity, & Michael McCarthy. *English Idioms in Use*.**
Cambridge, England: Cambridge University Press. 2010. Pp. 1, 202.
ISBN: 978-0521744294 (Advanced), 978-0521789578 (Intermediate).

*Rating:* 4.5

*Overview and Content*
This textbook presents the most significant idioms from the CAN-CODE corpus. The first sections of the book describe aspects of defining and using idioms. The next sections organize new idioms according to their origin, the topic in which the idioms are used, the written or spoken contexts of their use, and finally keywords that occur in many idioms. Each chapter presents idioms in different formats, including conversations, advertisements, pictures, and written texts.

*Teacher Uses*
The chapters are very short, and most of the exercises are brief fill-in-the-blank, matching, or short-answer activities. This textbook would be ideal for supplementing a core vocabulary or speaking textbook, with mini-lessons easily organized around each chapter.

*Student Uses*
This is perhaps the best textbook for self-study because a wide variety of information on many aspects of idioms is provided, and the exercises can all be completed because an answer key is provided.

*Critique*
The textbook combines some of the best aspects of other books by drawing on corpus research into the most useful idioms, providing information on how idioms function, offering examples of idioms from around the world, and organizing chapters in a variety of ways that keep learners interested. Few of the activities, however, are interactive.

**McPartland-Fairman, Pamela. *Take It Easy*, 2nd ed.**
White Plains, NY: Pearson Longman. 2000. Pp. viii, 200.
ISBN: 978-0136608127.

*Rating:* 4

*Overview and Content*
The book primarily introduces phrasal verb idioms in 10 chapters organized around themes such as fashion, love, and immigration. The

introduction notes the six grammatical patterns that the idioms follow (e.g., "intransitive verb + particle" for *hold on*), and exercises in each chapter draw attention to the grammatical patterns of the new terms. Each chapter contains many authentic listening and reading examples of the idioms, including a dialogue at the beginning.

*Teacher Uses*
The chapters offer a variety of interactive exercises and activities that can be easily adapted in the classroom, but the range of idioms and the focus on phrasal verbs make this book more useful as a supplementary text than the main textbook.

*Student Uses*
There are many explanations and examples, and there is an answer key for the 166 idioms introduced, making it useful for self-study. Most of the activities, however, are for classroom use.

*Critique*
The book's focus on grammatical structure and authentic examples provide both quality input and linguistic insight into the structure of verbal idioms. The book is limited by the narrow focus on phrasal verbs, but it could be useful as a supplementary textbook.

**Watkins, Dana. *The Idiom Advantage.***
White Plains, NY: Pearson Longman. 2001. Pp. xiii, 197.
ISBN: 978-0201619928.

*Rating:* 4.5

*Overview and Content*
This textbook organizes a variety of idioms from binomials such as *pros and cons*, to phrasal verbs such as *get a leg up*, to general themes such as effort and leisure. The distinctive feature of this textbook is the use of advertisements to introduce and practice new idioms. In addition to interactive exercises, role-plays, and debates, *The Idiom Advantage* offers extended reading sections using authentic texts in which the new idioms are used. The chapters also include critical thinking sections such as "Interpreting the Ads" and "Using the Idioms in Writing," in which students write everything from reports to new advertisements.

*Teacher Uses*

The variety of activities in the textbook allows it to be a main textbook, and teachers could easily expand each chapter into writing, speaking, listening, and presentation activities.

*Student Uses*

The additional listening activities and large amount of reading text lend themselves to self-study, but many of the exercises require at least a partner or small group to conduct the debate.

*Critique*

The textbook is a bit dated as there has not been a new edition since 2001, and some of the advertisements appear dated, as do some of the idioms, such as *feather one's nest*. But the authentic materials and use of advertisements is very engaging for students at an intermediate level and above.

**Collis, Harry. *101 American English Idioms: Understanding and Speaking English Like an American!***
Chicago, IL: Passport Books. 1987. Pp. vi, 104. ISBN: 0-8442-5446-0.

*Rating:* 4

*Overview and Content*

*101 American English Idioms* is divided into nine themed categories with an average of 11 idioms per chapter, such as "It's a Zoo Out There" which features animal-related idioms like *go to the dogs*, *take the bull by the horns*, and *cat got your tongue?* The majority of the idioms are informal but very useful and helpful for ELLs. Each idiom is introduced in five parts: (1) it is featured at the top of each page, (2) a very helpful cartoon is given to help explain the idiom, (3) a meaning is offered, (4) a dialog or narrative is given which uses the idiom, and (5) the idiom is explained in detail in either the dialog or narrative.

*Teacher Uses*

Teachers can use this book as is for their lessons due to the simple yet useful and practical nature of the page setup. With copyright approval, they can make photocopies of each page for class use, even using the pictures as flash cards to review the idioms once they have been learned.

*Student Uses*

This textbook is most useful for students as a source from which to copy important everyday idioms. They could then compile these idioms and create their own pocket idiom dictionary, complete with personal example sentences. Students can ask their teachers to check these for grammar and register.

*Critique*

This is a fantastic book for high-intermediate to advanced ELLs. One drawback might be the fact that most of the idioms are informal and not academic. However, the idioms in this volume are practical, useful, and necessary to know.

**McMordie, W., and Jennifer Seidl. *English Idioms:
A Fifth Edition of English Idioms and How to Use Them.***
Oxford, England: Oxford University Press. 1995. Pp. 1, 267.
ISBN: 0-19-432775-2.

*Rating:* 4.5

*Overview and Content*

*English Idioms* was first published in 1909 by W. McMordie and has since gone through five revisions, with many new idioms and phrasal verbs added to each edition. The book offers a concise introduction to idioms with a history of English vocabulary, a section on different aspects of the English idiom, an explanation of two kinds of idioms, and a small explanation on where and when to use English idioms.

The book itself is divided into nine categories for users: (1) key words with idiomatic uses such as *a big fish in a little pond* and *in a big way*; (2) idioms with nouns and adjectives such as *a cog in the machine* and adjective + noun idioms like *a close shave*; (3) idiomatic pairs such as pairs of adjectives, *cut and dried* and *spick and span,* or identical pairs like *bit by bit* and *through and through*; (4) idioms with prepositions such as *above board* or *after a fashion*; (5) phrasal verbs such as bi- and tri-part phrasal verbs like *act up* and *come up with*; (6) verbal idioms such as *burn the midnight oil* and *speak volumes*; (7) idioms from special subjects such as banking, business and travel; (8) idioms with key words from special categories such as animals, colors, numbers, body parts, and time; and (9) idioms with comparisons such as similes like *as fit as a fiddle* and *work like a Trojan.*

In addition, entries in the volume offer stress markers, give alternative words for certain idioms (e.g., *fresh* and *new* for the idiom *break fresh ground*), contain clear and concise definitions, and provide brief example sentences or short dialogs demonstrating the idioms.

*Teacher Uses*
Teachers of ELLs can use this book either to supplement a vocabulary lesson or teach theme-based lessons on a multitude of categories—from the use of preposition-headed idioms for a grammar class to the use of colors in idioms for a culture-based lesson. They can also assign a set number of idioms and have students research their idioms' meanings and uses and then conduct interviews with native speakers to reinforce the application of the terms. (See "Idioms in Action Activities" in Chapter 5.)

*Student Uses*
ELLs can use this book to enhance their knowledge of English vocabulary and their understanding of the various English-speaking host cultures in which they might study or live. Because they literally have hundreds of idioms to choose from, students can easily create a manageable list of 5 to 10 idioms from each category in the book. They can then make their own idiom usage dictionaries, complete with categories—grammatical and thematic—and write working example sentences or mini-dialogs.

*Critique*
Overall, this is a fabulous book for English language teachers and ELLs at the intermediate to advanced levels of study. In fact, it is so comprehensive, even the average native speaker of English can pick up new idioms for his or her own vocabulary. One drawback is the lack of actual exercises or activities in the book; however, *English Idioms* offers a companion exercise book on idioms, and a second book for phrasal verb practice is also available. Users should also note that the idioms are based on British English, so certain prepositional uses and meanings of idioms differ from those in American English.

**Niergarth, Hal, and Elizabeth Niergarth.** *The Idiom Book: 1010 Idioms in 101 Two-Page Lessons.*
Brattleboro, VT: Pro Lingua Associates. 2007. Pp. iv, 204.
ISBN: 0-86647-259-2.

*Rating:* 3

*Overview and Content*
*The Idiom Book* is written for high-intermediate to advanced ELLs. As the cover clearly expresses, there are 1,010 idioms covered in 101 two-page lessons. Each lesson offers 10 idioms and consists of four parts. Section A includes an informal dialog which introduces the 10 idioms. This can be both read and listened to on the CDs that accompany the text. Section B offers the first active use of the idioms through fill-in-the-blank exercises. These sections are in the form of journal entries, emails, or memos. Section C gives students a chance to match the idioms with their definitions. The last part, Section D, requires students to create their own example sentences using the 10 idioms. Answers for Sections C and D are available on the Pro Lingua website, which also includes the complete list of the idioms from the textbook.

*Teacher Uses*
The textbook offers four useful activities for each set of 10 idioms, so instructors can almost set up entire lessons around the format of the chapters. Section A can easily be used to introduce the idioms. Teachers could display this on a document camera and have students guess the meanings of the idioms. This can be done in pairs, in small groups, or as a class. We recommend skipping to Section C to have students confirm the definitions with the idioms. Again, this could be done in pairs or groups and then, as a class, check the answers. Sections B and D could be used as homework.

*Student Uses*
Given the format of this textbook, students could easily use this as a self-study text. However, they would still need the help of either a teacher or a very knowledgeable native speaker to understand the nuances, register, and possible multiple meanings of some of the idioms in the book. For optimal understanding, then, we suggest that students use this book in an ESL/EFL classroom environment.

*Critique*

*The Idioms Book*, in general, is a great book in terms of the quantity of idioms offered to the teacher and student and the easy-to-follow format of the chapters. The initial dialogs in each chapter, however, often seem forced and too simplistic to help learners understand how the idioms are actually used. Further, the sections do not follow a logical order for learner acquisition. If one does use this text, we recommend revising the order and do A, C, and then B and D. It makes more sense to confirm the meanings of the idioms before using them in the fill-in-the-blank exercises. Finally, Section D does not really give students much room to create and explore the idioms. They are essentially replacing one phrase with another without going deep into its register, nuance, or cultural ramifications.

## Part 2: Website Reviews

**The Free Dictionary: www.idioms.thefreedictionary.com**

*Rating:* 2.5

*Overview and Content*

The idiom portion of this website is compiled from two main sources: the *Cambridge International Dictionary of Idioms* and the *Cambridge Dictionary of American Idioms*. The site contains over 7,000 current American, Australian, and British idioms. Its primary goal is to facilitate understanding and use. Thirty-nine random idioms are placed on the homepage as examples. The site also offers the following free tools: for web surfers, free toolbar and extensions, a word of the day, a bookmark, and help; for webmasters, free content, linking, a lookup box, and double-click lookup.

*Teacher Uses*

Teachers can essentially use this like a book on idioms. They can simply type a particular idiom in the search box and find its definition.

*Student Uses*

Students can use the site in the same way as teachers can. But the students' use would be limited to high-intermediate and advanced learners of English.

*Critique*

Although a wide variety of idioms are listed with good definitions and example sentences, you need to know the specific idiom you are looking for before typing it in, so it requires a solid preexisting knowledge of English idioms. Moreover, the idioms are not classified in any special order aside from being alphabetical.

**UE Using English.com: www.usingenglish.com/reference/idioms**

*Rating:* 3.5

*Overview and Content*

Usingenglish.com offers a number of language tools and helpful resources for English language teachers and learners. To access the idioms and phrasal verbs, use the dropdown menu under Reference on the homepage. The English Idioms & Idiomatic Expressions portion of the site is very useful in that it provides basic definitions of 3,793 idiomatic expressions.

The idioms are listed alphabetically from A to Z in a search bar in the upper third of the screen. In addition, the site offers an Idioms Discussion Forum and a link to Suggest an Idiom. The idioms page includes a Recently Added section, and there is also a Members Get More feature that allows users to get access to additional idiomatic and slang expressions.

*Teacher Uses*

Instructors can find a number of idioms here, and the added feature of a discussion forum is nice. Moreover, they can become active participants by contributing to the website.

*Student Uses*

Students can access a wide variety of informal and formal idioms, and they can easily access the Idioms Discussion Forum and the English Phrasal Verbs Forum.

*Critique*

The site provides many tools for both English language teachers and learners. The Idiom Categories link is particularly useful. It offers 36 categories of idioms from animals to weather. The phrasal verb section of the site gives both good definitions and useful example sentences for each of the terms. The idiom section, however, provides only definitions and links to Google for random samples of usage that contain both good and bad examples of the terms.

**The Idiom Connection: www.idiomconnection.com**

*Rating:* 4.5

*Overview and Content*

The Idiom Connection provides language learners and teachers with a vast array of idioms from A to Z, a link to the 100 most frequent idioms, 26 separate categories of idioms (e.g., arm, hand, and finger idioms; color idioms), and a link to proverbs and sayings. This site also gives students a nice explanation of idioms, phrasal verbs, and proverbs. What makes this site stand out among the others is its very simple layout coupled with its rich content. For example, each letter category has a number of subsets. If you click on A, you get "A Idioms," "After Idioms," "All Idioms," "As Idioms," "At Idioms," and "Quizzes."

*Teacher Uses*

Instructors can use this site for lesson plans on idioms from prepositional-headed idioms such as *at a standstill* to topic-based idioms for special days or events such as love and relationship idioms for Valentine's Day. Whether it is a more grammar-based idioms class or a topic-based class, this site can be of great use.

*Student Uses*

The best features of this site for students are the detailed categories, clear example sentences, and self-quizzes they can take to develop a detailed understanding of idioms.

*Critique*

Like EnglishClub.com, this site has a nice, simple layout and yet a very detailed web of useful idioms. The categories are useful and well structured. The fact that each category has quizzes for language learners is an added plus. There are also good review segments at the end of each section.

**English Club: www.englishclub.com/ref/idioms**

*Rating:* 4.5

*Overview and Content*
The layout of this site is easy to follow and provides a number of idioms—25 on average—per letter in the alphabet. For example, when you click on A, it gives you 26 idioms that start with the letter A. In addition, it offers 22 categories of idioms; for instance, it supplies 90 idioms based on the body. A clear and simple definition is offered for each idiom along with one to two example sentences. Quizzes are offered for each idiom, complete with answers. You can enter a discussion of any of the idioms with a link to their discussion forum, which is usually found after each quiz. EnglishClub.com also offers links for formal versus informal idioms, links to both American and British idioms, and links to daily terms highlighted for its users.

*Teacher Uses*
The alphabetizing and categorizing of idioms help instructors save time, and they can have students take any of the 480 quizzes offered on the website.

*Student Uses*
The expressions of the day, the vast number of quizzes, and the categories of region and register help reinforce students' understanding and use of idioms.

*Critique*
The fact that the site has a great many categories makes it easy to use. The particular idioms chosen or highlighted are also quite useful and more common than some of the other idioms used on similar websites. Another beneficial aspect of this website is that it generally supplies two examples per idiom, giving language learners a better chance of developing a clearer understanding of its use and meaning.

**Dave's ESL Cafe: www.eslcafe.com**

*Rating:* 2

*Overview and Content*
The ESL Idiom Page on this website offers some basic idioms for ELLs and teachers. It is organized in two ways: (1) an alphabetical list

of idioms from A to Z and (2) the same list with meanings and example sentences for each idiom. The content is basic and there are no additional perks like quizzes or forums.

*Teacher Uses*
This site can be used to retrieve both informal and formal English idioms for class use. But because there are no categories, it will take time to hunt through the list.

*Student Uses*
Student uses would be virtually the same as teacher uses. They can hunt for useful idioms to enhance their vocabulary. This site, however, would be limited to high-intermediate or advanced ELLs.

*Critique*
The idioms on this website are a nice selection of formal and informal expressions. However, it is essentially a list, with limited definitions and examples. Some examples are informative, others are not. The lack of self-quizzes and discussion forums limits the functionality and use of this site.

## Idiom Site: www.idiomsite.com

*Rating: 2*

*Overview and Content*
This is a basic idiom website with a number of common and useful English idioms and proverbs. The list is alphabetized. There are no categories of idioms based on topics or regional use.

*Teacher Uses*
Idiom Site has a number of basic idioms composed of both phrases and single words. These are mostly informal in nature. There are also common proverbs listed among the idioms that teachers can use to enhance students' vocabulary.

*Student Uses*
The use for students is limited because there are no example sentences to help them secure the idiom's meaning and usage. But the list could be used to familiarize students with various idioms that they will hear in and out of their academic environments.

*Critique*

This site provides a basic introduction to a number of idioms. One major problem is that it mixes idioms with proverbs without any explanation. Moreover, it does not offer example sentences but merely supplies minimal definitions. A common problem with some of these is that they use certain idiomatic expressions or phrasal verbs within the definitions, further complicating the issue. Other drawbacks of this website are its lack of forums, discussion sections, quizzes, and categories for idioms.

## Self-Study Idiom Quizzes: www.a4esl.org/q/h/idioms.html

*Rating:* 4

*Overview and Content*

This student-centered website offers a whole gamut of quizzes on different levels of idioms and phrasal verbs. There are five quizzes based on idiom categories (e.g., Animal Idioms, Idioms with Body Parts, Idioms with Numbers). Seventeen phrasal verb quizzes are also offered which focus on specific themes tied to the phrasal verbs (e.g., Phrasal Verbs—Emotions, Phrasal Verbs—Thinking). This is followed by more advanced levels of idioms, with another 27quizzes related to an alphabetized list of idioms. The site also has a good quiz section on slang expressions.

*Teacher Uses*

This site could primarily be used for either homework or in-class activities in a lab. It might also be helpful for nonnative-English-speaking teachers as a way to brush up on their English.

*Student Uses*

This site provides, albeit for more advanced learners, a wonderful way to prepare for the TOEFL or the IELTS. It is also a nice way to naturally find various synonyms for common idioms and phrasal verbs.

*Critique*

This is a useful site for intermediate and advanced learners of English. It is effective in that it is one of the more interactive websites. In essence, it is like other sites, supplying examples and definitions, but it also allows students to check their understanding through the numerous quizzes. It also offers grammar and vocabulary quizzes. Perhaps a downside to this site, as with many others, is its lack of specialized categories for teacher and student use.

**Eye on Idioms: www.readwritethink.org/files/resources /interactives/idioms/index.html**

*Rating:* 4

*Overview and Content*
Eye on Idioms is a relatively simple website with great visuals for seven English idioms. It takes you through seven 4-part questions about each idiom. First, it presents a picture which is a "literal representation" of the idiom featured on that page. Next, it provides a sentence with a dropdown box for learners to choose the correct idiom that completes the sentence related to the picture. Third, it asks what the "metaphorical meaning" of the idiom is. And finally, it asks learners to use the idiom in an original sentence. Students can then print the page with their completed work and have their teacher check it.

*Teacher Uses*
Teachers can use this as an actual lesson, provided they explain the literary terms like *literal, representation*, and *metaphor*.

*Student Uses*
Students can complete the seven idiom pages and provide original ideas in answer to the questions about the idioms.

*Critique*
Although its use is limited to essentially one class, the idioms presented on this site are common and useful to know. The distinctive aspect of this site is that students are able to create their own sentences and actively participate in using the idioms.

**Vocabulary.co.il: www.vocabulary.co.il**

*Rating:* 4

*Overview and Content*
This fun-filled idiom website for intermediate to pre-advanced learners of English is brimming with various language games, from antonyms to word play games. The idiom section has All Ages Idioms

Games with eight kinds of idiom-meaning related activities: Animal Slang Game, Food Slang Game, Money Slang Game, Similes Fill in the Blank, Feelings Slang Game, Idioms Game-Slang Game, More Idioms, and Sentence Similes Slang Game. Although they use the term *slang*, most of these activities contain informal idioms.

*Teacher Uses*
Instructors could use these game-quizzes as homework or in class as actual lessons.

*Student Uses*
Students can use these to develop their idiom knowledge in an enjoyable and exciting way. They can learn and review these idioms by playing the games either by themselves or with a classmate.

*Critique*
Although this website appears to be geared more toward beginners, the idioms introduced are actually relatively advanced. The idioms are common among native speakers and useful in terms of developing ELLs' vocabulary knowledge.

As mentioned above, don't let the word *slang* deter you from using the game-quizzes for class; most of the terms are actually idioms. The advantage of this site is it teaches through games versus merely listing the idioms with meanings. Moreover, it categorizes idioms better than most sites via the game format.

## Learn English Today: www.learn-english-today.com /idioms/idioms-proverbs/html

*Rating:* 4

*Overview and Content*
This is a very well-organized and well-structured site for intermediate to advanced ELLs. It provides vocabulary games, quizzes, and links to phrasal verbs in addition to the link to idioms. The site offers an extensive A-to-Z detailed list of idioms along with links to 60 categories of idioms (e.g., Actions-Behavior, Food and Drink, Sports). These categories make it a great reference for teachers and a wonderful aid for lesson planning.

*Teacher Uses*

Instructors can literally plan lessons around the categories provided by the site. The idioms offered are all useful and beneficial for all levels of English language students.

*Student Uses*

Students will find the category lists more useful than the alphabetized list. The definitions and example sentences are also helpful for student use.

*Critique*

This is a practical and user-friendly site for idioms. One significant problem, however, is that it claims that idioms are not used in formal exchanges, which is not necessarily true. Another drawback is that its alphabetized lists are a bit confusing. For instance, *more by accident than design* and *hold all the aces* are under A, which might lead to confusion. Another point to keep in mind is that the site seems to adhere to British English pragmatics, hence the note about the rules of formality and English idioms. In the United States, idioms are very commonly used in formal speeches and academic writing. That being said, overall, this is a good website for idioms.

## ESL Bits: www.esl-bits.net/idioms

*Rating:* 4.5

*Overview and Content*

This site is a copy of the material from the book *English Idioms: Sayings and Slang* (Magnuson, 2001). It is very easy to use as it has three major categories: (1) look for idioms by section: A–Z, (2) look for idioms containing a specific word: A–Z, and (3) look for idioms explained by a specific word: A–Z. Each letter contains a link to a number of common and useful idioms. Each idiom is well defined with clear example sentences. In addition, some definitions link to other idiomatic terms.

*Teacher Uses*

Instructors can make great use of this site while they create lesson plans on specific topics. Moreover, they can have students go to the site and study the definitions and uses.

*Student Uses*
This site is for intermediate to advanced learners of English. It is user-friendly because each term is clearly defined and has anywhere from one to two example sentences. Students can use this site for hours of self-study.

*Critique*
This is a wonderful site for motivated and creative instructors and students. There are thousands of examples ranging from one-word to multiword idioms. The examples and definitions are clear and concise. One drawback is the lack of interactive activities such as quizzes or forums. However, students can use this site for self-study and create their own example sentences, which can be checked by their instructors. We recommend this site for ELLs due to its volume of idioms and the clarity with which they are explained.

**Everyday Idioms!!!: www.everyday-idioms.blogspot.com**

*Rating:* 4

*Overview and Content*
Everyday Idioms!!! is a very useful website, with 199 idioms and counting. On average, two new idioms are posted each week. The setup is simple, visual, and practical. For example, the site offers representative pictures or photos for the idioms of the week. As discussed earlier, teachers should confirm whether these images represent the correct meanings of the idioms.

*Teacher Uses*
Teachers can have students guess the meaning from the picture or photo and then give them the sample conversations. With the help of the visuals and examples, most students will be able to guess the meanings of the idioms.

*Student Uses*
This site is primarily for intermediate to advanced ELLs. They can practice the sample dialogs and get a true sense of how the idioms are used in conversation. They can then record the meanings segment in their notebooks and create their own idiom dictionaries.

*Critique*

The attractive feature of this website is the manageable number of idioms. The visuals are quite effective, as are the two sample dialogs for each idiom. In addition, the explanations of the idioms are clear, concise, and communicative. The only real drawback is the lack of interactive drills. However, the presentation is complete enough for most teachers, and they can create their own drills based on the information given on the website.

**Learn English Feel Good.com: www.learnenglishfeelgood.com/americanidioms/index.html**

*Rating:* 3

*Overview and Content*

This is an easy-to-use alphabetized list of American English idioms. The lists also include English proverbs. The idioms included range from short hyphenated idioms such as *all-out* to phrases such as *apple of someone's eye*. Definitions are given for all idioms, but examples are limited and are not necessarily given for each idiom.

*Teacher Uses*

Instructors can use this site to supplement their classes with a vast number of common and useful idioms. There are no themes or categories, but the idioms provided can be used in just about any unit, from business to psychology. Moreover, there are both informal and formal idioms to meet the academic as well as nonacademic needs of students.

*Student Uses*

This site, like many, is best for advanced ELLs. They can categorize the idioms in a personalized dictionary and create their own example sentences. They can then check the correct usage of these sentences with their instructors.

*Critique*

Learn English Feel Good.com is a basic idiom site with a vast collection of useful and common idioms. Unfortunately, not all the terms covered have example sentences for mastery and understanding. The site also lacks interactive tasks for students, such as question forums, quizzes, or self-tests. However, it does offer a significant number of common and beneficial idioms for university-bound students.

**English Daily: www.englishdaily626.com/idioms.php**

*Rating:* 4

*Overview and Content*
This site, in addition to a colossal number of idioms, offers links to English proverbs, slang, common English mistakes, and TOEFL vocabulary. It is a fantastic site for any ELL or English language teacher. It also has a link to a separate category of Business Idioms. All terms are explained by either a short narrative or a short dialog.

*Teacher Uses*
Teachers can use these narratives and dialogs to introduce the idioms in a fun and practical way. First, they can show the initial part of the dialog to the class and see if students can guess the meaning. Then teachers can show the second part of the dialog to confirm the meaning of the idiom in question.

*Student Uses*
This site is mainly for advanced ELLs, but with the help of instructors, intermediate or pre-advanced ELLs could use it effectively. Students can use the natural dialogs to study the use and meanings of idioms. They can then write their own dialogs and have them checked by their teacher. As with other sites, students can use this one to create their own idiom reference book.

*Critique*
This is a wonderful site for intermediate to advanced learners of English. The fact that it uses a more inductive approach to define the terms is refreshing and useful. One drawback to this site is the lack of quizzes and other activities, but the method used to introduce the idioms is a legitimate reason to use English Daily.

**The Idiom Jungle: www.autoenglish.org/jungle.html**

*Rating:* 4.5

*Overview and Content*
Bob Wilson has put together a user-friendly site that is organized by a number of easy-to-use categories. There is an Essential Idioms section which organizes idioms in 11 categories such as Advice, Business, Decisions, and Emotions. This is followed by a Fun Idioms and

Sayings section that is organized into 9 categories such as Animal—Fish, Insects and Reptiles, and Work Sayings. This site also offers a Varieties of English section that includes Irish Idioms, London Slang, and South African Slang. The Idiom Jungle also provides 18 additional links to sites such as Australian Idioms and Jamaican English.

*Teacher Uses*
Teachers can use this site to supplement a number of lessons as it offers useful idioms from more than 20 categories or themes.

*Student Uses*
This is a wonderful site for students because it is well organized, offers situations in which the idioms can be used, and contains a list of similar phrases for the idiom in question. Moreover, it offers an interactive quiz section and the option to print the quizzes.

*Critique*
We highly recommend this site because it is well organized, interactive, and user-friendly. The layout and information included are very practical for ELLs. In terms of level, this site would best fit the needs of intermediate to advanced ELLs. Although example sentences are not given after each definition like in other sites, the interactive portion offers effective usages of the idioms.

**Voxy: www.voxy.com/blog**

*Rating: 2.75*

*Overview and Content*
Voxy has 21 posts for English idioms and will offer more in the future; these include such posts as It's a Dog-Eat-Dog World and Other Animal Idioms, After Sandy: Seven Storm Idioms, Five Common Fishing Idioms, Most Common Baseball Idioms, and Top 10 Most Common Idioms in English.

*Teacher Uses*
Teachers can use this site to build an online library of idioms and their definitions. They can also have advanced students study theme-related idioms for corresponding units of study; for example, this site could be used to supplement units on weather or aspects of U.S. culture.

This site would be limited to advanced students who wish to read about the definitions and uses of English idioms.

*Critique*
This site provides helpful visuals, explanations, and definitions for a number of English idioms. One drawback is the limited use of example sentences. Another point of contention is the frequent use of other idioms or phrasal verbs in the example sentences. This is great for very advanced learners, but may prove to be challenging for the average student trying to use this site. Moreover, there are no quizzes or interactive sections to help students master the idioms on the website.

## Part 3: Brief Descriptions of Recommended Dictionaries, Workbooks, and Other Reference Materials

### *Collins COBUILD Idioms Dictionary*, 3rd ed.
Glasgow, Scotland: HarperCollins. 2012. Pp. xvi, 526.
ISBN: 978-0007435494.

Described in Chapter 4, this useful dictionary is often our go-to dictionary for use in class because of the information and examples of how and where the idioms are used. This 3rd edition has many of the new idioms from a variety of Englishes from around the world. It also contains a self-study section that helps students learn on their own.

### *Collins COBUILD Idioms Workbook*, 2nd ed.
Glasgow, Scotland: HarperCollins. 2002. Pp. 65. ISBN: 978-0007134007.

This companion to the *Collins COBUILD Idioms Dictionary* contains in-depth exercises for practicing 100 common idioms. Even more extensive than the dictionary, the units provide usage information from the Bank of English corpus that helps learners understand the context of how the idioms are used in everyday speech.

### *Oxford Idioms Dictionary for Learners of English*.
Oxford, England: Oxford University Press. 2006. Pp. vi, 469.
ISBN: 978-0194317238.

This well-known and extremely useful dictionary contains a wide range of idioms primarily from British and American English. As discussed in Chapter 4, entries include the history of the idioms, and the newer edition also has useful information such as links to related idioms, pronunciation information (including stress), antonyms, and study pages.

**Gairns, Ruth, and Stuart Redman.** *Oxford Word Skills Idioms and Phrasal Verbs.*
London, England: Oxford University Press. 2011. Pp. xiv, 203.
ISBN: 978-0194620130 (Advanced), 978-0194620123 (Intermediate).

These popular books are part of the *Oxford Word Skills* series. They contain 60 thematic units such as Thinking, Learning, Knowledge, and Communicating With People, each of which is full of activities for practicing more than 1,000 idioms and phrasal verbs, including extensive information on the history of the idioms. Links to online activities and reviews for each unit are particularly useful for learners.

**Gooden, Philip, and Peter Lewis.** *Idiomantics: The Weird and Wonderful World of Popular Phrases.*
London, England: Bloomsbury. 2012. Pp. x, 246. ISBN: 978-1408151440.

*Idiomantics* is not a textbook or dictionary but a book aimed at a general audience that presents the etymology and unique origins of idioms and idiomatic language from many languages, but primarily from English. The book is organized around 12 themes such as idioms referring to "gastronomic delights" and "the daily grind." We have found this book useful both for personal reading and in adding extra information for students when presenting new idioms, including connections between English idioms and idioms in other languages.

**Hart, Carl A.** *The Ultimate Phrasal Verb Book.*
Hauppauge, NY: Barron's Educational. 1999. Pp. vi, 410.
ISBN: 0-7641-1028-4.

This is an excellent book featuring 400 phrasal verbs. There are wonderful definitions and example sentences for each term. The book also shows how these phrasal verbs are used in noun or adjective forms to create idiomatic expressions.

**Schneider, Meg F. *Kaplan Word Power*.**
New York, NY: Simon & Shuster. 2002. Pp. xx, 340. ISBN: 0-7432-4115-0.

This vocabulary guide teaches single-word lexical items. However, the example sentences are full of useful idiomatic expressions and phrasal verbs. Students can thus learn idioms and acquire important vocabulary terms.

**Reel, Daniel A. *Vocabulary Power Plus for the New SAT: Vocabulary, Reading and Writing Exercises for High Scores*.**
Cheswold, DE: Prestwick House. 2004. Pp. 246. ISBN: 1-58049-255xx.

Although this book focuses on single-word lexical items, it includes useful collocations and idiomatic expressions to define the terms. It's a good example of showing how idioms can be used to teach single-word items.

**Rogers, Bruce. *The Complete Guide to the TOEFL Test*.**
Boston, MA: Heinle & Heinle. 1998. Pp. xxvii, 840. ISBN: 0-8384-6789-x.

In the listening section of this guide, there are a number of useful and frequently used idioms and phrasal verbs. Concise definitions are given as well as activities in which to practice the items.

**Terban, Marvin. *Scholastic Dictionary of Idioms*.**
New York, NY: Scholastic. 1996. Pp. vii, 298. ISBN: 0-439-77083-1.

This is one of the few dictionaries and textbooks intended for younger, elementary school–aged learners. The dictionary contains more than 600 common idioms used in the United States. Entries include sample sentences and amusing illustrations geared toward a younger audience.

# CHAPTER 10

# Conclusion: Keep the Ball Rolling

## Strategies, Resources, and Tips for Developing Your Own Idiom Resources and Curriculum

> I keep turning over new leaves, and spoiling them, as I used to spoil my copybooks, and I make so many beginnings there will never be an end.
>
> —*Louisa May Alcott*

We started this book with the honest question: Who is afraid of teaching idioms? Our answer: We are. Now, however, after spending a full year working on this project and digging deep into the world of idioms, we have developed a different perspective. So let's ask the question again. Who is afraid of teaching idioms? Our answer: We were!

With all the exchange of ideas, the hours of daily research after teaching a full load of classes, being continually inspired by students and pleasantly surprised by the results of our survey data, we are no longer afraid of teaching idioms, but rather, we are ready to embrace them and further their wonder and intrigue in the classroom. We have turned over a new leaf and are ready to gear up, for with "so many beginnings there will never be an end" to our enthusiasm and awe regarding these linguistically challenging creatures.

A great deal of this energy comes from our own students' infectious desire to learn and acquire idioms. In Chapter 1, we offered the story about the students in one of Randolph's speech classes who consciously avoided using idioms in their speeches because they claimed that they were not "comfortable" using them, or they argued that they felt "safer" using the single-word equivalent because "risk-taking" was just too troublesome for them. There is, however, a "silver lining" to this incident. The inspirational ending to this story happened a few weeks after midterm.

In late autumn, Randolph announced to his class that they would be investigating their role as international students in their host culture. They were asked to interview their classmates and other fellow ELLs regarding how they felt about their experience so far in the United States: Were they satisfied? Why? Why not? What was it that made their lives fulfilling? Or what was it that was lacking? Were they fitting into the campus, the city, the culture? Did they feel at home in their home away from home?

It was this activity that turned out to be, for many in the class, a new beginning. A number of the students reported that *culturally* they were starting to feel at home, but *linguistically* they were frustrated because they claimed they didn't fit in. They still, despite being advanced learners of English, had a difficult time understanding native speakers and expressing themselves the way they wanted. They desired to sound "more native-like and not cavemen like" as one student reported.

This was addressed the next day in class. "So how can you 'fit in,' feel more comfortable, feel more at home?" Randolph asked. One Iraqi student raised his hand and answered, "I guess do what you told us the first day of class—use more idioms or phrasal verbs." A large contingent of the class agreed that the number of idioms that they heard but didn't understand—on a daily basis—was "mind-boggling." And when they would attend campus presentations or free lectures, it was worse.

These experiences helped them understand that idioms were not just tricky creatures used in poetry and novels, not just informal linguistic *decorations for conversation*, but lexical items found everywhere— from newspapers to lectures to conversations around campus—by faculty and students alike. Idioms were freshly perceived not as unnecessary informal parts of a language, but rather as core elements for understanding, communicating, and feeling at home.

The upshot of that one class was inspiring, for more than 90% of the students began to use the learned idioms and phrasal verbs in their speeches. But perhaps the most uplifting result of this *turning over a new leaf* came from a report in their writing class. These same students had a different lecturer for their research paper class. That lecturer came to Randolph because she was concerned that the students were plagiarizing. This concern was based on the students' "native-like" use of idioms and phrasal verbs! Randolph read the passages and assured the writing lecturer that they were in fact the students' own work; they had simply put the terms to use in their writing class and done so in a very impressive manner. What more motivation could a teacher need to continue spreading the word on idioms?

## The Language Personality

For the group above, their change came about through a need, as it were, to find ways to express themselves in English that would be accepted by other, primarily monolingual English speakers. Moreover, they wanted to find ways to speak English that represented their own sense of who they were—they wanted to develop their *language personality* in English.

Research about identity and personality development in language learning has considered multiple aspects: from the cognitive perspective of a language learner's **language ego** (Guiora, Beit-Hallami, Brannon, Dull, & Scovel,1972), to the sociocultural description of learners' **investment** in becoming multilingual citizens and members of local communities (Norton, 2000), to discourse analysis of the ways bi- and multilinguals talk about themselves as different people in a new language (Pavlenko, 2005), to poststructural theories of language learners as **multilingual subjects** who struggle to find their position among other multilingual and monolingual speakers (Kramsch, 2006, 2012).

As anyone who has intensively studied another language has probably felt, there is some sense of taking on different roles and even a new personality or personalities when we begin to use a new language. A key question in developing these new personalities is how much choice we have in how we use the new language forms that we learn, and when and where new language users choose to display their new language abilities. For example, Randolph's students should certainly be praised for their growing confidence in using idioms and sounding more "native-like" to their teachers, but desire for a new language personality can be conflicting and more complicated than simply moving between two separate personalities. As Kramsch (2006) writes:

> Desire can also be the urge to survive and to cling to the familiar. Many fossilized L2 [second language] learners have a deep desire not to identify with native speakers, even though they claim they want to improve their knowledge of the language. They maintain that learning a language is nothing more than giving other labels to the familiar furniture of their universe. Their resistance to the language is a measure of the threat it poses to their integrity as subjects. What drives them to learn the forms but retain their own accent and grammar is a deep desire to preserve what is theirs. (pp. 101–102)

Randolph's students and Kramsch's discussion of desire and resistance in language learning are reminiscent of a student in one of McPherron's graduate academic writing classes who told him after giving a class presentation in which fellow students critiqued her pronunciation, "I want to write like an American and sound like a Malaysian." Indeed, it seems that in addition to teaching students about the meanings and uses of idioms, we should also be aware that English language learners, as peripheral members of social and academic communities, are walking a fine line between different egos, personalities, and norms. As Ivan Stavans (2001) writes, "Changing languages is like imposing another role on oneself, like being someone else temporarily. . . . You know, sometimes I have the feeling I'm not one but two, three, four people. Is there an original person? An essence?" (cited in Kramsch, 2012, p. 486). We argue that teaching students about idioms and idiomatic language will help students navigate these identity processes while nurturing their various language personalities. In fact, many of the lesson plans and examples we presented in the previous chapters began with student discussions about what the idioms and metaphors in their other languages are and how specific idioms in English draw on certain conceptions of the world. Further, by drawing attention to both the meanings and pragmatic uses of idioms and also how students feel about using idioms or why they may not use idioms in a particular context due to their own desire to sound or not sound "American," we feel that our teaching of idioms draws student attention to their own language personalities and choices as speakers.

But we digress. As a way of wrapping up the various aspects of teaching idioms that we presented in the preceding pages, we now offer a summary of key themes on teaching idioms by way of the *five-E system*. We recommend incorporating this into as many lessons as you can. The five Es are *emotion*, *examples*, *energy*, *exercise*, and *euphoria*. Each has its own power to transform any class into a real learning and growing experience.

## The Five-E System of Learning

### Emotion

We cannot deny the impact and influence of such Western thinkers as Plato, Descartes, and Leibnitz; their influence on Western education still exists today—unfortunately. We say it is unfortunate, for most Western philosophers believed we need to keep emotion separate from thinking and the noble pursuits of the rational mind, and it is exactly this that has greatly hurt us as a civilization, particularly in the classroom. For without emotion in the learning process, most of us would not remember much at all. In fact, it is our emotional state that influences how we think and problem solve. If we are emotionally invested in the task at hand, chances are we will successfully solve the problem. Neuroscientist Antonio Damasio (1994) has argued, based on much research, that emotions are—contrary to popular belief— "indispensable" for optimal rational thought (p. xiii). And we may recall from Chapter 3 that emotions, as Medina (2009) claims, are attention-getters, for "emotionally charged events persist much longer in our memories and are recalled with greater accuracy than neutral memories" (p. 80).

Chemically speaking, emotions are healthy in that they actually do help facilitate learning. When we experience high positive emotions, our old friend the amygdala sends dopamine into our system. This, you may recall, is a positive reaction because the neurotransmitter dopamine helps secure memories and develops our ability to process information. Oxytocin is also produced during healthy emotional experiences. And a classroom that nurtures an emotionally happy atmosphere stimulates more oxytocin. Further, researchers have found that oxytocin encourages feelings of trust. As Horstman (2009) writes, "it literally feels good when someone seems to trust you, and this recognition motivates you to return that trust" (p. 116). For example, Randolph takes every opportunity in class to encourage students to laugh and play, bringing in a steady stream of humor and jokes that draw on the day's vocabulary or theme.

At the same time, without discounting the need for a trusting and happy environment, recent work on emotions in the language classroom has pointed out that there is much more to emotions in the classroom than simply instilling trust in students and lowering the affective filter (cf. Krashen, 1982). As Benesch (2012) argues,

> By aiming to reduce what are viewed as negative emotions, so as to get on with the business of language teaching, cognitive approaches have the potential to trivialize or dismiss students' appropriate reactions to unfavorable situations and conditions, in the name of emotional intelligence. This tendency to legislate correct emotions or urge students to abandon what are perceived to be negative feelings also sabotages a possibly dynamic source of learning. (p. 35)

We would add that the neuroscience backs up this call for using all emotions and emotional experiences or "emotionally charged events" as sources of idiom learning. In fact, as illustrated in many of the lesson plans in Chapter 8, many idioms describe very troubled, sad, angry, and frustrating experiences, and we can think of no better way to introduce these new vocabulary items than starting with the full range of emotions and experiences of students' daily lives.

All of this adds up to one simple thing: In order to help students find their language personality and simultaneously keep them on track with incorporating as many idioms into their evolving sense of self in English, we must integrate the use of emotions into the classroom and the learning process as a whole. When we teach, we are usually concerned about simply conveying content and how students' minds absorb that content. It's probably safe to say that we devote 95% of our energy to their minds. What we should be doing, however, is devoting 40% to teaching their brains and 60% to nurturing their hearts, emotions, and ability to draw on their own emotional experiences as learning experiences. In other words, often the best teacher is a motivator and empathetic analyst of student emotions, not just a mere conveyor of knowledge.

With that in mind, let's return to our original question: How can we help students learn new idioms and navigate their new or evolving personality in English? The answer includes emotion and the other four Es of learning: examples, energy, exercise, and euphoria. These are the five elements that we use to help students retain idiom knowledge long after they have left the classroom.

## Examples

One of the most obvious ways to help students learn idioms and evoke their emotions in the process is by having them create example sentences in class. This gets them to *play* with the idioms, *use* them, *make mistakes* with them, and finally become *comfortable* with them. We both have found this simple activity to be extremely beneficial. Moreover, if we look at the data from the survey in Chapter 6, "Making sentences using idioms" came in at the top of the list at 69.4% for "most useful activities for teachers." They found the activity very useful or extremely useful.

We recommend that teachers have volunteers give example sentences in class, but make sure you correct any misuse immediately as noted in Chapter 4. This will help students get on the right track. Example sentences can be done as homework for idioms covered in class. The next day, select a few undaunted volunteers or pairs to share their sentences with the class. The likelihood that students will personalize these is very high. This, as addressed in the brain chapter, will evoke both emotion and personal interest in the material, therefore making it all the more likely that students will retain the information and safely guard it in their long-term memories. And finally, having students create examples will naturally inspire them to take "safe" risks in class, which hopefully will pave the way to more natural risk-taking down the road.

## Energy

The energy and excitement level at which idioms are introduced is also crucial. Recall in Chapter 3, we explained that the moment of encoding is crucial; it is often the deciding factor in whether enough neurons fire together to start the process of memory and learning. So we need to pay attention to the volume of our voice, our use of gestures, and our illustration of excitement. Our eyes need to be intense and scan each and every learner, albeit for a brief *augenblick* in time (i.e., quick snapshot of the class). The eyes are a great bridge of energy for teachers and students, and that energy and excitement may last a lifetime in the learners' memory.

The level of energy and excitement will also get a number of those needed neurotransmitters flowing in the brain, and the more they flow, the better chances we have of helping students retain and embrace the information.

## Exercise

Perhaps this should have been first on our list due to its ever-important presence in our lives. We stressed the significance of exercise in Chapter 3 and revisited its importance in Chapter 8 with the idea of its use in the lesson plans. The simple fact that such helpful memory and learning neurotransmitters like acetylcholine, dopamine, epinephrine, norepinephrine, and serotonin are the result of minimal physical exercise is truly inspiring.

We recommend that each instructor help keep students focused by making exercise before and during class a daily routine. A recent 13-year study shows that for every minute you walk, you add 1 to 2 minutes to your life (Cool, 2012). If just walking can do that for your longevity, think what it can do to help students focus and learn in the classroom.

## Euphoria

In 1993, just 2 months before dying of cancer, former North Carolina basketball coach Jimmy Valvano gave a memorable speech at the ESPY Awards. A moment from that speech is particularly inspiring: "If you laugh, you think, and you cry, that's a full day. That's a heck of a day. You do that seven days a week, you're going to have something special."[1]

Emotions are a powerful source of life, and we need them to fulfill our lives. The last point in our five-E system is euphoria. It's

---

[1] See http://www.youtube.com/watch?v=HuoVM9nm42E.

absolutely no surprise that "teachers who smile, use humor, have a joyful demeanor, and take genuine pleasure in their work generally have high-performing learners" (Jensen, 2008, p. 98). Being happy and helping students mirror that will obviously help them feel good, produce more levels of oxytocin, and give you their trust. And where there is trust in the classroom, only spectacular things can occur.

There is also the idea that laughter and humor help keep us focused on the task at hand; they produce oxygen for the brain and create the optimal environment for learning and using idioms.

But the most important consequence of euphoria and humor is that they help students feel at home in their new environment, whether that be a new class or a new city or country. It relieves them of stress and helps them learn.

There is no doubt about the fact that we want students to succeed, feel at home, and develop their new language personality with new exciting thoughts, laughter, and tears. As Coach Valvano said, "You do that seven days a week, you're going to have something special." In order for students to turn over a new leaf, we must encourage them to use idioms while also seeing just how necessary they are as language tools for understanding and communication. Using the five-E system will help instructors expedite the learning process and keep the ball rolling toward idiom acquisition.

## Theorists *and* Practitioners

> There is no clear point in human development when it can be said that idioms have been mastered. (Nippold, 1991, p. 101)

Nippold was discussing first language users, so we can only imagine the challenges of using idioms faced by students learning a new language, and thus we should not feel that we must teach students to recognize and use every idiom and idiomatic phrase in English. As numerous vocabulary specialists have pointed out, no one knows every term, phrase, or nuance of meaning in a language, and in many ways we are all constantly learning and relearning all of the languages that we claim to speak and write. And it is this spirit of viewing learning as a never-ending process that we end our book on a note about teaching as a never-ending process of learning and relearning, theorizing and practicing—in short, a postmethod view of the classroom.

In his popular and often-used teacher education book, Brown (2006) writes, "we are all practitioners and we are all theorists. We are all charged with developing a broadly based conceptualization of the process of language learning and teaching" (p. 309). Unfortunately, as Brown himself notes, the ELT community has for too long been divided by researchers (mostly based in Western universities) who theorize and practitioners (located around the world) who teach. In our splitting the book between chapters summarizing the theories and research behind idioms and juxtaposing them with the latter chapters focused more on classroom practices, we too adopted the artificial theory/practice divide. However, we also attempted throughout the book to connect these two perspectives, as we truly agree with Brown that new insight into teaching languages can occur when we all take up roles as both researchers and practitioners.

Thus, we have contributed a small perspective from a variety of classrooms and research studies about what idioms are, how we use them, how we remember them, how we teach them, and how we learn them. It is now up to us as a community of TESOL practitioners and researchers to continue these investigations, but we wonder if the charge should not be to develop one, unitary conceptualization, method, or group of activities for idiom teaching, as Brown (2006) notes, or even one grand language learning theory for teaching and learning English for that matter. Instead, we argue that we must continue to look for more un-unified and often very local conceptions of English teaching and idiom learning, what has often been referred to as the *postmethod condition* (cf. Kumaravadivelu, 2003, 2006) in which we view teaching not as simply the search for and application of the best method but a continual process of *principled pragmatism* in which teachers shape classroom learning in TESOL as a result of critical appraisal of what works in their context and with their students.

Following from this postmethod and sociocultural approach to the classroom and continuously striving to implement findings from new research on how the brain functions, as described in multiple places in the book, including the five-E system, we look forward to creating and re-creating more lessons and classroom activities for learning and teaching idioms. And most important, we look forward to reading more examples from your unique and ever-dynamic classrooms.

# Appendix A: Glossary of Key Terms

**amygdala:** This is a pivotal part of the limbic system, and it houses the center for emotions, motivation, emotional behavior, and emotional memory. The amygdala is also highly involved with various cognitive functions such as attention and perception.

**brain-derived neurotrophic factor (BDNF):** This protein is a potent neurotrophin that literally strengthens communication between our neurons. It also helps create new neurons in the hippocampus. BDNF is additionally responsible for activating genes that produce other proteins that create stronger and healthier synaptic connections in the brain.

**compositionality:** Linguists use this term to describe one of the key differences between idioms and other words and phrases. A word or phrase is considered compositional if its meaning can be determined based on knowing its smaller words or morphemes (i.e., smaller units of meaning). For example, the meaning of the term *unhappy* can be determined by the meaning of its component parts (i.e., *un* attaches to adjectives and verbs to mean "the opposite or reverse," and happy means "joy" or "a pleasurable state"). Linguistics classify idioms as varying in degrees of noncompositionality because phrases such as "cat got your tongue" are not easily understood based on their smaller components (i.e., morphemes).

**computer-assisted language learning (CALL):** Consolidating numerous terms related to technology use for learning language—both inside and outside the classroom—Levy (1997) offers one of the most widely cited and succinct definitions of CALL as "the search for and study of applications of the computer in language teaching and learning" (p. 1). In particular, research studies in CALL have offered numerous insights and innovations for learning and teaching vocabulary.

**corpus linguistics:** This is a branch of linguistics as well as a method of analysis that draws insight into language usage and word meanings based on a collection of natural, "real" texts or corpora. Beginning with handmade collections of words and examples, corpus linguistics draws almost entirely on computer programs and software to code and analyze large amounts of spoken and written texts. Studies in corpus linguistics offer particular insights for vocabulary teachers into how words and phrases are used in speech and writing, and corpus linguistics software programs and corpora are very useful as learning and teaching tools.

**encoding:** This is the first stage in the memory process by which one "takes in" or encodes new information. How information is encoded is crucial in the learning process.

**exercise stations:** These are designated corners of a classroom where individual students can go to do their own oxygen-boosting exercises. After refreshing themselves physically, they return to their seats better prepared to learn.

**fixedness:** Along with compositionality, this is a key attribute of idioms that distinguishes them from other words and phrases. Linguists define fixedness as the ability to alter the syntax by changing the aspect (e.g., present perfect to simple present), mood (e.g., subjunctive vs. conditional), or voice (e.g., active vs. passive). Linguists offer the common example of many idioms that cannot be used in the passive once they have become "fixed" in the present. For example, you can say, "The cat got my tongue and I was speechless," but it is extremely awkward to say, "My tongue was gotten by the cat and I was speechless."

**hippocampus:** This part of the limbic system is responsible for a number of functions, one of the primary ones being to convert short-term information from working memory to long-term memory. It is highly significant, then, in memory and learning. Another key aspect is its ability to generate new neurons.

**idiom, idiomatic expression, idiomatic language:** These words and phrases are the main topic of our book. Definitions of idioms range from those that include any type of formulaic language or fixed colocations (e.g., one-word terms such as *dough*, meaning "money"; greetings such as *What's up?*) to those that limit idioms to only "purely" figurative expression, such as *red herring*, in which the meaning of the term is completely independent from its constituent parts.

**investment:** Bonny Norton (2000) uses this term to help describe the complex motivations of language learners that do not easily fit into traditional theories of intrinsic and extrinsic motivation. Through detailed ethnographic description of immigrant English language learners, Norton reveals how language learning is intimately tied to the imagined identities and communities of English speakers and how much access learners may or may not have to these communities and identities.

**language ego:** Guiora Beit-Hallami, Brannon, Dull, and Scovel (1972) refer to a language learner's new language identity as a *language ego*: "Similar to the concept of the body ego, language ego too is conceived as a maturation concept and refers to a self-representation with physical outlines and firm boundaries. . . . Thus a child can assimilate native-like speech in any language. Once ego development is concluded, flexibility will be sharply restricted forever" (p. 112).

**lexical chunks:** This refers to groups of words that are commonly used together. The chunks include idioms, idiomatic language, and other formulaic routines, but they also include collocations such as the classic example from linguist Michael Halliday, who pointed out that we prefer to say *strong tea* in English and not *powerful tea*, even though both would make sense. Teaching lexical chunks is the basis of the lexical approach to vocabulary instruction since this knowledge and the use of the appropriate collocations and chunks are what often differentiate fluent speakers of a language from learners.

**metaphor:** In literature, a metaphor is a figure of speech in which an author figuratively asserts that one item is, in some way, the same as another object in a way that is readily apparent. In examining the definitions and attributes of idioms, linguists describe core concepts as the metaphors on which groups of idioms are based. For example, an idiom such as *I see the light* is based on a core metaphor that associates light with knowledge (i.e., light = knowledge).

**metonymy:** Similar to metaphor, metonymy is a literary device in which an author uses one attribute or physical part of an item to stand in and refer to the other item or word for which it is closely associated. Common examples include using *the White House* to refer to the president of the United States or saying *the Crown* in reference to the British monarchy. In linguistics, metonymy is a concept used to show the underlying organization and similarities between groups of idioms. For example, the metonymy that *the hand stands for the person* is the basis for idioms such as *all hands on deck*.

**mirror neuron:** This is a specialized kind of neuron that fires at the sight or sound of seeing or hearing someone do something, and the observer's brain simulates these events. Mirror neurons thus "mirror" the world around them. They are also informally referred to as *empathy neurons*; *monkey see, monkey do neurons*; and even *Gandhi neurons*.

**multilingual subjects:** Claire Kramsch (2006) uses this term to highlight how language, as a symbolic system, "creates and shapes who we are, as subjects" (p. 100). In other words, unlike cognitive and mentalist perspectives that view language as neutral and learning as an individual, psychological process, Kramsch's use of this term highlights the social and emotional experiences of language learning, "its embodied dimensions, its links with memory, emotion and the imagination, multilinguals' relationship to other multilingual or monolingual subjects, and their struggle to find satisfactory subject positions" (p. 101).

**multiple intelligences (MI):** Moving away from purely intellectual views of intelligence as narrowly defined according to IQ testing, Howard Gardner proposed a theory in which people can have varying degrees of ability on a number of intelligences, including linguistic, logical-mathematical, interpersonal, and others. Critics have noted that his theory lacks empirical evidence, is too broad, and simply describes personality traits. Further, recent research in neuroscience points out that the brain is much more complex than the categories in the theory reveal. Regardless, MI can be a useful starting point for planning lessons for learners with diverse abilities and interests.

**neuron:** A neuron is a nerve cell that helps transmit information throughout the brain and the body. A neuron does this via both chemical and electrical forms. A neuron has three basic parts: the dendrites, the cell body, and the axon. There are approximately 100 billion (100,000,000,000) neurons in the human brain.

**neurotransmitters:** These are neural chemicals that communicate various kinds of information through the brain and body. For instance, the brain uses neurotransmitters to tell the stomach to digest food and to tell the brain to be attentive. Examples of neurotransmitters are acetylcholine, dopamine, epinephrine, and serotonin.

**phrasal verb:** Grammarians generally define phrasal verbs as verbs that are formed by joining a verb with a verb particle (typically an adverb or a preposition). The verb particle is essential to the meaning of the verb and is clearly attached to the verb as one unit of meaning. For example, compare "ran up" in the following sentences: (1) She ran up the bill; (2) She ran up the hill. In the first sentence, "the bill" is an object of the phrasal verb "ran up." In the second sentence, "up the hill" is a prepositional phrase, and "ran up" is not a phrasal verb. Some linguists include phrasal verbs in their definitions of idioms because they are formulaic collocations. We have included them throughout the book, but other books offer more in-depth activities for teaching phrasal verbs to English language learners.

**postmethod approach; postmethod condition:** As described by Braj Kumaravadivelu and others, the postmethod condition describes the current situation in ELT in which no one method or approach to teaching is advocated; rather, language teachers must develop their own effective strategies and techniques that work well in their particular social and political context. More than simply describing an eclectic teacher, the notion of postmethodology places practicing teachers at the center of ELT theory and practice, and it is an attempt to reframe the focus in TESOL from grand theories and methods to more attention to small-scale processes of everyday classrooms.

**retrieval:** This is the third stage in the memory process. It is concerned with how we get information out of storage and use it.

**storage:** This is the second stage in the memory process. It deals with where and how the information is stored.

**systemic functional linguistics (SFL):** SFL is a model of language, literacy, and education that is often described as an *applicable linguistics* in that its theories are centered on the linguistic choices that a speaker has in a given context. Unlike earlier Chomskyian linguistic accounts of language that attempted to map the underlying structures of languages, SFL has focused on mapping how language is actually used in different contexts and among different speakers. Work in SFL has been particularly useful for vocabulary teaching because it has offered insights into the functions of idioms in conversation and writing.

# Appendix B:
# Idioms With Definitions
# and Example Sentences

The following contains lists of idioms in eight categories based on what we often teach and the results from the surveys discussed in Chapters 6 and 7.

## Part 1: Figurative Idioms

1. *a chip on one's shoulder*: a sense of inferiority

   **Example:** Because Josh had *a chip on his shoulder*, he seemed to work harder than anyone else.

   **Register:** This is normally used in informal situations.

2. *be all thumbs*: be very awkward and clumsy, especially with one's own hands

   **Example:** We usually don't invite Alex to play football. He's *all thumbs* and can't catch even the easiest pass.

   **Register:** This is normally used in informal situations.

3. *burn the candle at both ends*: work extremely hard all day and stay up late to continue working

   **Example:** Phil is *burning the candle at both ends* this week. He's working 24/7.

   **Register:** This is normally used in informal situations.

4. *cold turkey*: in a sudden and abrupt manner (as an adverb)

   **Example:**  Isabel: Is your husband still smoking?

   Akina: No, he stopped *cold turkey*!

   **Register:** This is normally used in informal situations.

5. *a flash in the pan*: briefly successful or briefly popular; something transient

   **Example:** "Most modern rock groups are just a mere *flash in the pan*," said Paul.

   **Register:** This is normally used in informal situations.

6. *head over heels* (in love): to be very much in love with someone

   **Example:** Marjorie is *head over heels* in love with Albert. She hasn't slept for a week now.

   **Register:** This is normally used in informal situations.

7. *in the doghouse*: in trouble; in disfavor

   **Example:** The manager is *in the doghouse* after all of his financial cover-ups.

   **Register:** This is normally used in informal situations.

8. *turn over a new leaf*: to begin again; fresh; to reform and begin again

   **Example:** Shizuka has decided to *turn over a new leaf* and start exercising every day before work.

   **Register:** This is normally used in informal situations.

9. *tie the knot*: to marry

   **Example:** Davide and Claudia just *tied the knot* this summer in England.

   **Register:** This is normally used in informal situations.

10. *hit the books*: to study hard or in a concentrated way; to cram

    **Example:** Aylene is *hitting the books* hard this week. She hasn't slept a wink.

    **Register:** This is normally used in informal situations.

## Part 2: Transparent Idioms

11. *a blessing in disguise*: something that initially seems bad, but later turns out to be very good

    **Example:** The class that Mark failed was *a blessing in disguise*. When he retook it a year later, he met his wife to be.

    **Register:** This is used in both formal and informal situations.

12. *a drop in the bucket*: an insufficient amount as compared to what is required

    **Example:** The work Lyle did was *a drop in the bucket*. His boss was expecting him to do so much more.

    **Register:** This is used in both formal and informal situations.

13. *spread oneself too thin*: to become involved in too many activities and not be able to do any of them well; to do too many things at the same time

    **Example:** Zain *spread herself too thin* at work and, as a result, wasn't able to successfully accomplish any of her projects.

    **Register:** This is usually used in informal situations, but there are exceptions to its common use.

14. *a slap on the wrist*: a light punishment for doing something wrong

    **Example:** Unfortunately, even though many politicians commit serious crimes, they only get *a slap on the wrist*.

    **Register:** This is usually used in informal situations.

15. *bend/bent over backwards*: try very hard to please someone; exert oneself to the fullest extent; try very hard to do something

    **Example:** Gamze *bent over backward* to make Patrick as happy as she could on his birthday.

    **Register:** This is used in both formal and informal situations.

16. *burn the midnight oil*: to work very hard into the night

    **Example:** Yuko *burnt the midnight oil* to prepare for her nursing exam.

    **Register:** This is usually used in informal situations.

17. *in over one's head*: too deeply involved with something; beyond what one can deal with or handle

    **Example:** George has way too much work this month. He is *in over his head*.

    **Register:** This is used in both formal and informal situations.

18. *on pins and needles*: be in a state of anxiety or anticipation

    **Example:** Wisam and Kristi are *on pins and needles* as they wait to hear back from their last job interview.

    **Register:** This is typically used in informal situations.

19. *the best of both worlds*: a situation in which one can simultaneously enjoy the advantages of two very different things

    **Example:** People who can teach and travel have *the best of both worlds*.

    **Register:** This is used in both formal and informal situations.

20. *word of mouth*: information received by spoken rather than written form; informal verbal communication

    **Example:** We decided to go to the Thai restaurant based on *word of mouth*.

    **Register:** This is used in both formal and informal situations.

## Part 3: Tri-part Phrasal Verbs

21. *be up on*: know about something; be informed about something; have current information about something

    **Example:** Dylan is really *up on* all the latest technology in his field. He seems to know about everything.

    **Register:** This is used in both formal and informal situations.

22. *come up with*: to produce; create; make; invent; think up; discover

    **Example:** Erol *came up with* a fantastic new method to learn English idioms.

    **Register:** This is used in both formal and informal situations.

23. *get back to*: to return to something; contact someone at a later time because one couldn't earlier

    **Examples:** Yin finally *got back to* spending more time with her family after she finished her project.

    Ran *got back to* her client after researching more about her competitors.

    **Register:** This is used in both formal and informal situations.

24. *get out of*: to leave somewhere; escape from somewhere; avoid doing something that you should do or that you said you would do

    **Examples:** Jose *got out of* California just in time before the rains hit.

    Maria *got out of* working the late-night shift after she heard how dangerous it was.

    **Register:** This is used mainly in informal situations.

25. *get through to*: to make someone understand what you want to express; make contact by phone, email, and so forth.

    **Examples:** Sachiko *got through to* her parents, and they finally let her come to the United States.

    Despite the phone lines being busy on New Year's Day, Minako *got through to* her family.

    **Register:** This is used in both formal and informal situations.

26. *look back on*: recall a past event; think about a past event

    **Example:** When Kaitlin *looks back on* her first week in college, she realizes how much she has learned.

    **Register:** This is used in both formal and informal situations.

27. *look forward to*: to anticipate something with great pleasure or excitement

    **Example:** Patrick *looks forward to* seeing his wife, daughter, and cat after work every day!

    **Register:** This is used in both formal and informal situations.

28. *look up to*: to admire and respect

    **Example:** Darlene *looks up to* Joe with great affection, and she has done so for a great many years.

    **Register:** This is used in both formal and informal situations.

29. *live up to*: to meet someone's standards or expectations

    **Example:** Ayfer has *lived up to* Haluk's idea of being the perfect wife.

    **Register:** This is used in both formal and informal situations.

30. *run out of*: use/exhaust the supply of something

    **Example:** The head chef *ran out of* eggs early and had to run to the store before all the customers left his café.

    **Register:** This is used in both formal and informal situations.

    This phrasal verb could also appear in Part 7 (B): Top Everyday Idioms.

## Part 4: Bi-part Phrasal Verbs

31. *deal with*: to take action to do something; accept/control a difficult situation

    **Examples:** Ayano is *dealing with* quite an arduous problem at her new job.

    Hiroki has *dealt with* being homesick now for over a month.

    **Register:** This is used in both formal and informal situations.

32. *end up*: to become eventually; turn out to be; finally be or do something

    **Example:** Phyllis *ended up* staying longer in New York to be with her grandson.

    **Register:** This is used in both formal and informal situations.

33. *figure out*: to understand; solve

   **Example:** Kelly and Diana *figured out* how to learn Spanish with minimal effort.

   **Register:** This is used in both formal and informal situations.

34. *find out*: to discover or confirm the truth

   **Example:** Amirah was so very excited when she *found out* her grade in writing class.

   **Register:** This is used in both formal and informal situations.

35. *get through*: to succeed in something; come to a destination, often after overcoming problems

   **Examples:** Javier *got through* the exam with time to spare.

   Maria de la Vega *got through* the storm and arrived safely home.

   **Register:** This is used in both formal and informal situations.

36. *go over*: to review; check; survey something

   **Example:** Robbie *went over* the contract with a fine-tooth comb.

   **Register:** This is used in both formal and informal situations.

37. *run into*: meet or find someone by chance

   **Example:** Deanna *ran into* her old college roommate in Paris.

   **Register:** This is used in both formal and informal situations.

   *This phrasal verb could also appear in Part 7 (B): Top Everyday Idioms.

38. *show up*: to arrive at a place; appear; reveal

   **Example:** Joseph *showed up* early to the party, so he studied for an hour in his car.

   **Register:** This is used in both formal and informal situations.

39. *turn out*: prove; shown to be; develop in a particular way

   **Example:** The answer to the question *turned out* to have endless possibilities.

   **Register:** This is used in both formal and informal situations.

40. *used to*: expresses habitual past actions

   **Example:** Jessica *used to* run at 4:30 a.m. every day before she got married.

   **Register:** This is used in both formal and informal situations.

## Part 5: Proverbs and Sayings

*Note:* The register for these proverbs and sayings is usually informal in both spoken and written English. However, there are situations, such as formal speeches and academic articles, in which a speaker or writer will use them to either enhance his or her statements or pull the audience in at particular points in the course of the speech or article.

41. *Absence makes the heart grow fonder*: One appreciates someone more when he or she is away; when people are apart, their love grows stronger.

    **Example:** Ali can't wait to get home from his business trip to see his wife, Muazzez. *Absence makes the heart grow fonder.*

42. *Actions speak louder than words*: What people actually do is more important than what they say they will do.

    **Example:** "Don't just talk about it. Do it. *Actions speak louder than words*," said Gable.

43. *Great minds think alike*: Wise individuals tend to come up with the same ideas at the same time (usually said to someone just after you have heard that he or she has the same idea as you).

    **Example:** "Let's let the rain wash the car," said Mark.

    "Just what I was thinking. I guess *great minds think alike*," replied Tom.

44. *Haste makes waste*: Often when one tries to do something too quickly, he or she makes mistakes and the result is a waste.

    **Example:** "Why did the secretary send these memos out in such a rush? There are a hundred typos! *Haste makes waste!*"

45. *It's a small world*: This is used when individuals find out that people or events in different places are somehow connected.

    **Example:** Ayça: Who did you say your boss was?

    Sibel: Mr. Pamuk!

    Ayça: Goodness! That's my brother! *It's a small world* indeed!

46. *Let sleeping dogs lie*: It is best to leave things alone if they may cause trouble.

    **Example:** Cedric:: Should we let Mr. Chips know about this error?

        Majken:: Hmm . . . I think we should *let sleeping dogs lie*.

47. *Let the cat out of the bag*: to disclose confidential secrets

    **Example:** "I shouldn't have told her about the surprise party. I really *let the cat out of the bag*."

48. *Six of one, half dozen of the other*: The alternatives are basically the same. This is used to compare/state two things that are the same.

    **Example:** "We can take either the umbrella or the rain coats. It's really *six of one, half dozen of the other*."

49. *When it rains, it pours*: often used when both good and bad things happen; used when a lot of good or bad things happen at the same time

    **Example:** "Hayder got a call from Sheri. Then he heard from Sophie, Maria, and Min. I guess *when it rains, it pours!*"

50. *Every cloud has a silver lining*: Every difficult situation has a positive outcome.

    **Example:** "Don't worry about failing that test. *Every cloud has a silver lining*, OK?"

    This phrasal verb could also appear in Part 7 (A): Top Most Difficult Idioms to Learn.

## Part 6: Idiomatic Greetings

*Note:* The register for these common greetings is informal. All are used between acquaintances or friends.

51. *Long time no see*: This is equivalent to *It's been a long time since I've seen you.*

    **Example Exchange:**

        Sang Sook: *Long time no see!*

Yin: Yes! How have you been?

52. *It's been ages*: This is equivalent to *It's been so long since I last saw you.*

    **Example Exchange:**

    > Sean: *It's been ages!*
    >
    > Davide: Yes, it has. How ya been?

53. *What's the good word?*: This is equivalent to *Do you have any good news to report?*

    **Example Exchange:**

    > Boram: Hey Juseon, *what's the good word?*
    >
    > Juseon: Oh, not much. How are you?

54. *What's up?*: This is equivalent to *How are you? What have you been doing lately?*

    **Example Exchange:**

    > Victor: *What's up?*
    >
    > Pablo: Not much. What about you, man?

55. *What's shaking?*: This is equivalent to *What is going on with you? How is everything with you?*

    **Example Exchange:**

    > Mike: Hey, *what's shaking*, Wang?
    >
    > Wang: Not much. Just busy these days.

56. *What's cooking?*: This is equivalent to *What is going on with you?*

    **Example Exchange:**

    > Doug: *What's cooking*, honey?
    >
    > Linda: Well, dear, we need to go shopping if you want dinner tonight.

57. *What's new?*: This is equivalent to *What is new in your life? How is everything in your life?*

    **Example Exchange:**

    > Ali:: Hey, Don, *what's new?*
    >
    > Don: Not much. I start back to work again on Monday.

58. *How is life?*: This is equivalent to *How is life treating you? How is everything with you?*

**Example Exchange:**

> Edna: Hey, *how is life?*
>
> Norm: Oh, it's great. We go on vacation next Wednesday.

59. *Look at what the cat dragged in*: This is equivalent to *Look who is here!* A good-humored way of showing surprise at someone's presence in a place.

**Example Exchange:**

> Akiko: Wow! *Look at what the cat dragged in*!
>
> Sarah: Hey, long time no see!

60. *Howdy, stranger!*: This is equivalent to *Long time no see.* A humorous way to greet an old friend whom one hasn't seen for a while.

**Example Exchange:**

> Gary: *Howdy, stranger!*
>
> Chad: Hey! What's up with you?

## Part 7: The Most Difficult Idioms for Students to Learn (from the student survey)

61. *a red herring*: something (an argument or idea) intended to divert attention from the real matter at hand

    **Example:** The senator used *a red herring* to keep voters from thinking poorly about him.

    **Register:** This is used in both formal and informal situations.

62. *safe and sound*: to be out of danger and unharmed by anything

    **Example:** We are glad that Bethany is home *safe and sound*. Her flight was a long and arduous one.

    **Register:** This is predominantly used in informal situations, but formal use is not uncommon.

63. *come across as*: to give an impression of being a certain way

    **Example:** Daniel, Owen, and Anna *came across as* little angels.

    **Register:** This is used in both formal and informal situations.

64. *dog days* (often *dog days of summer*): the hottest part of summer; a period of inactivity

    **Example:** No one feels like working during the *dog days of summer*. It's just too hot and humid.

    **Register:** This is most commonly used in informal situations.

65. *a stepping stone*: any means of advancement; something that provides progress toward a goal

    **Example:** Isabel used her years in the local orchestra as *a stepping stone* to become one of the state's best musicians.

    **Register:** This is used in both formal and informal situations.

66. *throw in the towel*: to give up; admit defeat

    **Example:** No student should ever *throw in the towel*. They must find the desire to continue.

    **Register:** This is most commonly used in informal situations, but it may appear in a formal presentation or speech.

67. *pull someone's leg*: to playfully trick someone

    **Example:** Brett is always *pulling our leg*. He is a real jokester.

    **Register:** This is most commonly used in informal situations.

**Top Everyday Idioms (from the student survey)**

68. *out of the blue*: something unanticipated; at an unexpected time

    **Example:** Yu's friend surprised her *out of the blue* and appeared at her door.

    **Register:** This is typically used in informal situations.

69. *break a leg*: a theatrical term which means good luck

    **Example:** Faisal: I've got an exam in 20 minutes.

    Dave: Hey, man, *break a leg*.

    **Register:** This is typically used between friends or close acquaintances in informal situations.

70. *a change of pace*: a temporary shift in a normal routine

    **Example:** As *a change of pace*, Kamden decided to take her family out to dinner.

    **Register:** This is used in both formal and informal situations.

71. *the bottom line*: the final result; the upshot; the main/essential point

    **Example:** I think *the bottom line* is you need to be more serious about your work.

    **Register:** This is used in both formal and informal situations.

72. *play with fire*: to take part in dangerous or risky activity

    **Example:** Nate thinks that writing that op-ed would be *playing with fire*.

    **Register:** This is most typically used in informal situations.

73. *put something off*: to postpone or delay

    **Example:** Catherine *put her trip off* until the end of the semester.

    **Register:** This is most commonly used in informal situations.

74. *ring a bell*: something that reminds a person of something he or she has heard before; evoke a memory

    **Example:** Özlem: Have you ever heard of Pamukkale?

    Nozomi: Yes, the name *rings a bell*.

    **Register:** This is most commonly used in informal situations.

75. *save one's breath*: to refrain from talking, explaining, arguing; to not say anything (because argument is pointless)

    **Example:** "Just *save your breath*. They won't listen to you anyway."

    **Register:** This is most commonly used in informal situations.

76. *rain cats and dogs*: to rain very heavily; storm

    **Example:** It was *raining cats and dogs* last night. The front lawn looks like a lake.

    **Register:** This is most commonly used in informal situations.

## Part 8: The Most Difficult Idioms for Students to Learn (from the teacher survey)

77. *Where there's a will, there's a way*: If people are determined enough, they can find a way to achieve their goal.

    **Example:** "Hey, Irene, don't give up. *Where there's a will, there's a way.*"

    **Register:** This can be used in both formal and informal situations, but typically it is used in informal dialog and writing.

78. *in your face*: be blatantly aggressive; defiant attitude of aggression

    **Example:** That old professor in the philosophy department really has an *in-your-face* attitude. I guess that's why he's not so popular.

    **Register:** This is used in informal situations.

79. *take a shower*: to have a shower; bathe

    **Example:** Most Americans *take a shower* every day before work.

    **Register:** This is used in both formal and informal situations.

    Students also noted other phrasal verbs that involve *take* as difficult to learn.

80. *run for office* (e.g., president): to stand or campaign as a candidate for a public political office

    **Example:** I wish John had *run for president*. He would have been a true philosopher-king.

    **Register:** This is used in both formal and informal situations.

    Students also noted other phrasal verbs that involve *run* as difficult to learn.

81. *be all set*: be ready; prepared

    **Example:** Akiko *is all set* for her job interview.

    **Register:** This is typically used in informal situations.

82. *set off an alarm/set alarm bells off*: starting to feel worried, suspicious

    **Example:** The high cost of gas *set alarm bells off* all over the city.

    **Register:** This is used in both formal and informal situations.

    Students also noted other phrasal verbs that involve *off* as difficult to learn.

83. *tip of the iceberg*: a small, evident part of something much larger; only a small part of something bigger

**Example:** The unemployment problem in America is just the *tip of the iceberg*.

**Register:** This is used in both formal and informal situations.

84. *make up*: to do or give something to compensate for something else

**Example:** Students will have to *make up* the quiz next week if they do not take it today.

**Register:** This is used in both formal and informal situations.

Students also noted other phrasal verbs that involve *up* as difficult to learn.

# Appendix C: Teacher Survey

1. Where do you currently teach? Please describe the student level (K–12, university, etc.), setting (U.S. institution, international setting, etc.), and levels (beginners, intermediate, advanced, etc.).

2. What classes do you teach? Please list the titles of the classes that you typically teach and a brief description, if possible. Please note if you have ever taught a class focused on learning idioms and/or vocabulary in general.

3. In total, how many years have you taught English as a second or foreign language courses?

   | 0–1 | 2 | 3 |
   |-----|---|---|
   | 4 | 5 | more than 5 |

4. How often do you teach students about idioms and/or idiomatic language in the classes you teach?

   I never address idioms in the courses I teach.

   I rarely address idioms in the courses I teach.

   I address idioms in the courses I teach every other week.

   I address idioms in the courses I teach at least once a week.

   I address idioms in the courses I teach almost every class.

5. Below is a list of common difficulties teachers mention about teaching idioms in the classroom. Check all that you have experienced.

It is difficult to find a good idiom book that I can use along with my main textbook.

Not many texts have useful idioms in them, but instead focus on more "academic"-related lexical items.

Students question whether idioms are useful to their overall English language learning.

It is difficult to know which idioms are important to teach and which ones students will need.

I have too little time in class to cover core class topics and skills.

The textbooks I use do not address idioms or idiomatic language.

I am not familiar with methods and/or activities to teach idioms or idiomatic language.

There is not a useful definition of idioms that will help students learn to use them.

Please explain your above choices and add any further difficulties.

6. Please check all of the materials that you have used before or would use to teach idioms.

Textbooks that focus on idioms and idiomatic language

Supplemental lists of idioms that you prepare for students

Lists of idioms collected by your students from authentic sources

Textbooks that include sidebars or descriptions of idioms

Websites that introduce idioms with definitions, examples, and quizzes

Idiom dictionaries

7. Below is a list of different definitions of idioms from linguistics research papers and ESL/EFL textbooks. Rank each definition from 1 (*not useful at all*) to 5 (*extremely useful*) for students when learning idioms.

Idioms have a meaning that is completely different from the literal meaning of the individual word or words (i.e., idioms are completely noncompositional).

Idioms have a meaning that extends from the literal meaning of the individual word or words (i.e., idioms are figurative).

Idioms break or stretch the rules of grammar, word order (syntax), and semantics to a certain degree.

Idioms change meaning when translated word for word into another language.

Idioms are set expressions (i.e., if one word is substituted or the word order is altered, the phrase's meaning may change or become meaningless).

Idioms include full sentences and sayings such as "It's a small world" or "Don't put all of your eggs in one basket."

8. Do you include phrasal verbs (bi-, tri-, or multi-part) as idioms or put them in a separate category? For example, some textbooks consider verbs such as *get over* or *be up on* as idiomatic language in the same category as idioms such as *dog and pony show*.

9. Below is a list of categories that are commonly used to group idioms in ELL textbooks as adapted from Liu (2008). Rank each definition from 1 (*not useful at all*) to 5 (*extremely useful*) for students when learning idioms.

By grammatical structure; for example: prepositional phrases (*at the moment, in a hurry*), phrasal verbs (*give in, look up*), verb + noun structure (*jump the gun, toe the line*)

By grammatical function (part of speech); for example: nouns (*backseat driver*), verbs (*kick the can*), adverbs (*by and large*)

By motivating concept; for example: knowledge is light (*see the light, it dawned on me*)

By origin or source; for example: from sports (*hit a home run*), from body parts (*hold their feet to the fire*), from food (*dough, go nuts*)

By activity for which the idiom is used; for example: dating (*go steady, hit it off*)

By key words; for example: ball (*drop the ball, have a ball, the ball is in your court*)

By semantics; for example: opposites (*it's a long shot, it's in the bag*)

By degree of literalness (i.e., pure/semiliteral/literal); for example: *kick the bucket, fat chance, throw away*

10. Below is a list of activities for teaching idioms adapted from Liu (2008). Rank each definition from 1 (*not useful at all*) to 5 (*extremely useful*) for students when learning idioms.

Reading and identifying idioms in a passage

Identifying and comparing idioms in L1 and L2

Conducting searches for idiom examples from an online corpus

Hypothesizing and then finding the origin of the idioms

Guessing the meaning of the idioms from context

Guessing the meaning of the idioms using pragmatics, conceptual knowledge, and imagination

Guessing the meaning of the idioms based on knowledge of L1 idioms

Identifying idioms' meanings from motivating concepts or sources (e.g., *up* means more in idioms such as *speed up*)

Filling in the blanks with appropriate idioms

Playing idiom games such as Pictionary or charades

Making sentences using idioms

Keeping a list of idioms from readings outside of class

Writing and performing skits using idioms

11. Please comment on any further activities, definitions, or categories that you find or would find useful for teaching idioms in your classes.

12. List any idioms or idiomatic language that students often ask you about or you feel is potentially difficult for students.

13. Please add any further comments or ideas about teaching idioms.

# Appendix D:
# Student Survey

1. What is the highest level of school you have completed?

   Elementary school (K–8)     Master's degree (MA or MS)

   High school (9–12)     Doctorate (PhD)

   Undergraduate degree
     (BA or BS)

2. In the past, where have you taken English classes? Please check all that apply.

   In my elementary school     At my university

   In my high school     At an adult/community center

   At my office/work

3. In total, how many years have you studied English?

4. What is/are your first language or languages?

5. In your own words, how would you describe what an idiom is? What are some examples?

6. In the past, have idioms been discussed in your English classes?

   Never     Rarely     Sometimes

   Often     Very often

7. Please check the type of classes where your teachers specifically taught or discussed idioms.

   Speaking                        Reading

   Listening                       Grammar

   Writing                         Culture/special topics

8. Please check all of the materials that you have used in your classes to learn idioms.

   Textbooks that focus on idioms and idiomatic language

   List of idioms that your teacher prepared

   List of idioms that students prepared

   Textbooks that include sidebars or descriptions of idioms

   Websites that introduce idioms with definitions, examples, and quizzes

   Idiom dictionaries

9. Below is a list of activities for learning idioms adapted from Liu (2008). Please rank each activity according to how useful you think the activity is for you. Use the scale provided: 1 (*not useful at all*) to 5 (*extremely useful*).

   Identifying and guessing the meaning of idioms in a reading passage

   Comparing idioms in English with your first language

   Conducting searches for idiom examples from online sources

   Guessing and then finding out the origin of the idioms

   Filling in the blank words in a passage with the correct idioms

   Playing idiom games such as Pictionary or charades

   Making up example sentences using idioms

   Keeping a list of idioms from readings outside of class

   Writing and performing skits using idioms

   Taking quizzes (either online or in class)

10. How difficult do you feel the following idioms are to learn? Please use the scale provided: 1 (*not very difficult*) to 5 (*extremely difficult*). Note that the definition of each idiom is in the parentheses that follow. Definitions adapted from http://idioms.thefreedictionary .com.

"Red herring" (something that draws attention away from the central issue)

"Come across as" (to appear to have a particular attitude or character)

"Be in the driver's seat" (to be in control of a situation)

"The dog days" (the hottest days of the summer)

"Safe and sound" (unharmed and whole or healthy)

"An eye for an eye" (if someone does something wrong, they should be punished by having the same thing done to them)

"Every cloud has a silver lining" (You can derive some benefit from every bad thing that happens to you)

"As good as gold" (being positive or desirable in nature)

"Stepping stone" (a circumstance that assists progress toward some goal)

"Throw in the towel" (to signal that one is going to quit; to quit)

"Pull someone's leg" (subject someone to a playful hoax or joke)

11. How important is it for you to learn and use idioms?

Not important at all        Important

Not important              Very important

Somewhat important

12. What additional materials, including websites, do you recommend for English language learners who wish to improve their English vocabulary and use of idioms?

13. Please add any further comments or ideas about learning idioms.

# Appendix E: Images of Key Parts of the Brain

**(Images courtesy of http://pixabay.com)**

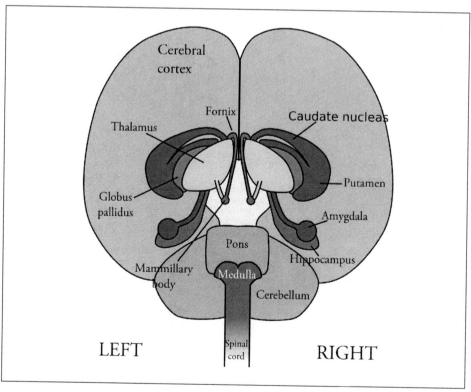

*Image 1. Front View of the Brain*

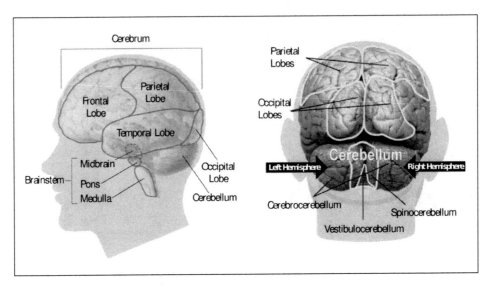

*Image 2. Side and Rear Views of the Brain*

# References

Abel, B. (2003). English idioms in the first language and second language lexicon: A dual representation approach. *Second Language Research, 19,* 329–358.

Adams, G. (2011, January 20). *How to increase oxygen to your brain with exercise.* Retrieved from http://www.livestrong.com

Adams, T. W., & Kuder, S. R. (1994). *Attitudes through idioms* (2nd ed.). Boston, MA: Heinle.

Akbarov, A. (2010). A cross-linguistic application on idioms rendering a conceptual schema. *Journal of Linguistic Intercultural Education, 3,* 137–146.

Arbib, M. A. (2002). The mirror system, imitation, and evolution of language. In K. Dautenhahn & C. Nehaniv (Eds.), *Imitation in animals and artifacts* (pp. 229–280). Cambridge, MA: MIT Press.

Armstrong, A. C., Stokoe, W. C., & Wilcox, S. E. (1995). *Gesture and the nature of language.* Cambridge, England: Cambridge University Press.

Ayto, J. (Ed.). (2009). *Oxford dictionary of English idioms* (3rd ed.). Oxford, England: Oxford University Press.

Aziz-Zadeh, L., Wilson, S. M., Rizzolatti, G., & Iacoboni, M. (2006). Congruent embodied representations for virtually presented actions and linguistic phrases describing actions. *Current Biology, 16,* 1818–1823.

Bachmann, D., Elfrink, J., & Vazzana, G. (1999). E-mail and snail mail face off in rematch. *Marketing Research, 11*(4), 11–15.

Bagheri, M. S., & Fazel, I. (2010). Effects of etymological elaboration on the EFL learners' comprehension and retention of idioms. *Journal of Pan-Pacific Association of Applied Linguistics, 14*(1), 45–55.

Balu, D. T., & Lucki, I. (2009). Adult hippocampal neurogenesis: Regulation, functional implications, and contribution to disease pathology. *Neuroscience & Biobehavioral Reviews, 33,* 232–252.

Balunda, S. A. (2009). Teaching academic vocabulary with corpora: Student perceptions of data-driven learning (Unpublished master's thesis). Indiana University Purdue University, Indianapolis, IN.

Bellanca, J., Fogarty, R., & Pete, B. (2012). *How to teach thinking skills within the common core: 7 key student proficiencies of the new national standards.* Bloomington, IN: Solution Tree Press.

Benesch, S. (2012). *Considering emotions in critical English language teaching: Theories and praxis.* New York, NY: Routledge.

Berendt, E. (2008). Introduction. In E. Berendt (Ed.), *Metaphors for learning: Cross-cultural perspectives* (pp. 1–12). Amsterdam, Netherlands: John Benjamins.

Biber, D., Conrad, S., & Leech, G. (2002). *Longman student grammar of spoken and written English.* White Plains, NY: Pearson Education ESL.

Biber, D., Johansson, S., Leech, G., Conrad, S., & Finegan, E. (1999). *Longman grammar of spoken and written English.* Harlow, England: Pearson Education ESL.

Blakeslee, S. (2006, January 10). Cells that read minds. *New York Times.* Retrieved from http://www.nytimes.com

Bobrow, S. A., & Bell, S. M. (1973). On catching on to idiomatic expressions. *Memory and Cognition, 1,* 342–346.

Boers, F. (2001). Remembering figurative idioms by hypothesising about their origins. *Prospect, 16,* 35–43.

Boers, F., & Demecheleer, M. (2001). Measuring the impact of cross-cultural differences on learners' comprehension of imageable idioms. *ELT Journal, 55,* 255–262.

Boers, F., Demecheleer, M., & Eyckmans, J. (2004). Cross-cultural variation as a variable in comprehending and remembering figurative idioms. *European Journal of English Studies, 8,* 375–388.

Boers, F., Eyckmans, J., & Stengers, H. (2007). Presenting figurative idioms with a touch of etymology: More than mere mnemonics? *Language Teaching Research, 11*(1), 43–62.

Boers, F., & Lindstromberg, S. (2005). Means of mass memorization of multi-word expressions, part one: The power of sounds. *Humanising Language Teaching, 7*(1). Retrieved from http://www.hltmag.co.uk/index.htm

Boers, F., & Lindstromberg, S. (2008a). From empirical findings to pedagogical practice. In F. Boers & S. Lindstromberg (Eds.), *Cognitive linguistic approaches to teaching vocabulary and phraseology* (pp. 375–393). Berlin, Germany: Mouton de Gruyter.

Boers, F., & Lindstromberg, S. (2008b). How cognitive linguistics can foster effective vocabulary teaching. In F. Boers & S. Lindstromberg (Eds.), *Cognitive linguistic approaches to teaching vocabulary and phraseology* (pp. 1–61). Berlin, Germany: Mouton de Gruyter.

Boers, F., Lindstromberg, S., Littlemore, J., Stengers, H., & Eychkmans, J. (2008). Variables in the mnemonic effectiveness of pictorial elucidation. In F. Boers & S. Lindstromberg (Eds.), *Cognitive linguistic approaches to teaching vocabulary and phraseology* (pp. 189–216). Berlin, Germany: Mouton de Gruyter.

Boers, F., Píriz, A. M. P., Stengers, H., & Eyckmans, J. (2009). Does pictorial elucidation foster recollection of idioms? *Language Teaching Research, 13,* 367–382.

Bortfeld, H. (2003). Comprehending idioms cross-linguistically. *Experimental Psychology, 50,* 217–230.

Brenner, G. (2011). *Webster's new world American idioms handbook.* New York, NY: Houghton Mifflin Harcourt.

Brown, D. (2006). *Principles of language learning and teaching* (5th ed.). White Plains, NY: Pearson.

Buccino, G., Binkofski, F., Fink, G. R., Fadiga L., Fogassi, L., Gallese, V., . . . Freund, H. J. (2001). Action observation activates premotor and practical areas in a somatotopic manner: A FMRI study. *European Journal of Neuroscience, 13,* 400–404.

Cacciari, C., & Glucksberg, S. (1991). Understanding idiomatic expressions: The contribution of word meanings. In G. B. Simpson (Ed.), *Understanding word and sentence* (pp. 217–240). Amsterdam, Netherlands: Elsevier.

Cacciari, C., & Tabossi, P. (1988). The comprehension of idioms. *Journal of Memory and Language, 27,* 668–683.

Cacciari, C., & Tabossi. P. (Eds.). (1993). *Idioms: Processing, structure, and interpretation.* Hillsdale, NJ: Lawrence Erlbaum.

Casolini, P., Kabbaj, M., Leprat, F., Piazza, P. V., Rouge-Pont, F., Angelucci, L., . . . Maccari, S. (1993). Basal and stress-induced corticosterone secretion is decreased by lesion of mesencephalic dopaminergic neurons. *Brain Research, 622,* 311–314.

Celce-Murcia, M. (2013). An overview of language teaching methods and approaches. In M. Celce-Murcia (Ed.), *Teaching English as a second or foreign language* (pp. 2–14). Boston, MA: Heinle Cengage Learning.

Chomsky, N. (1980). *Rules and representations.* New York, NY: Columbia University Press.

Cieślicka, A. (2006). Literal salience in on-line processing of idiomatic expressions by second language learners, *Second Language Research, 22,* 115–144.

Clark, J. M., & Paivio, A. (1991). Dual coding theory and education. *Educational Psychology Review, 3,* 233–262.

*Collins COBUILD idioms dictionary* (3rd ed.). (2012). Glasgow, Scotland: HarperCollins.

*Collins COBUILD idioms workbook* (2nd ed.). (2002). Glasgow, Scotland: HarperCollins.

Cool, L. C. (2012, September 11). The easiest way to live longer. *Yahoo! Health.* Retrieved from http://health.yahoo.net

Cooper, C. (2002). *Individual differences* (2nd ed.). London, England: Arnold.

Cooper, T. C. (1998). Teaching idioms. *Foreign Language Annals, 31,* 255–266. doi:10.1111/j.1944-9720.1998.tb00572.x

Cooper, T. C. (1999). Processing of idioms by L2 learners of English. *TESOL Quarterly, 33,* 233–262.

Corballis, M. C. (2002). *From hand to mouth: The origins of language.* Princeton, NJ: Princeton University Press.

Corbett, J. (2010). *Intercultural language activities.* Cambridge, England: Cambridge University Press.

Craik, F. I. M., & Lockhart, R. S. (1972). Levels of processing: A framework for memory research. *Journal of Verbal Learning and Verbal Behaviour, 11,* 671–684.

Craik, F., & Tulving, E. (1975). Depth of processing and the retention of words in episodic memory. *Journal of Experimental Psychology: General, 104,* 268–294.

Crayton, P. W. (2011). A corpus-based study of the linguistic features and processes which influence the way collocations are formed: Some implications for the learning of collocations. *TESOL Quarterly, 45*, 291–311.

Croft, W., & Cruse, D. A. (2004). *Cognitive linguistics.* Cambridge, England: Cambridge University Press.

Cytowic, R. E., & Eagleman, D. M. (2011). *Wednesday is indigo blue.* Cambridge, MA: MIT Press.

Dagut, M., & Laufer, B. (1985). Avoidance of phrasal verbs: A case for contrastive analysis. *Studies in Second Language Acquisition, 7*, 73–79.

Damasio, A. (1994). *Descartes' error: Emotion, reason, and the human brain.* New York, NY: HarperCollins.

Davies, M. (n.d.). *The corpus of contemporary American English (COCA).* Retrieved from http://www.americancorpus.org

DeCarrico, N. (2001). Vocabulary and teaching. In M. Celce-Murcia (Ed.), *Teaching English as a second or foreign language* (3rd ed., pp. 285–300). Boston, MA: Heinle.

Doidge, N. (2007). *The brain that changes itself: Stories of personal triumph from the frontiers of brain science.* New York, NY: Penguin Books.

Dörnyei, Z. (2001). *Motivational strategies in the language classroom.* Cambridge, England: Cambridge University Press.

Dörnyei, Z. (2003). Attitudes, orientations, and motivations in language learning: Advances in theory, research, and applications. *Language Learning, 53*, 3–32. doi:10.1111/1467-9922.53222

Dörnyei, Z. (2007). *Research methods in applied linguistics: Quantitative, qualitative, and mixed methodologies.* Oxford, England: Oxford University Press.

Drew, P., & Holt, E. (1998). Figures of speech: Figurative expressions and the management of topic transition in conversation. *Language in Society, 27*, 495–522.

Drew, P., & Holt, E. (2005). Figurative pivots: The use of figurative expressions in pivotal topic transitions. *Research on Language and Social Interaction, 38*(1), 35–61.

Duranti, A. (2004). *Linguistic anthropology.* New York, NY: Cambridge University Press.

Duranti, A., & Goodwin, C. (1992). *Rethinking context: Language as an interactive phenomenon.* New York, NY: Cambridge University Press.

Eagleman, D. M. (2011). *Incognito: The secret lives of the brain.* New York, NY: Pantheon Books.

Ebbinghaus, H. (1913). *Memory: A contribution to experimental psychology* (H. A. Ruger & C. E. Bussenius, Trans.). New York, NY: Teachers College. (Original work published 1885)

Eerdmans, S. L., & Di Candia, M. (2007). Watching paint dry: The sequentiality of idiomatic expressions in NS-NS and NS-NNS talk-in-interaction. *Discourse Studies, 9,* 579–595.

Elley, W. (1989). Vocabulary acquisition from listening to stories. *Reading Research Quarterly, 24*(2), 174–187.

Fadiga, L., Craighero, L., Buccino, G., & Rizzolatti, G. (2002). Speech listening specifically modulates the excitability of tongue muscles: A TMS Study. *European Journal of Neuroscience, 15,* 399–402.

Feare, R. E. (1980). *Practice with idioms.* Oxford, England: Oxford University Press.

Feare, R. E. (1997). *Everyday idioms for reference and practice.* Reading, MA: Addison Wesley Longman.

Fernando, C. (1996). *Idioms and idiomaticity.* Oxford, England: Oxford University Press.

Fernando, C., & Flavell, R. (1981). *On idiom: critical views and perspectives.* Exeter, England: University of Exeter.

Folse, K. S. (2004). Myths about teaching and learning second language vocabulary: What recent research says. *TESL Reporter, 37*(2), 1–13.

Fragiadakis, H. K. (1992). *All clear: Idioms in context* (2nd ed.). Boston, MA: Heinle ELT.

Francis, E. (2010). *A year in the life of an ESL student: Idioms you can't live without.* Tucson, AZ: Wheatmark.

Gardner, H. (1983). *Frames of mind: The theory of multiple intelligences.* New York, NY: Basic Books.

Gass, S. M., & Selinker, L. (2001). *Second language acquisition.* Mahwah, NJ: Lawrence Erlbaum.

Gee, J. P. (2003). *What video games have to teach us about learning and literacy.* New York, NY: Palgrave MacMillan.

Gee, J. P. (2006). Why game studies now? Video games: A new art form. *Games & Culture, 1*(1), 1–4.

Gee, J. P. (2012). Forward. In H. Reinders (Ed.), *Digital games in language learning and teaching* (pp. xii–xiv). New York, NY: Palgrave.

Gibbs, R. W. (1980). Spilling the beans on understanding and memory for idioms in conversation. *Memory and Cognition, 8,* 149–156.

Gibbs, R. W. (1994). *The poetics of mind: Figurative thought, language, and understanding.* New York, NY: Cambridge University Press.

Gibbs, R. W., & Nayak, N. P. (1989). Psycholinguistic studies on the syntactic behavior of idioms. *Cognitive Psychology, 21,* 100–138.

Gibbs, R. W., Nayak, N. P., & Cutting, C. (1989). How to kick the bucket and not decompose: Analyzability and idiom processing. *Journal of Memory and Language, 28,* 576–593.

Giora, R. (2003). *On our mind: Salience, context, and figurative language.* Oxford, England: Oxford University Press.

Glucksberg, S. (1993). Idiom meanings and allusional content. In C. Cacciari & P. Tabossi (Eds.), *Idioms: Processing, structure, and interpretation* (pp. 3–26). Hillsdale, NJ: Lawrence Erlbaum.

Grant, L. E. (2007). In a manner of speaking: Assessing frequent spoken figurative idioms to assist ESL/EFL teachers. *System, 35,* 169–181.

Grant, L., & Bauer, L. (2004). Criteria for re-defining idioms: Are we barking up the wrong tree? *Applied Linguistics, 25*(1), 38–61. doi:10.1093/applin /25.1.38

Guiora, A. Z., Beit-Hallami, B., Brannon, R. C., Dull, C. Y., & Scovel, T. (1972). The effects of experimentally induced changes in ego states on pronunciation ability in second language: An exploratory study. *Comprehensive Psychiatry, 13,* 421–428.

Halliday, M. A. K. (1973). *Explorations in the functions of language.* London, England: Edward Arnold.

Heacock, H. (Ed.). (2003). *Cambridge dictionary of American idioms.* Cambridge, England: Cambridge University Press.

Heigham, J., & Croker, R. (2009). *Qualitative research in applied linguistics: A practical introduction.* New York, NY: Palgrave.

Hewes, G. W. (1973). Primate communication and the gestural origin of language. *Current Anthropology, 14*(1–2), 5–24.

Hippocrates. (1931). *Regimen* (W. H. S. Jones, Trans.). Cambridge, MA: Harvard University Press. (Original work published 380 BCE)

Holt, E., & Drew, P. (2005). Figurative pivots: The use of figurative expressions in pivotal topic transitions. *Research on Language and Social Interaction, 38*(1), 35–61.

Horstman, J. (2009). *The scientific American day in the life of your brain.* San Francisco, CA: Jossey-Bass.

Howard, J. (1987). *Idioms in American life*. New York, NY: Pearson Education ESL.

Hulstijn, J. H., & Laufer, B. (2001). Some empirical evidence for the involvement load hypothesis in vocabulary acquisition. *Language Learning, 51,* 539–558.

Hunston, S. (2002). *Corpora in applied linguistics*. Cambridge, England: Cambridge University. Press.

Hutchby, I., & Wooffitt, R. (2002). *Conversation analysis*. Malden, MA: Blackwell.

Iacoboni, M. (2009). *Mirroring people: The science of empathy and how we connect with others*. New York, NY: Picador.

Iacoboni, M., Woods, R. P., Brass, M., Bekkering, H., Mazziotta, J. C., & Rizzolatti, G. (1999). Cortical mechanisms of human imitation. *Science, 286,* 2526–2528.

Irujo, S. (1986). A piece of cake: Learning and teaching idioms. *English Language Teaching Journal, 40,* 236–242. doi:10.1093/elt/40.3.236

Jacobs, A. (2010, May 2). Shanghai is trying to untangle the mangled English of Chinglish. *New York Times*. Retrieved from http://www.nytimes.com

Jaeger, J. (1999). *The nature of idioms: A systematic approach*. Berlin, Germany: Peter Lang.

Jefferson, G. (1984). On stepwise transition from talk about a trouble to inappropriately next-positioned matters. In J. M. Atkinson & J. Heritage (Eds.), *Structures of social action: Studies in conversation analysis* (pp. 191–222). Cambridge, England: Cambridge University Press.

Jensen, E. (2008). *Brain-based learning: The new paradigm of teaching*. Thousand Oaks, CA: Corwin.

Joe, A. (1995). Text-based tasks and incidental vocabulary learning. *Second Language Research, 11,* 149–158.

Johnson-Laird, P. N. (1993). Introduction. In C. Cacciari & P. Tabossi (Eds.), *Idioms: Processing, structure and interpretation* (pp. v–x). Mahwah, NJ: Lawrence Erlbaum.

Kandel, E., & Hawkins, R. (1992, September). The biological basis of learning and individuality. *Scientific American*, pp. 79–86.

Kane, J., & Anderson, R. (1978). Depth of processing and interference effects in the learning and remembering of sentences. *Journal of Educational Psychology, 70,* 626–635.

Kapur, S., Craik, F. I., Tulvig, E., Wilson, E. E., Houle, S., & Brown, G. M. (1994). Neuroanatomical correlates of encoding in episodic memory: Levels of processing effect. *Proceedings of the National Academy of the United States of America, 91*(6), 2008–2011.

Katz, J. J. (1973). Compositionality, idiomaticity, and lexical substation. In S. Anderson & P. Kiparsky (Eds.), *A festschrift for Morris Halle* (pp. 357–376). New York, NY: Holt, Rinehart & Winston.

Katz, J. J., & Postal, P. (1963). The semantic interpretation of idioms and sentences containing them. *MIT Research Laboratory of Electronic Quarterly Progress Report, 70,* 275–282.

King, K. (1999). *The big picture: Idioms as metaphors.* New York, NY: Houghton Mifflin.

Knecht, S., Breitenstein, C., Bushuven, S., Wailke, S., Kamping, S., Flöel, A., . . . Ringelstein, E. B. (2004). Levodopa: Faster and better word learning in normal humans. *Annals of Neurology, 56,* 20–26.

Kohler, E., Keysers, C., Umiltà, M. A., Fogassi, L., Gallese, V., & Rizzolatti, G. (2002). Hearing sounds, understanding action: Action representation in mirror neurons. *Science, 297,* 846–848.

Kolb, D. (1984). *Experiential learning: Experience as the source of learning and development.* Englewood Cliffs, NJ: Prentice Hall.

Korol, D. L., & Gold, P. E. (1998). Glucose, memory, and aging. *American Journal of Clinical Nutrition, 67,* 7645–7715.

Kövecses, Z. (1990). *Emotion concepts.* New York, NY: Springer.

Kövecses, Z. (2002). *Metaphor: A practical introduction.* Oxford, England: Oxford University Press.

Kövecses, Z., & Szabó, P. (1996). Idioms: A view from cognitive semantics. *Applied Linguistics, 17,* 326–355.

Kramsch, C. (2006). The multilingual subject. *International Journal of Applied Linguistics, 16*(1), 97–110.

Kramsch, C. (2012). Imposture: A late modern notion in poststructuralist SLA research. *Applied Linguistics, 33,* 483–502.

Krashen, S. (1982). *Principles and practice in second language acquisition.* Oxford, England: Pergamon.

Krashen, S. (1989). We acquire vocabulary and spelling by reading: Additional evidence for the input hypothesis. *Modern Language Journal, 73,* 440–464.

Krashen, S. (2004). *The power of reading: Insights from the research* (2nd ed.). Westport, CT: Libraries Unlimited.

Kumaravadivelu, B. (2003). *Beyond methods: Macrostrategies for language teaching*. New Haven, CT: Yale University Press.

Kumaravadivelu, B. (2006). *Understanding language teaching: From method to post-method*. Mahwah, NJ: Lawrence Erlbaum.

La France, M. (1982). Posturing, mirroring and rapport. In M. Davis (Ed.), *Intention rhythms: Periodicity in communicative behavior* (pp. 279–298). New York, NY: Human Sciences Press.

Lakoff, G. (1987). *Women, fire and dangerous things: What categories reveal about the mind*. Chicago, IL: University of Chicago Press.

Lakoff, G., & Johnson, M. (2003). *Metaphors we live by* (2nd ed.). Chicago, IL: University of Chicago Press.

Lange, E., & Lane, J. (2011). *Writing clearly: An editing guide* (3rd ed.). New York, NY: Heinle.

Laufer, B., & Hill, M. (2000). What lexical information do L2 learners select in a CALL dictionary and how does it affect word retention? *Language Learning & Technology, 3*, 58–76.

Laufer, B., & Shmueli, K. (1997). Memorizing new words: Does teaching have anything to do with it? *RELC Journal, 28*, 89–108. doi:10.1177/003368829702800106

Levinson, S. C. (2003). *Pragmatics*. New York, NY: Cambridge University Press.

Levy, M. (1997). *CALL: context and conceptualisation*. Oxford, England: Oxford University Press.

Levy, M., & Stockwell, G. (2006). *CALL dimensions: Options and issues in computer assisted language learning*. Mahwah, NJ: Lawrence Erlbaum.

Lewis, M. (1993). *The lexical approach*. Boston, MA: Heinle ELT.

Lewis, M. (2002). *Implementing a lexical approach: Putting theory into practice*. Boston, MA: Heinle ELT.

Lightbown, P., & Spada, N. (2006). *How languages are learned* (3rd ed.). Oxford, England: Oxford University Press.

Liu, D. (2003). The most frequently used spoken American English idioms: A corpus analysis and its implications. *TESOL Quarterly, 37*, 671–700.

Liu, D. (2008). *Idioms: Description, comprehension, acquisition, and pedagogy*. London, England: Routledge.

Mack, D., & Ojalvo, H. E. (2010, May 10). Are you a fish out of water? Learning English idioms. *New York Times*. Retrieved from http://learning .blogs.nytimes.com

Magnuson, W. (2001). *English idioms: Sayings and slang*. Calgary, Alberta, Canada: Prairie House Books.

Makkai, A. (1972). *Idiom structure in English*. The Hague, Netherlands: Mouton.

Martin-Chang, S. Y., & Gould, O. N. (2008). Revisiting print exposure: Exploring differential links to vocabulary, comprehension and reading rate. *Journal of Research in Reading, 31*, 273–284.

Mateu, J., & Espinal, M.T. (2007). Argument structure and compositionality in idiomatic constructions. *Linguistic Review, 24*, 33–59.

McCarthy, M. (1998). *Spoken language and applied linguistics*. Cambridge, England: Cambridge University Press.

McCarthy, M., McCarten, J., & Sandiford, H. (2006). *Touchstone*. Cambridge, England: Cambridge University Press.

McGlone, M. S., Glucksberg, S., & Cacciari, C. (1994). Semantic productivity and idiom comprehension. *Discourse Processes, 17*, 167–190.

McLay, V. (1988). *Idioms at work*. New York, NY: Heinle ELT.

McPartland, P. (1989). *What's up? American idioms*. New York, NY: Prentice Hall Regents.

McPherron, P., & Randolph, P. T. (2013). Thinking like researchers: An ESL project that investigates local communities. *TESOL Journal, 4*, 312–331. doi:10.1002/tesj.80

Medina, J. (2009). *Brain rules*. Seattle, WA: Pear Press.

Merriam-Webster. (2014). *Idioms*. Retrieved from http://www.learners dictionary.com/search/idiom

Middleton, F., & Strick, P. (1994). Anatomical evidence for cerebellar and basal ganglia involvement in higher cognitive function. *Science, 266*, 458–461.

Miller, J. (2006). English learners' dictionaries: An undervalued resource. *TESOL in Context, 15*(2), 30–37.

Miller. J. (2012). Dictionaries without borders: Expanding the limits of the academy. *Journal of Learning Design, 5*(1), 43–51.

Milton, J. (2009). *Measuring second language vocabulary acquisition*. Tonawanda, NY: Multilingual Matters.

Moon, R. (1998). *Fixed expressions and idioms in English: A corpus-based approach*. Oxford, England: Clarendon Press.

Nation, P. (2001). *Learning vocabulary in another language*. Cambridge, England: Cambridge University Press.

Nattinger, J., & DeCarrico, J. (1992). *Lexical phrases and language teaching*. Oxford, England: Oxford University Press.

Niergarth, H. (2007). *The idioms book: 1010 American English idioms in 101 two-page lessons*. Brattleboro, VT: Pro Lingua Associates.

Nimoy, L. (Director). (1986). *Star Trek IV: The voyage home*. United States: Paramount Pictures.

Nippold, M. A. (1991). Evaluating and enhancing idiom comprehension in language-disordered students. *Language, Speech, and Hearing Services in Schools, 22,* 100–106.

Norton, B. (2000). *Language and identity in language learning*. London, England: Longman.

Nunberg, G., Sag, I., & Wasow, T. (1994). Idioms. *Language, 70,* 491–538.

O'Dell, F., & McCarthy, M. (2010). *English idioms in use*. Cambridge, England: Cambridge University Press.

Osnos, E. (2008, April 28). Crazy English: The national scramble to learn a new language before the Olympics. *New Yorker.* Retrieved from http://www.newyorker.com

Paivio, A. (1986). *Mental representations*. Oxford, England: Oxford University Press.

Paolo, A., Bonaminio, G., Gibson, C., Partridge, T., & Kallail, K. (2006). Response rate comparisons of e-mail- and mail-distributed student evaluations. *Teaching and Learning in Medicine, 12*(2), 81–84.

Parkinson, D., & Francis, B. (Eds.). (2006). *Oxford idioms dictionary for learners of English* (2nd ed.). Oxford, England: Oxford University Press.

Pavlenko, A. (2005). *Emotions and multilingualism*. Cambridge, England: Cambridge University Press.

Percy, B. (2013). The realm of realia: The use of authentic materialism in the English language classroom. *Global Education Review, 1*(3), 14–18.

Pereira, A. C., Huddleston, D. E., Brickman, A. M., Sosunov, A. A., Hen, R., McKhann, G. M., . . . Small, S. A. (2007). An in vivo correlate of exercise-induced neurogenesis in the adult dentate gyrus. *Proceedings of the National Academy of Sciences of the United States of America, 104,* 5638–5643.

Piirainen-Marsh, A., & Tainio, L. (2009). Other-repetition as a resource for participation in the activity of playing a video game. *Modern Language Journal, 93*(2), 153–169. doi:10.1111/j.1540-4781.2009.00853.x

Pimenova, N. (2011). Idiom comprehension strategies used by English and Russian language learners in a think-aloud study (Unpublished doctoral dissertation). Purdue University, West Lafayette, IN.

Plato. (1985). *The republic* (R. W. Sterling & W. C. Scott, Trans.). New York, NY: W. W. Norton. (Original work published 360 BCE)

Prodromou, L. (2003). Idiomaticity and the non-native speaker. *English Today, 19*(2), 42–48.

Ramachandran, V. S. (2006). *Mirror neurons and imitation learning as the driving force behind "the great leap forward" in human evolution.* Retrieved from http://www.edge.org/3rd_culture/ramachandran/ramachandran_index .html

Randolph, P. T. (2013a). Breaking the Ebbinghaus curse: Strengthening memory, enhancing learning. *CATESOL News, 45*(1), 17–19.

Randolph, P. T. (2013b). The magic of movement: Exercise's phenomenal impact on the language learner's brain. *ITBE Link, 41*(2), 1–7.

Randolph, P. T. (2013c). Mirror neurons in the ESL classroom: The power of imitation, attitude, and gestures in learning. *ITBE Link, 41*(1), 4–9.

Randolph, P. T. (2013d). What's in a name? Personalizing vocabulary for ESL learners. *CATESOL News, 44*, 12–13.

Ratey, J. J. (2001). *A user's guide to the brain: Perception, attention, and the four theaters of the brain.* New York, NY: Pantheon Books.

Ratey, J. J. (with Hagerman, E.). (2008). *Spark! How exercise will improve the performance of your brain.* London, England: Quercus.

Reeves, G. (1985). *The new idioms in action.* New York, NY: Newbury House.

Reinders, H. (Ed.). (2012). *Digital games in language learning and teaching.* Basingstoke, England: Palgrave Macmillan.

Reppen, R. (2010). *Using corpora in the language classroom.* Cambridge, England: Cambridge University Press.

Reppen, R. (2011). Using corpora in the language classroom. In B. Tomlinson (Ed.), *Materials development in language teaching* (pp. 35–50). Cambridge, England: Cambridge University Press.

Reynolds, G. (2011, November 30). How exercise benefits the brain. *New York Times.* Retrieved from http://well.blogs.nytimes.com

Richards, K. (2003). *Qualitative inquiry in TESOL.* New York, NY: Palgrave.

Riding, R. (2002). *School learning and cognitive style*. New York, NY: David Fulton.

Rizzolatti, G. (2005). The mirror neuron system and its function in humans. *Anat Embryol, 210*, 419–421.

Rizzolatti, G., & Arbib, M. A. (1998). Language within our grasp. *Trends in Neurosciences, 21*, 188–194.

Rizzolatti, G., & Craighero, L. (2004). The mirror neuron system. *Annual Review of Neuroscience, 27*, 169–192.

Rizzolatti, G., Fadiga, L., Matelli, M., Bettinardi, V., Paulesu, E., Perani, D., & Fazio, F. (1996). Location of grasp representation in humans by PET:1. Observation versus execution. *Experimental Brain Research, 111*, 246–252.

Ruhl, C. (1989). *On monosemy: A study in linguistic semantics*. Albany, NY: SUNY Press.

Sacks, H. (1995). *Lectures on conversation*. Malden, MA: Blackwell.

Sapolsky, R. M. (2004). Is impaired neurogenesis relevant to the affective symptoms of depression? *Biological Psychiatry, 56*, 137–139.

Schmitt, N. (Ed). (2004). *Formulaic sequences: Acquisition, processing and use*. Amsterdam, Netherlands: John Benjamins.

Schweigert, W. A. (1986). The comprehension of familiar and less familiar idioms. *Journal of Psychological Research, 15*, 33–45.

Seashore, R. H., & Eckerson, L. D. (1940). The measurement of individual differences in general English vocabularies. *Journal of Educational Psychology, 31*, 14–38.

Shams, L., & Seitz, A. R. (2008). Benefits of multisensory learning. *Trends in Cognitive Sciences, 30*, 1–7.

Shaw, E. M. (2011). *Teaching vocabulary through data-driven learning*. Retrieved from http://corpus.byu.edu/coca/files/Teaching_Vocabulary_Through _DDL.pdf

Simpson, R., & Mendis, D. (2003). A corpus-based study of idioms in academic speech. *TESOL Quarterly, 37*, 419–441.

Sinclair, J. M. (1987). Collocation: A progress report. In R. Steele & T. Threadgold (Eds.), *Language topics: Essays in honour of Michael Halliday* (Vol. II, pp. 319–331). Amsterdam, Netherlands: John Benjamins.

Sinclair, J. (1991). *Corpus, concordance, collocation*. Oxford, England: Oxford University Press.

Sinclair, J. (2003). *Reading concordances: An introduction*. New York, NY: Pearson.

Sinclair, J. M., & Moon, R. E. (1995). *Collins COBUILD dictionary of idioms.* London, England: Collins.

Skehan, P. (2002). Theorising and updating aptitude. In P. Robinson (Ed.), *Individual differences and instructed second language acquisition* (pp. 69–93). Amsterdam, Netherlands: John Benjamins.

Sousa, D. A. (2011). *How the brain learns.* Thousand Oaks, CA: Corwin.

Squire, L. R., & Kandel, E. R. (1999). *Memory: From mind to molecules.* New York, NY: W. H. Freeman.

Stanovich, K. E., & Cunningham, A. E. (1993). Where does knowledge come from? Specific associations between print exposure and information acquisition. *Journal of Educational Psychology, 85,* 211–229.

Strässler, J. (1982). *Idioms in English: A pragmatic analysis.* Tübingen, Germany: Gunter Narr Verlag.

Streck, R. (2013). Portugal will licht am ende des tunnels sehen. *Teleopolis.* Retrieved from http://www.heise.de/tp/blogs/8/153627

Sundqvist, P., & Sylvén, L. K. (2012). World of VocCraft: Computer games and Swedish learners' L2 English vocabulary. In H. Reinders (Ed.), *Digital games in language learning and teaching* (pp. 189–208). New York, NY: Palgrave.

Sünram-Lea, S. I., Dewhurst, S. A., & Foster, J. K. (2008). The effect of glucose administration on the recollection and familiarity components of recognition memory. *Biological Psychology, 77,* 69–75.

Szczepaniak, R., & Lew, R. (2011). The role of imagery in dictionaries of idioms. *Applied Linguistics, 32,* 323–347.

Thornbury, S. (2002). *How to teach vocabulary.* Essex, England: Pearson Education.

Waterhouse, L. (2006). Multiple intelligences, the Mozart effect, and emotional intelligence: A critical review. *Educational Psychologist, 41,* 207–225.

Willis, J. (2006). *Research-based strategies to ignite student learning: Insights from a neurologist and classroom teacher.* Alexandria, VA: Association for Supervision and Curriculum Development.

Winter, B., Breitenstein, C., Mooren, F. C., Voelker, K., Fobker, M., Lechtermann, A., . . . Knecht, S. (2007). High impact on running improves learning. *Neurobiology of Learning and Memory, 87,* 597–609.

Wong, L. H., & Looi, C. K. (2010). Vocabulary learning by mobile-assisted authentic content creation and social meaning-making: Two case studies. *Journal of Computer Assisted Learning, 26,* 421–433.

Wray, A. (2002). *Formulaic language and the lexicon.* Cambridge, England: Cambridge University Press.

Wright, J. (2002). *Idioms organiser: Organised by metaphor, topic and key word.* New York, NY: Language Teaching.

Yeh, Y., & Wang, C. (2003). Effects of multimedia vocabulary annotations and learning styles on vocabulary learning. *CALICO Journal, 21*(1), 131–144.

Young, S. N. (2007). How to increase serotonin in the human brain without drugs. *Journal of Psychiatry & Neuroscience, 36,* 396–399.

Zechmeister, E. B., Chronis, A. M., Cull, W. L., D'Anna, C. A., & Healy, N. A. (1995). Growth of a functionally important lexicon. *Journal of Reading Behavior, 27,* 201–212.

Zyzik, E. (2009). Teaching and learning idioms: The big picture. *Clear News, 13*(2), 3–6.

Zyzik, E. (2011). Second language idiom learning: The effects of lexical knowledge and pedagogical sequencing. *Language Teaching Research, 15,* 413–433.

# Index

Page numbers ending in *t* or *f* indicate table or figure.

## G

Games with idioms, 128*f*, 143, 144*f*, 150
Gestures, 61, 172–174
Glial cells, 44–45
Graded salience hypothesis, 51
Grammatical patterns
  history of vocabulary teaching, 68–72
  organizing new idioms and, 78
  presenting new idioms in the classroom, 87
Grammaticalized lexis, 68–72
Guessing the meaning of idioms, 128*f*, 129, 144*f*
Guessing the origin of idioms activities, 144*f*

## H

Hippocampus. *see also* Brain functioning
  definition, **238**
  images of key parts of the brain, 267–268
  memory and, 54
  overview, 42–43
  stress and, 57
Hypothalamus, 42–43. *see also* Brain functioning
Hypothesizing activities, 128*f*, 129

## I

Id, 40
Ideational function of language, 31–32. *see also* Functions of language
Idiom acquisition. *see* Acquisition of idioms
*The Idiom Advantage* (Watkins, 2001), 205–206
*The Idiom Book: 1010 Idioms in 101 Two-Page Lessons* (Niergarth & Niergarth, 2007)
  presenting new idioms in the classroom, 80*t*
  review of, 209–210
The Idiom Connection (website), 212–213
Idiom decomposition model, 50
The Idiom Jungle (website), 221–222
Idiom list hypothesis, 49, 50
Idiom Site (website), 214–215
*Idiomantics: The Weird and Wonderful World of Popular Phrases* (Gooden & Lewis, 2012), 224
Idiomatic expression, **239**
Idiomatic greetings, 251–253
Idiomatic language, **239**
Idiomatic meaning, 23. *see also* Noncompositional function
Idioms in action activities, 107–108. *see also* Classroom strategies
*Idioms in American Life* (Howard, 1987), 81–82
Idioms in general
  definition, **239**
  "fuzzy" category of, 32–37, 33*f*, 34*t*–35*t*, 36*f*
  mythos and logos of language, 11–12
  overview, 1–4, 6–9, 15–21
Idioms of decoding, 21–23
Idioms of encoding, 21–23
Idioms of restricted variance. *see* Restricted variance
Immediate memory, 54. *see also* Memory
Impulsivity, 60
Informal functions of language, 37
Information processing, 49–56
Instruction. *see also* Classroom strategies; Lesson plans
  choosing and developing materials, 89
  choosing new idioms for, 72–76, 74*t*
  cognition and brain-based activities, 92–96, 93*f*, 95*t*
  Five-E System of learning, 231–235
  history of vocabulary teaching, 68–72
  language personality, 229–231
  organizing new idioms and, 76–79

Nonconscious memory, 55. *see also*
	Memory
Nondeclarative memory, 55. *see also*
	Memory
Norepinephrine, 60

## O

Occipital lobes, 43–44, 268. *see also*
	Brain functioning
*101 American English Idioms:*
	*Understanding and Speaking*
	*English Like an American!* (Collis,
	1987), 206–207
Online activities
	digital media activities and, 106–107
	results from survey of students, 144*f,*
		145, 147*f*
	results from survey of teachers, 128*f,*
		129, 130*f*
Opacity, 22, 36*f. see also*
	Noncompositional function
Origins
	Digging Out the Origins of Idioms
		(Lesson 2), 157–159
	results from survey of teachers, 128*f,*
		129
*Oxford Dictionary of English Idioms*
	(Ayto, 2009), 77–78, 83
*Oxford Idioms Dictionary for Learners of*
	*English* (2006), 223–224
*Oxford Word Skills Idioms and Phrasal*
	*Verbs* (Gairns & Redman, 2011),
	224
Oxytocin, 231–232

## P

Pantomiming idioms, 61
Parietal lobes. *see also* Brain functioning
	images of key parts of the brain, 268
	memory and, 54
	overview, 43–44
Passages, idioms in, 128*f,* 143
Permutations, 25–26
Personalizing the material, 64
Phonological structures, 68–72

Phrasal verbs, 19, **241**
Physical activity
	brain functioning and, 58–62
	Let's Get Physical—Idiom Use and
		Exercise (Bonus Lesson Plan),
		193–196
	R.E.S.T. and, 62–65
Pictionary game, 93–94, 143
Pictorial depictions, 82–85
Planning, 43–44
Play
	Five-E System of learning, 233
	Play With Idioms (Lesson 4),
		163–164
	results from survey of students and,
		150
Postmethod approach, 10, **241**
Postmethod condition, **241**
*Practice With Idioms* (Feare, 1980), 79
Pragmatic resources, 29–32, 34*t*–35*t*
Pragmatics, 128*f*
Prefrontal cortex, 54. *see also* Brain
	functioning
Problem solving, 43–44, 59–60
Procedural memory, 55. *see also*
	Memory
Processing theory, 82–83
Professional corpus, 73–74, 74*t*
Pronunciation tips, 87, 104–105
Proverbs, list of, 250–251
Pure idioms, 22. *see also* Categorization
	of idioms

## Q

Quizzes, 130*f,* 143, 144*f*

## R

Reading, 81–82
Reading and identifying idioms
	activities, 128*f*
Reasoning, 59–60
Reference materials. *see also* Materials;
	Resources, reviews of, 223–225
Repetition, 64